THE
TUDOR
EMPIRE

To Jon,
who introduced me to the world of the Tudors

THE
TUDOR
EMPIRE

DAVID J WILDMAN

PEN & SWORD
HISTORY

AN IMPRINT OF PEN & SWORD BOOKS LTD.
YORKSHIRE – PHILADELPHIA

First published in Great Britain in 2023 by
PEN AND SWORD HISTORY
An imprint of
Pen & Sword Books Ltd
Yorkshire – Philadelphia

ISBN 978 1 39908 922 7

Typeset in Times New Roman 11.5/14 by
SJmagic DESIGN SERVICES, India.
Printed and bound in the UK by CPI Group (UK) Ltd.

Pen & Sword Books Limited incorporates the imprints of After the Battle, Atlas,
Archaeology, Aviation, Discovery, Family History, Fiction, History, Maritime,
Military, Military Classics, Politics, Select, Transport, True Crime, Air World,
Frontline Publishing, Leo Cooper, Remember When, Seaforth Publishing, The
Praetorian Press, Wharncliffe Local History, Wharncliffe Transport, Wharncliffe
True Crime and White Owl.

For a complete list of Pen & Sword titles please contact
PEN & SWORD BOOKS LIMITED
George House, Units 12 & 13, Beevor Street, Off Pontefract Road,
Barnsley, South Yorkshire, S71 1HN, England
E-mail: enquiries@pen-and-sword.co.uk
Website: www.pen-and-sword.co.uk

or

PEN AND SWORD BOOKS
1950 Lawrence Rd, Havertown, PA 19083, USA
E-mail: uspen-and-sword@casematepublishers.com
Website: www.penandswordbooks.com

Contents

Preface

The coronation procession of Henry VIII in 1509 included 'nine children of honour' who were placed on horses that were adorned on 'velvet with embroidery' with the title of a region claimed by the English monarch: 'England, France, Gascony, Guienne, Normandy, Anjou, Cornwall, Wales, Ireland'.[1] The message was loud and clear: Henry was no mere king limited to one realm, he was a ruler who oversaw an empire.

History is filled with examples of empires rising and falling. The Roman Empire stretched across the ancient world for centuries, its imperial eagle on display in countless sites in Europe; the Mongol Empire spread throughout the Asian continent, impacting countless societies; and the British Empire, on which the sun never set, ruled the waves of the world's oceans into the twentieth century. Then there are those fictional empires in pop culture, notably that of the Seven Kingdoms of Westeros in the world of *Game of Thrones*, or the dark and sinister Galactic empire of the *Star Wars* universe. All share similarities, with each empire expanding their domains to rule over others, through warfare, economic domination and subterfuge.

However, despite the common use of the word 'empire', there is nothing uniform in the manner in which these empires operated. The Romans centralised power under an emperor in Rome; however, the British Empire had no recognisable singular head, despite the creation of the largely ceremonial title for Queen Victoria as Empress of India in 1876. The Victorian writer J.R. Seeley commented that there was no over-arching plan or structure for the British Empire, and that 'half the world' was conquered 'in a fit of absence of mind'. This is at odds with the popular perception of a strong central leader, such as that of Caesar Augustus, Genghis Khan, or Emperor Palpatine. Furthermore, there are a multitude of other empires that are not labelled as such; the Americans would not call themselves imperial; however, they have stretched across the world in terms of economic influence and political control of places such as Hawaii and Puerto Rico, all of which sits them firmly within the definition of an empire. The historian Niall Ferguson once commented on this issue by suggesting that if something walks like a duck and talks like a duck, then we must view it as a duck.

So, how are we to view and understand the Tudor empire? The imperial expansion during the Tudor period of 1485–1603, particularly the reign of Elizabeth I, is traditionally understood as sowing the seeds of the later British Empire, rather than existing and operating as an empire itself. This is due, in part, to the perception that 'empire' is something that happens in far-away places; more specifically, actions taken to other peoples across a sea or ocean. There is plenty of evidence within the Tudor period of imperial attempts and expansion within this mould, particularly with the voyages of John Cabot in the 1490s, of Francis Drake on reaching California, and of the attempt to establish a colony in North America. Furthermore, there are other imperial transactions during the Tudor era, including the engagement of Sir John Hawkins in the slave trade, connecting England to West Africa and then again to the New World. However, empire cannot be simply defined as one power taking control of land and people across a divide as large as a sea or an ocean. Noam Chomsky has promoted this concept as the 'salt-water fallacy', stressing that the central factor of imperialism is when one nation or group of people exerts their influence, through military force or economic influence, over another. As such, the geographical divide of a sea can be disregarded. Therefore, the British Empire did not simply begin when Jamestown was established in 1607; it is firmly rooted in the attempts of Anglo domination of the British Isles in the medieval period, particularly in controlling Celtic regions such as Wales. Using Chomsky's logic, if a sea separated England from the Celtic corner of Cornwall rather than the Tamar river we would be able to recognise the act of imperialism far more clearly.

The Tudor empire, then, must be fully recognised within this context. Our modern conception of empire is far different to how it would have been perceived in the past; we must view the Tudors not with a twentieth-century or twenty-first-century lens, but rather with fifteenth- or sixteenth-century eyes. Their empire was not just their attempts to expand into the New World, but also their schemes and policies to control people closer to home within the orbit of the British Isles: the Welsh, the

Irish, the Northern English and the Cornish. This is highlighted by the Tudor-era historian Polydore Vergil, who wrote that Britain was:

> divided into four parts; whereof the one is inhabited of Englishmen, the other of Scots, the third of Welshmen, and the fourth of Cornish people, which all differ among themselves, either in tongue, either in manners, or else in laws and ordinances.[2]

Of course, we must also view the Tudor dynasty not simply as a political unit, but as a family. In this light, the Tudor empire was a family business, forever searching to expand their power and might in a similar manner to other family-owned business empires, such as the Murdochs in media, the Waltons controlling Walmart, or the Rockefellers. Furthermore, there are similar analogies with underworld crime family business empires; after all, the Tudors used a range of violent methods to vanquish their rivals. Henry VII shares a striking resemblance to that of Michael Corleone of *The Godfather* movies: attempting to balance the advancement of their family alongside the expansion of their business operations. The personal and the business elements were one and the same, and if blood had to be spilt, then that was the price of maintaining family prestige.

The chapters in this book focus on key events within the Tudor period, assessing how each of the Tudor monarchs faced problems in an attempt to push forward and promote their rule. The first Tudor monarch, Henry VII (r: 1485–1509), faced questions of legitimacy across his kingdom, resulting in numerous rebellions and threats. His son, Henry VIII (r: 1509–47), focused on European affairs, particularly the pursuit of the throne of France, while also strengthening the power of the Crown within the British Isles. The third generation of Tudors (such as Edward VI, r: 1547–53, and Mary I, r: 1553–8) dealt with the legacy of their father, leading to notable failures. The final Tudor monarch, Elizabeth I (r: 1558–1603), experienced the greatest threats of the period while promoting a new expansive view of empire.

The Tudor period was vital in paving the way to what would eventually become the British Empire; there was a clear change in England's perception, from operating within a corner of Europe to thinking in global terms. But this period was much more than simply sowing the seeds of the later empire; the whole course of British history changed due to the interventions of Tudor monarchs in areas such as Wales, Ireland and the North of England. Power and prestige were thought about, fought for and sought after, resulting in the formation of a distinct Tudor empire.

Chapter 1

The Plantagenet Inheritance

The rise of the Tudors and their imperial domains

It is the twenty-second day of August 1485. Henry Tudor stands on a field in the middle of the English kingdom facing King Richard III in battle, with the royal army outnumbering his own men. He is the invader in a country that was largely unknown to him, having left it in his childhood. His own force is a fragile coalition comprising different elements: Lancastrian loyalists, Yorkist dissidents, Welsh rebels and French soldiers. Henry Tudor's claim to the throne – and English history – hangs on a thread. If he is victorious, a new dynasty will emerge, but if he is defeated, the Tudor name will become nothing more than a mere footnote in history. These are the stakes; the line between triumph and disaster is paper thin. But Henry Tudor is prepared. In many ways, his whole life has been building up to this moment.

The Rise of Henry Tudor

The story of Henry Tudor's rise to prominence can be traced back three decades to 1455 – two years before his birth – and another military clash: the Battle of St Albans.

The king at this time was Henry VI and his opponent was Richard's father, the Duke of York. An opposition Yorkist faction had emerged due to the king's failed policies, of which there was a long list: evil counsellors, misuse of funds, and defeat against the French in the final phase of the Hundred Years' War. It had all been enough to send the king into literal madness and England itself became riven with division. The Duke of York had determined that enough was enough, and he advocated wholesale reform of the government; this led him down the path of taking military action and waging war on the king.

St Albans – the first of many battles in the period known as the Wars of the Roses – was a victory for the Yorkists. However, this action led to the creation of a rival faction: the Lancastrians. Over the next thirty years, in a generational conflict, the two groups fought for control of the throne. The central players came and went, with the wheel of fortune constantly spinning; the Duke of York held great influence in the 1450s, but by 1460 he was killed. His sons continued his legacy, with the eldest claiming the crown to become Edward IV in 1461. Then, Edward himself lost the throne and fled England in 1470 due to the collapse of the Yorkist faction; his mentor – the Earl of Warwick – achieved a reputation as a 'Kingmaker' by throwing his support in with the Lancastrians, leading to Henry VI's restoration. However, this all collapsed in 1471 when Edward triumphantly returned to England, leading to the deaths of his enemies, including Warwick, the Prince of Wales, and Henry VI. Turn, turn, turn, went the wheel of fortune, with the Wars of the Roses proving to be, as noted originally in *Ecclesiastes*, 'a time to love and a time to hate, a time for war and a time for peace'.

Within the backdrop of this wider war and changing fortunes were the Tudors; a family of little note before the middle of the 1400s. Owen Tudor – grandfather to Henry – was a member of the gentry who caught the eye of the widowed queen of Henry V – and mother of Henry VI – Catherine of Valois. Their affair and later marriage was kept secret due to Owen not being of royal or noble stock, with the relationship creating two children: Edmund and Jasper. Both were half-brothers to King Henry VI, and so it was natural that they would reap more than their fair share of patronage and mouth-watering titles (Edmund was created Earl of Richmond, while Jasper was made Earl of Pembroke). It was also natural that they would support the Lancastrians in their feud with the Yorkists. Edmund was married to a distant relative, Margaret Beaufort, whose own family included the dukes of Somerset, whom the Yorkists despised. Despite her young age – she was only 12 years old – the pair married in 1455, and soon Margaret fell pregnant. However, Edmund never saw the birth of his son, Henry; he was captured by Yorkist forces at Carmarthen Castle and died of bubonic plague while in captivity.

The early years of Henry's life were disrupted due to the uncertainty and shifting sands of politics in the kingdom. His mother Margaret remarried several times to maintain a notable position in society, while Henry was moved around and taken as a ward by various nobles. His uncle Jasper had gone into hiding in opposition to the new Yorkist regime, and for a time it seemed as if Henry would become reconciled with this new dynasty. His guardian, the Yorkist supporting William Herbert, even had plans to marry Henry to his own daughter.

However, the wheel of fortune spun again, bringing an end to Henry's time with the Herberts; in 1469, during the period of Yorkist division, Herbert was executed by the Earl of Warwick. The Lancastrian restoration of 1470–71 provided Henry with a short snapshot of what life could have been like; he was reunited with his mother and uncle, with the family fortunes of the Tudors elevated once again. This brief restoration was shattered in 1471 with the Yorkist Edward IV's return; Jasper feared for his nephew's life, and so he took possession of Henry and fled England for the safety of Europe.

For the next thirteen years Henry and Jasper lived in exile in the ducal court of Francis II, Duke of Brittany. During this time they became forgotten figures, isolated from the cut-and-thrust events of English politics. Edward IV half-heartedly attempted to retrieve them on an occasion or two, but due to the stability of his rule the wars – and the Tudors – became a distant memory.

Then came 1483. And everything turned once more.

1483

Edward IV entered the year of 1483 as a relatively young man of 41 years of age. After the trials and tribulations of the Wars of the Roses, he had brought peace and stability to the kingdom, and it might have been expected that he would endure on the throne into the new sixteenth century. However, this young warrior king had become idle and developed an indulgent lifestyle that, coupled with ill health, led to his premature death on 9 April 1483.

The death reopened the divisions in the kingdom and reignited a new – and final – phase in the Wars of the Roses. Many mistrusted Edward's wife – Elizabeth Woodville – due to her extended family's greedy consumption of patronage. There was a growing fear that the Woodvilles would dominate the kingdom due to having control of the new king: Edward V, a mere boy not yet 10 years of age. And so, those in opposition turned their attention to Edward IV's brother, Richard of Gloucester. Richard was the remaining son of York, and his entire career had been spent in dedication to the Yorkist project, particularly in standing with Edward during the problems of 1470–71. He had been rewarded handsomely, particularly in being provided with control of the North of England. But his brother's death had stirred him to action.

Richard decided on a pre-emptive strike: he had Edward V's maternal uncle, Earl Rivers, arrested, before taking control of the boy king himself. On entering London, Richard ensured that he took control of the major organs of government, while his sister-in-law, Elizabeth Woodville, fled to sanctuary with her family and her youngest son, Prince Richard, Duke of York. Richard convinced Elizabeth to hand over little Richard, leading to both princes being kept together in the Tower of London. Then, nobody saw any more of them. It was as if the two boys simply vanished. However, there were to be repercussions for Richard's swift, brutal actions. His harsh treatment of his former allies – such as Lord Hastings and the Duke of Buckingham – and the rumours of his involvement in the likely murder of his nephews had led many to reconsider their options. And so, many started to look elsewhere for a rival claimant to remove Richard from the throne.

There was a key problem with this search: an absence of men with a suitable claim, due to three decades of fighting having removed dozens of lords who had royal blood. Within the Yorkist camp there was only the son of Richard's brother, George, Duke of Clarence; however, this young earl – Edward, Earl of Warwick – was too young to rule and for people to rally behind. Meanwhile, other sons – such as the de la Poles of Richard's older sister Elizabeth – had accommodated themselves to the new regime. Even strong Lancastrian claimants were non-existent; the family line of Henry V and his heirs were gone, and other possible links – such as those of the Beauforts – had been killed off in various battles and executions. All, that is, but for one: Margaret Beaufort. Margaret's son Henry, by her first husband Edmund Tudor, became a valid, rival claimant for Richard's crown.

Henry Tudor's claim to the throne was, as he was well aware, fragile and weak. For starters, he did not derive a claim based on the Tudor blood from his father. Although the Tudors did have a link to royal stock, it was to that of French royalty through Henry's grandfather – Owen – marrying Catherine of Valois. Therefore, his link to the English crown could only be traced through the ancestry of his mother; a hundred years into the past brings this line back to John of Gaunt, the son of Edward III. John of Gaunt married three times during his life, and the union with his final wife – Katherine Swynford – created the royal line of the Beauforts.

But the Beauforts themselves had a chequered history, for Katherine Swynford was originally a mistress of John of Gaunt and their affair had produced several children two decades before their actual marriage. These children were later legitimised; however, the family itself was subsequently disbarred from ever declaring a legal claim to the throne of England. Yet, despite this limitation, the Beauforts were notable players in the events of fifteenth-century politics and were key Lancastrian leaders during the Wars of the Roses. But their misfortune during the battles of this conflict had led to a quick succession of dukes, until the final one perished at the Battle of Tewkesbury in 1471.

Despite the limitations in his claim, more and more came to Henry's camp from the period of 1483 to 1485. This forgotten noble became the focal point of dissenters from the English kingdom, with a ragbag coalition forming of old Lancastrians, dissatisfied Yorkists and outraged Woodvilles. Momentum started to build and on Christmas Day 1483, Henry entered the church of Rouen in Brittany and declared that he would fight for the English throne. This statement outlined how Henry could be the one – finally – to restore peace and prosperity to England. The division of the Wars of the Roses, between Lancastrian and Yorkist, would be healed with Henry's marriage to Elizabeth of York, the daughter of Edward IV.

But there was one problem. He had to solve the conundrum of how to sail across the Channel and to beat Richard for the throne.

Bosworth

The years 1484 and 1485 were spent plotting and preparing, while King Richard became more impatient in England. In 1484 he put pressure on Duke Francis to serve up his guests, leading to Henry and Jasper fleeing Brittany for France. This, however, turned out to be a blessing in disguise, for the French royal court of Charles VIII was willing to offer men, money and ships to destabilise the English kingdom. Furthermore, Henry's cause was boosted with the arrival of new supporters, none more impressive than the military strategist Earl of Oxford. Oxford had been languishing in a Calais prison for the past decade due to his undying support for the Lancastrians; however, on hearing of Henry's rise he managed to convince his gaoler that joining this new camp would be a better option than sticking with Richard.

Henry's invasion force landed in south Wales at the start of August 1485. Wales was chosen because it was Jasper's old stomping ground, and it was hoped that the Tudors could take advantage of their old Welsh connections. And it worked, with various local nobles, such as Rhys ap Thomas, joining Henry rather than preventing his march through the principality. The invasion force moved northwards before crossing into Shrewsbury, and then on into the heart of England. The final destination was Bosworth.

The Battle of Bosworth has gone down in history as one of the most pivotal conflicts in British history. It began with King Richard appearing the more likely victor; after all, it was Richard who had the experience of campaigns against the Lancastrians, in fighting against the Scots, and in controlling the North. He had the necessary skills to see off this threat, whereas Henry was a mere rookie in military affairs. More importantly, Richard had the numbers; it was judged that he had 10,000 soldiers to Henry's 5,000. On paper, the battle was nothing more than a foregone conclusion – but for three crucial points.

First, although Henry was a novice, he had the expertise of several tacticians. There was Uncle Jasper, who had fought more than his fair share of campaigns, as well as the Earl of Oxford. Like Richard, Oxford had plenty of experience on the battlefield during earlier conflicts in the Wars of the Roses. Second, Richard had not inspired the men of England to fight for him. Many feared him, rather than respected him, and the accusations of him being a nephew-murderer had not abated. This can be seen in the contingent of the Earl of Northumberland, who had men and had come to fight, but used the excuse of boggy terrain to prevent him from getting to the battlefield. Northumberland was a Percy – old friends of the Lancastrians – and it appears that he was hedging his bets and hoping for a Tudor victory.

Third, and perhaps most importantly, was the role of the Stanleys. The Stanleys were two brothers – the older Thomas Lord Stanley and the younger William Stanley – who had profited greatly from the Wars of the Roses by simply switching sides to the winning team at the right moment. Ostensibly they had come to Bosworth to fight for Richard; however, they had other irons in the fire. Thomas Stanley was married to Margaret Beaufort, thereby making him step-father to Henry. Henry attempted to use this card to convince Lord Stanley to switch sides, and both had met a couple of days before the battle to discuss this proposition. However, Lord Stanley had not elevated his position through succumbing to emotion; he remained distant and would await the battle itself before making his final decision. Such was the military force of the Stanleys, the fates of both Henry and Richard rested on them. But if Lord Stanley needed any motivation to fight for Richard it came in the form of his son, Lord Strange, who was held hostage by Richard's men. Either Lord Stanley would fight for the king or his son would have his throat slit.

This was the shifting, volatile dynamic of Bosworth on 22 August 1485. The battle began when the Earl of Oxford led his men into the melee against the Duke of Norfolk. Norfolk was a keen Ricardian, no doubt due to the elevation of his dukedom by Richard; however, he was slain in the fight, while his son – the Earl of Surrey – was viciously wounded, leading some of Norfolk's men to retreat. Richard saw the need to plug the gap and ordered in Northumberland's force, but his men remained rooted to their positions.

And then came the key decision of the battle. Richard spotted an opportunity to seize the initiative by charging at Henry to take him out and end the battle in his favour. Although dangerous, this tactic had worked in previous battles; it was the true test of a proud, valiant knight. Richard flew into the thick of it, with him and his men slaying Henry's guardians. He was within distance of his rival, with Henry's standard bearer killed by Richard's sword. It seemed as if Henry had gambled and lost. However, Richard's charge had finally pushed the Stanleys to act. Sir William Stanley entered the fray on the side of Henry, not Richard. This sizeable force swung the battle in favour of Tudor, with Richard being cut down and killed.

At the battle's conclusion, Richard's broken body was placed on the back of a donkey, with instructions for it to be ridden through the streets of nearby Leicester; it was not seen again until being found beneath a carpark in the twenty-first century. Legend has it that Lord Stanley picked up Richard's fallen crown and placed it on Henry Tudor's head. He was 27 years old and had become the King of England. It was the beginning of the new Tudor dynasty.

The Plantagenet Inheritance

At sundown, after the battle ended, Henry may have reflected on the full extent of what he had won that day. He was now King of England, but also much more. The possessions attached to the English Crown were an interesting, numerous and diffuse hodgepodge collection, and at that point in 1485 the wider imperium was in danger of collapsing. Henry would spend the majority of his twenty-four-year reign retaining and strengthening this fragile empire.

England, by far, was the most notable and sizeable of Henry's new possessions. In 1485 the population of the English stood between two and three million, and was still recovering from the impact of the Black Death more than a century earlier. The main organs of Henry's government were centred in the capital of London, a city that completely overshadowed all other settlements in the British Isles. Henry was very much aware of England's importance; on the eve of Bosworth, he announced to his men:

> We have without resistance penetrated the ample region and large country of Wales … If we had come to conquer Wales and achieved it, our praise had been great and our gain more; but if we win this battle, the whole rich realm of England shall be ours, the profit shall be ours and the honour ours.[1]

The English state had developed over a thousand years, with it initially originating in the aftermath of the withdrawal of Roman legions. Various Germanic tribes – such as the Angles, the Saxons, the Jutes – migrated to Britain from the 400s onward, leading to the establishment of a variety of Anglo-led territories. Prominent kingdoms included Northumbria in the North, Mercia in the Midlands and Wessex in the South. The Wessex monarch Alfred the Great declared himself King of the Anglo-Saxons in the late ninth century, providing a political and administrative unity for a developing English kingdom. This was further enhanced by Alfred's successors, with other Saxon territories, such as Northumbria, being absorbed. However, this fertile kingdom was coveted by the eyes of many others, including the Danes and the Normans. William the Conqueror's successful invasion and victory at Hastings in 1066 established a new dynasty on the throne that would eventually lead to further expansion and domination of the British Isles.

However, despite the kingdom boasting a long history, the English themselves were not strictly united. There were many regional differences that Henry needed to be aware of if he intended to retain his throne. The North of England – roughly comprising the modern-day counties of Yorkshire, Lancashire, Durham, Northumberland and Cumbria – was distinct from the southern section centring on London. These differences can be traced back to the divisions within the old Anglo-Saxon kingdoms and in the various policies employed by successive monarchs to reduce the North to submission. The disturbances of the Wars of the Roses in the fifteenth century provided lords in the North with greater powers and autonomy. The monarchs in London struggled with controlling the northern reaches of the kingdom, particularly with the powerbases of the northern lords who were able to retain their own armies. The rise of the Yorkists could be seen, in many ways, as a victory for the North; they supported the claims of Richard Duke of York, and then placed their trust in the reigns of his sons Edward IV and Richard III. However, Richard's death at Bosworth led to fears that the North would resurrect their voice and autonomy. The Yorkist sympathies within the region meant that they cast a suspicious eye toward the new Tudor regime. The North was the refuge of many Yorkist supporters, and as such, Henry Tudor soon realised that he would need to tread carefully in terms of dealing with a potential volcanic eruption from that region.

In the West Country, the Cornish were a distinctive people who were proud of their culture and history. The early sixteenth-century historian Polydore Vergil noted how the Cornish comprised one part of the people who inhabited Britain, alongside the English, the Welsh and the Scots. The Cornish enjoyed a level of autonomy during the rise of the Anglo-Saxon kingdoms, but by 937 their border was fixed at the River Tamar and their position was submerged within the growing English kingdom. The Earldom of Cornwall – and later, the Duchy – was dominated by England; however, by 1485 the Cornish remained a distinct people with their own language, customs and even their own political institution in the tin-mining Stannary Parliament.

The Cornish shared many similarities with the Welsh, both being Celtic peoples who had been pushed back with the rise of the Anglo-Saxon kingdoms. But the Welsh were a stronger, more united people, retaining their own political autonomy into the medieval age. In the later 1200s, King Edward I conquered Wales and redefined its status; it was transformed into 'the Principality', connecting the land to the English royal family. The construction of castles was a clear reminder of Anglo-imperial rule, with the Council of Wales based in Ludlow to oversee regional affairs. The early fifteenth century had witnessed a series of rebellions against English rule, notably under the leadership of Owain Glyndwr. It seemed, for a brief time, that Welsh national identity would be able to reassert itself; however, the English government was able to re-establish control. The passing of the Penal Laws prohibited Welsh people from having influence over policy and forbade them from buying arms. It was clear that the laws were intended to reduce the status of the Welsh to demonstrate the difference with the controlling English. The Anglo-Welsh political relationship was a difficult one, with Wales remaining distinct to England and not yet fully absorbed, but yet politically neutered.

By the time of Henry Tudor's arrival in South Wales in 1485, the Welsh appeared to have accommodated themselves with the Yorkist regime. But the Tudor name was enough to convince many to switch allegiance, as illustrated with the decision of Rhys ap Thomas to fight alongside Henry. Many Welsh soldiers fought at Bosworth, no doubt with the belief that Henry would bring about better times for their land. Nobody expected independence to come to Wales, but now that a man of Welsh blood sat on the English throne they at least hoped for greater freedoms and autonomy. However, some notable Yorkist links remained in Wales, as shown with the disturbances of 1486.

The other significant people in Britain were north of the border in Scotland. The English may have dominated everyone else in the Isles, but Scotland was a proud, independent kingdom that co-existed with England in an uneasy, fraught relationship. As with Wales, the late 1200s was a particularly difficult period; the Scottish king Alexander III died in 1286 with no clear successor, leading to the rise of thirteen competing claimants. The English king, Edward I, was asked to arbitrate the dispute, but he took full advantage to manipulate the situation for his own benefit. He chose John Balliol, but in return Balliol agreed to the principle of suzerainty; this placed the English monarch as the overlord of the Scottish crown, effectively making England supreme over all of Scotland. This led to the exploitation of the Scottish people, which eventually ruptured into the Wars for Scottish Independence in which national heroes were created, such as William Wallace and Robert the Bruce. The defeat of the English at the Battle of Bannockburn in 1314 reaffirmed Scotland's independence, and from that point onward the relationship remained strained.

The 1300s and 1400s saw constant border skirmishes, with Berwick continually changing hands. However, the fifteenth century was characterised by the English being too divided to focus on Scotland, while the Scottish crown was itself weakened through the succession of child kings (such as James II and James III). The Scottish border remained an important strategic area for the English Crown, as shown with the organisation of the Lord Warden of the Marches. Henry VII would have cast a cautious eye to Scotland. Having just installed himself on the English throne he was unlikely to dust off the old suzerainty claim, but he desired stability in Britain to provide a basis for the Tudor name to take root. Luckily for him, the Scottish king – James III – governed a country riven by factional divisions; eventually he would be killed in facing these rebels in battle. Therefore, the Scottish kingdom was weak and unlikely to cause Henry problems in the immediate future.

The same could not be said of the land that England controlled across the sea: Ireland. English domination of Ireland stretched back to the Norman incursion of the late 1100s, when the island was divided into a wide range of small kingdoms. Henry II was able to exploit this division to claim lordship over the entirety of the island, and in 1177 established the Lordship of Ireland for his son, John Lackland, the future King John. Henry II actually wanted Ireland raised as a kingdom for his son; however, Pope Lucius III did not consent. Henry tried his luck a second time with the next Pope – Urban III – who did relent; a crown of gold and peacock feathers was commissioned for John. However, after John's ill-fated visit to Ireland in 1185, plans for the raising of a kingdom were scuppered. When John became King of England in 1199, the lordship was joined with the English crown, with it remaining attached into the Tudor era.

Although Henry II and future English monarchs claimed lordship over all of Ireland, the reality was very different. First, the geographical distance was so vast that an English king could not expect to be physically present. Therefore, a representative – Lord Deput – was positioned in Ireland to oversee political matters. The Pale – the area securely controlled by the English – was the centre of Anglo administration, centring on Dublin Castle. Second, the English did not, and could not, rule all of

Ireland. The physical land controlled by the English was the Pale, and this land – centred on Dublin – grew or shrank over the centuries. The vast remainder – Gaelic Ireland – was controlled by various lords who had pledged fealty to the English Crown.

Over the course of time from the twelfth century the situation became blurred, particularly in the development of the Anglo-Irish lords: they were Norman in origin, but over time had embraced the customs and culture of the Irish. There were concerns about the assimilation of the English and the Irish, as shown with the Statutes of Kilkenny in 1366, which noted how 'many English of the said land, forsaking the English language, manners, mode of riding, laws and usages, live and govern themselves according to the manners, fashion, and language of the Irish enemies'. The statutes forbade English settlers from going native and taking up the Irish way of life; it was deemed important to retain a clear distinction between coloniser and colonised. However, it was clear that the English needed Irish cooperation to continue their enterprise; rebellions could frequently occur if these Irish lords became hostile. Unfortunately for Henry, many of these lords retained Yorkist sympathies.

The English Crown also had a variety of other territories attached to it, each of them scattered around the British Isles. The Isle of Man became a fiefdom of England during the reign of Henry IV, and as such it accepted Anglo suzerainty throughout the fifteenth century. It was governed on behalf of the Crown by the earls of Northumberland, and by the time Henry came to power in 1485 it was under the control of Thomas Stanley. Further south, the Channel Islands off the coast of France retained a level of autonomy. These islands – principally Jersey, Guernsey, Sark – were relics of the time when the English and Norman thrones were linked together.

The Channel Islands were, in many ways, a humiliating reminder of the wider dreams the English once had of controlling the entirety of the French kingdom. England and France regularly clashed in battle during the medieval era, particularly because of the Norman dukes also allowing allegiance to the French crown. Furthermore, at one point the English crown had other substantial holdings in France, principally due to Henry II's accession to the crown and his marriage to Eleanor of Aquitaine. The Angevin empire included Aquitaine, Gascony, Anjou, as well as significant influence over Brittany. However, King John's disastrous reign ended with these lands becoming separated from the

Crown in the early thirteenth century, although it did not erase the ambition of English monarchs to reclaim what they once owned.

In the fourteenth century, Edward III claimed that the entire French kingdom was legitimately his, thereby leading to the Hundred Years' War. The high point was undoubtedly Henry V's reign in the years 1413–22; England won a resounding victory at Agincourt, which ultimately led to the two crowns becoming united under the Treaty of Troyes. However, Henry V's premature death led to the succession of a baby king – Henry VI – and decades of defeats led to the expulsion of the English from France in the 1450s. After this point, the attention of the English kingdom was on the factional divides of the Wars of the Roses, thereby meaning that the Yorkist dynasty did not press forward the French claim. Edward IV invaded France in 1475 but was content to be pacified with a pay-off, thereby renouncing the claim. The French royal court of 1485 sponsored Henry Tudor in his invasion, thereby suggesting that a new era of Anglo-French relations was on the horizon. No doubt, the French believed that they had an ally – or at the very least a friend – in Henry; however, there were some in England who had not entirely abandoned the French imperial project. Whether Henry would dust off the French claim remained to be seen.

The only piece of territory in mainland France that remained from the reign of Henry V was the port of Calais. The English had been in control of the town since 1347, back in the early phase of the Hundred Years' War; the Pale of Calais was less than twenty square miles, and it was used primarily as a trading base. However, it also served an important military role, due to the army stationed there being England's only royal standing army. As such, the post of Constable of Calais was an important one. But problematically, Calais provided a seemingly irresistible temptation for English monarchs to meddle in European affairs; it could be used as an accessible base of operations on which to launch invasions in northern France. Along with the old French claim, would the allure of a French adventure be too much for Henry VII?

In total, this inheritance from the Plantagenet dynasty was an empire that consisted of the English state (with its varying levels of division), Wales, Ireland, the various smattering of islands, as well as the port of Calais. From the position of a virtual Breton vagabond, Henry's stock had risen considerably. He had won an empire on the battlefield; however, his most significant task would be ensuring that he held onto it. There were plenty of takers willing to prise it from his hands.

13

Chapter 2

The Ghost of York

Henry VII's consolidation of the North 1485–1489

The North had been the ruin of previous English monarchs. Far away from London, kings needed to empower and rely on the northern nobles to maintain peace and stability, while also hoping that the same nobles did not plot their downfall. The newly crowned Henry VII knew that he had to control the North if he had any intention of holding onto his wider domains. The first five years of his reign presented considerable problems that threatened to end the Tudor dynasty in its infancy.

Yorkist threats. Foreign meddling. Pretenders. Rebellion. Henry was to experience a sharp and troubled apprenticeship in the ways of kingship.

The Good, the Bad and the Untrustworthy

When Henry became King he faced a divided North; a region that had been split apart during the Wars of the Roses, with strong Yorkist sympathies remaining. As such, the new Tudor monarch had to quickly figure out who he could trust and who he had to keep an eye on.

The Percys were among the most distinguished of northern nobles, with the family being one of the earliest supporters of the first Lancastrian king, Henry IV, at the turn of the fifteenth century. The Wars of the Roses unleashed the Percy rivalry with the Nevilles, leading to the death of many of their leading members; their influence was initially reduced in the 1460s, before they accommodated themselves to the new Yorkist regime in the 1470s. Serving in the role of Earl of Northumberland, the head of the Percy family offered a strong, loyal powerbase to keep peace in the North, as well as the ability to protect the border with Scotland. However, Henry was cautious in trusting the current earl; Henry Percy had pledged fealty to Richard III and headed to Bosworth to fight against Henry, but did not commit his troops to battle. Reasons he did not engage suggest that Percy was a coward, incompetent, or secretly hoped for Henry to restore the Lancastrians once again. After the battle, Henry obtained Percy's allegiance, but he would have had reservations about whether he could rely on him in the testing times ahead.

The same could be said of the Percys' hated rivals: the House of Neville. Their original stronghold was Durham, but they expanded in the fifteenth century to become a powerful family, particularly due to beneficial marriages. During the Wars of the Roses, Richard Neville in his title as Earl of Warwick welded great influence; his support of the Yorkists helped Edward IV to the throne in 1461, and his switch to Henry VI led to his brief restoration in 1470–71. As such, historians have provided Warwick with the moniker 'Kingmaker'. However, 1471 saw the sharp decline of the Nevilles due to their treasonous actions; Edward IV reclaimed the throne, leading to Warwick and his brother being slayed at the Battle of Barnet. By 1485, the leading member of the family was Ralph Neville, Earl of Westmorland, who was disdainful of the Yorkists since his father's death in battle against them. Ralph Neville kept himself quiet during the 1470s, and when Henry became king he swore loyalty to him.

The Cliffords also played a key role during the Wars of the Roses; the eighth baron, Thomas Clifford, died at the first Battle of St Albans fighting for the Lancastrians, and the ninth baron, John 'Butcher' Clifford, was later killed in battle in 1461. The early life of the remaining claimant to the family fortune, Henry Clifford, is similar to that of Henry Tudor's; one legend suggests that he was hidden away and grew up in a rural location for fear of being targeted by the Yorkists. Due to his pedigree, the tenth baron became a useful, trusted servant of the new Tudor regime; however, his energetic actions and the scorn of former Yorkist supporters disrupted the fragile balance in the North.

The most powerful – and most dangerous – family was the one that helped Henry secure his crown at Bosworth: the Stanleys. This family grew in stature and power throughout the fifteenth century, particularly under the direction of Thomas Stanley and his brother William Stanley. The pair gained a reputation throughout the Wars of the Roses for picking the winning side, often sitting back and awaiting to see the most rewarding outcome before involving themselves and their men.

The Yorkists provided them with a key role in maintaining peace in the north-west of England and they were well rewarded for their service.

The fast-paced events of 1483 severely tested the Stanley policy of flip-flopping between rival camps. Thomas Stanley's initial intention on the death of Edward IV was in preserving balance between the Ricardian and Woodville factions; however, he was imprisoned during Richard's seizure of the throne. Clearly Richard suspected Stanley, no doubt due to his marriage – back in 1472 – to Henry Tudor's mother, Margaret Beaufort. However, Richard concluded that the Stanleys were more useful as friends rather than as foes, leading to Thomas Stanley's release and their incorporation into the new regime; Thomas bore the mace at Richard's coronation and was given the position of Lord High Constable of England, and William was provided with lands in North Wales. However, the growth of the Tudor candidacy led to developing tension in Richard mistrusting Margaret Beaufort, and then by extension, Thomas Stanley's loyalty. When Thomas Stanley asked to be excused from the royal court, Richard responded by demanding that his eldest son – Lord Strange – remain at the court; this would, by implication, guarantee the good behaviour of the Stanleys.

It is clear that the Stanleys were in communication with Henry during the period of his landing in early August 1485, his journey into mid-Wales, and then into England. Of course, Thomas Stanley had much to gain if his stepson was to take the throne. However, very true to form, neither of the Stanleys openly declared for Henry. Richard suspected that something was afoot: his order to intercept the Tudor rebellion went unheard, and he ordered Thomas Stanley to return to the court. Stanley said that he was not able to do so, claiming that the 'sweating sickness' provided a hurdle. No doubt it was at that moment that King Richard realised that the Stanleys were scheming, and so he highlighted his insurance policy: the life of Lord Strange. Stanley's response was boastful: 'Sire, I have other sons.' But despite the public confidence, internally Stanley must have feared that all that the previous generations had built would be undone in a single afternoon if the cards did not fall into place. The decisive actions of William Stanley at Bosworth on 22 August 1485 led to the death of Richard III, and the Stanleys were highly rewarded: Thomas was created the Earl of Derby, and William was given the post of Lord Chamberlain. However, there was a feeling that the Stanleys could never be satiated, and that their heads could be turned if another opportunity presented itself.

This, then, was the situation in the North of England when Henry took the throne in 1485: a disrupted region in which strong Yorkist support remained. The remoteness of the area meant that Henry had to rely on the northern lords; however, the tools that he had at his disposal were a fragmented patchwork of rebels, traitors and flip-floppers. Threats would undoubtedly rise their head, and it was in the North in which his throne and early budding empire could be lost.

First Blood

Anti-Tudor murmurs inevitably began before the dust had settled at Bosworth. The battle may have ended the life of Richard III and many of his key supporters, but there remained many Ricardians who were not happy at reconciling with the new regime. There was hope that the North would provide the key in unseating the new upstart Tudor monarch, just as it had in previous decades when turfing out other kings during the Wars of the Roses. One of those who yearned for a Yorkist restoration was Viscount Francis Lovell, who had been a devoted supporter of Richard III. He fought at Bosworth, and on realising that Richard had been killed, he fled the battlefield and sought sanctuary in Colchester where he licked his wounds and considered new plans throughout the winter.

During the same period, Henry consolidated his control of the kingdom: he married Elizabeth of York in January 1486 – who quickly became pregnant – and wisely secured supporters through gifting rewards, while imprisoning potential threats. He was clearly concerned about the volatility of the North and he planned a royal progress to the region in the hope that 'he might castigate the minds of men contaminated by the plague of factions', particularly the pulling power of the Yorkist cause.[1]

It was while arriving in Lincoln on his way to the North that Henry first heard that Lovell had escaped sanctuary and was on the loose. By the time Henry arrived at York more news was presented to him: Viscount Lovell now had an army and his associates – the Stafford brothers (Humphrey and Thomas) – were planning a rebellion in Worcestershire. Henry's fears of insurrection had arrived. What was more worrying was that he was now in potentially hostile terrain – the city of York 'in whose mind the memory of Richard's name remained fresh' – without the army that had won him his crown at Bosworth the summer before.[2] If the going got tough, Henry was 'doubtful' of raising the men needed to protect him and his new dynasty.

But despite appearing to have the momentum, the rebellion fell apart due to not having a clear strategy. Lovell was not presenting himself as a claimant to the throne (despite holding a distant claim), and it is likely that he intended to find and capture Henry to control the kingdom. The seizing of a monarch was an old, tried-and-tested tactic from the Wars of the Roses, and perhaps Lovell hoped that once he held control of the king he would then be able to bring about a restoration of Yorkist rule.

Henry's trusted uncle, Jasper – newly created as the Duke of Bedford – hastily put together a fighting force to counteract the rising. But what was most effective was the issue of a pardon for all rebels to disperse, which led to many of Lovell's men to reconsider their options and return home. Lovell wavered, with the historian Polydore Vergil believing that the viscount lost all confidence; he 'furtively absconded from his men in the night'.[3] The loss of their leader was all that was needed for the remaining rebels to have 'without delay cast themselves at Bedford's feet, begged for pardon, and surrendered themselves to the Crown'.[4] The collapse of Lovell's rebellion led to the disintegration of the cause of the Staffords in Worcestershire. Realising that the rebellion was crushed, they sought sanctuary, just as they had done after the events at Bosworth; however, Henry decided against recognising the tradition of respecting asylum, ordering the arrest of the pair. The eldest, Humphrey, was executed at Tyburn, while the youngest brother was spared in what Henry hoped would be an olive branch to the family.

What became of Lovell? He fled into Lancashire, before then leaving for the Continent where he found refuge at the ducal court of Burgundy, which became a safe haven for disgruntled Yorkists supporters. Their host, Margaret of Burgundy – a sister of Edward IV and Richard III – has been described by one historian in the early seventeenth century as 'having the spirit of a man and the malice of a woman'.[5] These Yorkists were intent on bringing down the Tudors, and they did not need to wait long for a new plan to rouse the North to action.

The Pretender

It would have been reasonable for Henry to have cast an apprehensive eye at the remaining Yorkists who held a claim to the throne. The generation of Edward IV and Richard III may have gone, but there were notable offspring from the former kings' siblings, notably their nephew, Edward, Earl of Warwick, who was the last surviving paternal Yorkist. However, Warwick was a mere boy 10 years of age when Henry Tudor came to the throne; his father – George, Duke of Clarence – was dead, and his mother – the daughter of the great 'Kingmaker' of the 1460s – had also passed. Henry did not waste a moment in securing the boy and placed him in the Tower, where he would remain for the following fourteen years. Despite the obvious problems, Warwick was the person who the remaining Yorkists could rally behind. Rather than be deterred in not having access to Warwick, a new, cunning plan was hatched: they would find another boy, an imposter, to pose as the real earl of Warwick. And so, the Yorkist conspirators found one boy who fit the bill: Lambert Simnel.

The true origins – or even name – of Simnel are not known. What is known is that he was groomed by a priest called Richard Symonds, who became involved in the wider Yorkist conspiracy. The boy was educated by Symonds in Oxford:

> where he studied letters and with wonderful zeal began to acquire royal manners, the goodly arts, and to memorize the royal pedigree, so that, when the need should arise, the common people might admire the boy's character and more readily believe this lie.[6]

It was decided that Simnel would make a plausible double for Edward, Earl of Warwick, thereby providing a person who an army and the nation could rally behind. However, the real puppet-master behind the whole operation was John de la Pole, the son of Elizabeth of York; yet another nephew of Richard III. The de la Poles were an influential family, and despite having made peace with the Tudors in 1485, John harboured a grudge. There was little wonder why; before Bosworth, John de la Pole was the heir to his uncle Richard. It is highly likely that de la Pole planned to use Simnel to have Henry deposed, before then taking the reins of power himself.

It was decided to use the edges of the Tudor kingdom to allow the rebellion to grow, which led to Simnel and Symonds heading to Ireland. It was a logical place: it was far away from London and the royal court, and even though the English claimed the island for themselves, the reality was that the English Crown only controlled the area around Dublin. Third, as with the North, many in Ireland held great affection for the Yorkist dynasty, primarily due to being provided with autonomy during the reign of Edward IV. Gerald Fitzgerald, the Earl of Kildare – the most significant and important noble in Ireland – welcomed the Yorkist rebels with open arms. Simnel was widely acclaimed, with a popular image showing him being carried on the shoulders of a giant of a man, Sir William Darcy, through the streets. In May 1487, Simnel was coronated in Christ Church Cathedral in Dublin, under the title of King Edward VI.

Meanwhile, John de la Pole obtained the financial support of his aunt in Burgundy, which resulted in 2,000 mercenaries under the leadership of the renowned Martin Schwartz. This force arrived in Ireland in May 1487, allowing them to combine with the Irish men to launch an invasion of England. History seemed to be repeating itself: in the summer of 1485, just two years prior, it was Henry Tudor who led a rag-tag alliance to the mainland; now in 1487 it seemed as if the momentum was with the Yorkists. This family had pulled off miraculous comebacks in both 1461 and 1471, and so perhaps it was their turn again to renew their glorious summer from a new son of York … albeit, a son of York in appearance only.

Henry was rattled. Less than two years into his reign his empire was straining at the seams. The Tudor monarch attempted to win a publicity campaign by having the real Earl of Warwick walked through the streets of London, but this did not deter the pretender gaining support. And so, the king gave the order to call up his troops, with the same key players of Bosworth reforming; the band was getting back together, including Uncle Jasper, the Earl of Oxford, and Rhys ap Thomas. But could Henry actually rely on his nobles? Similar to Richard III in 1485, he did not trust those, such as the Stanleys and other northern lords. Would they seize this opportunity to overthrow him for potentially greener grass? Perhaps Northumberland would sit back, as he did at Bosworth. Perhaps the Stanleys would wait and watch, before switching sides.

The rebels landed in Lancashire in early June as it was hoped that the North would rise and stand with them. No doubt, John de la Pole was disappointed when none of the major lords endorsed him. Polydore Vergil writes:

> But when he saw few men following him and that he had no reason for turning back, he nevertheless decided to try the fortunes of war, knowing that Mars is a god common to all, and mindful that two years previously Henry, with a small band of fighters, had conquered King Richard.[7]

The rebel army was now 8,000 strong and was heading south. There were a handful of clashes, with Lovell finally tasting a victory – after his bitter defeats in 1485 and 1486 – when he led an attack against an advanced royalist force. The Yorkist men eventually ended up in a village in Nottinghamshire, taking the decision to camp on Stoke Field. Henry's force moved in to bring about a final confrontation on 16 June 1487. The battle lasted three hours, with Polydore Vergil noting how 'both sides fought very stoutly and fiercely'; both the Germans and the Irish fought with great determination. However, Henry's superior resources determined the outcome, particularly with the Irish being poorly armed and clad.

The death toll for the Yorkist cause was high, with 4,000 men lost. Among them were John de la Pole, as well as Martin Schwartz. Richard Symonds was spared, on account of being a priest, as was the boy Lambert Simnel. The pretender was treated mercifully by Henry and was given a job in the royal kitchens where he 'turned the spit', before eventually working as a falconer for the king.[8] Margaret, however, remained a threat:

> as soon as she learned this from a rumour carried into Flanders, she began to be miserably afflicted, to mourn, grieve, and at the same time to scheme how she might hatch some more serious trouble for King Henry.[9]

Henry may have deemed the victory in 1487 sweeter than the success he experienced in 1485, for he had shown that he was no flash in the pan, and that the Tudors were here to stay. Furthermore, it also proved that the shaky, fragile alliance of 1485 – of die-hard Lancastrians, of dissident Yorkists, and spiteful Woodvilles – remained largely in shape. The whole Simnel rebellion suggested that although the North may not have loved Henry VII, it was not willing to go against him for the Yorkist cause.

The Pacification of the North

Within two years of suffocating the Yorkists at Stoke Field, the North was once again in revolt. However, in many ways, the central cause of the rebellion was Henry's own doing, rather than being stirred by a rival claimant. In early 1489, Henry signed a foreign agreement with Brittany, offering aid in their struggle against the French; Parliament voted the king £100,000 for his military endeavour, which would be paid for by the people of the country in a form of tax. There was little sympathy for Henry's foreign commitments in the North, particularly due to the impact of a poor harvest in 1488 and the feeling of being cheated due to having also to pay for taxation to ensure border control with Scotland.

In April 1489, a rebellion in Yorkshire started to form. The man tasked with dispersing the mob and bringing about peace was Henry's number one northern noble: the Earl of Northumberland. The rebels initially appealed to him, leading Northumberland to write to the royal court to ask for leniency. Henry, however, was clear: all of the tax was to be collected, particularly for fear that relenting in the North would lead to other regions also refusing to pay. The rebels did not react well to Henry's response, and at the end of April they attacked Northumberland and killed him.

By this point, Henry was not willing to let the situation simmer any longer. He sent Thomas Howard, Earl of Surrey, north with 8,000 men with the brief of dispersing the rebels and restoring order to the region. The chief cause of the rebellion may have been economic, but there were elements involved who believed that the rising could be the springboard of a new, more serious Yorkist plot. One of the leaders, John Egremont, was said to have 'borne an ill talent towards the King', and after the arrival of the royal army he left England for Margaret of Burgundy's court, the 'sanctuary and receptacle of traitors against the King'.[10]

To appease the North a general pardon was given to the rebel army. Henry paid a high cost, particularly in not being able to collect the taxes he had wanted for his Breton military adventure. The king headed North on a royal progress, using the opportunity to provide a visible presence and to make changes in the governance of the region; the Earl of Surrey was his new lieutenant, ensuring that stability was achieved. The North remained a fragile part of the Tudor empire and by the end of 1489, Henry would have been pleased that the region which had been an unsettling factor for so many past monarchs was, largely, pacified. One of his most important early challenges was achieved and his troubled apprenticeship had been served, allowing him to look beyond the North to the domains within the wider kingdom.

Chapter 3

The French Connection

The Breton Crisis and Henry VII's French war

Having signed the Treaty of Troyes in 1420, Henry V was set to rule over two kingdoms: both England and France. His ascent to such lofty heights had come in the short space of a handful of years, having ascended to the English throne in 1413, then winning the famous victory at Agincourt, before then marrying the French king's daughter and becoming accepted as the heir to the French throne.

However, this 'star of England', later wrote William Shakespeare in his play *Henry V*, was dead by the end of 1422. The union of the crowns unravelled during the reign of his son, Henry VI, leading to generations of English nobles regretting their place in the decline of England's powerbase in France. Henry V became forever known as the warrior king of the medieval age; a reign to which future English monarchs aspired.

France: The English Obsession

For generation after generation of English monarchs and lords, France was an undying obsession; it was a key driving force of many monarchs, particularly the likes of Edward III, and it was also the ruin of others, such as Henry VI. For centuries, the two countries regularly waged war, stretching back to that fateful year of 1066 when William of Normandy won all of England at the Battle of Hastings. This established an unsteady relationship due to the Norman dukes pledging fealty to the French Crown; their taking of the English kingdom created a highly unstable relationship, leading to French monarchs becoming more involved in English affairs due to the covetous desire to claim the Norman duchy.

Henry II's succession to the throne in 1154 ensured that the French obsession remained intact; during his reign the English kingdom was one part of the wider Angevin Empire of the Plantagenets. However, the reign of Henry II's son, John – in the years 1199 to 1216 – oversaw disastrous policies that led to Normandy becoming annexed by the French. By the 1300s, Edward III made a claim for the French lands via his ancestry, thereby initiating what would become known as the Hundred Years' War. Early victories at Crécy (1346) and Poitiers (1356) were celebrated; by the end of Edward's fifty-year-long reign in 1377, however, he was no closer to achieving his ambition. The war continued on, with triumphs and tragedies for both countries; the high point for England was Henry V's victory at Agincourt in 1415 that eventually led to the Treaty of Troyes, which set about linking the two crowns into one. However, Henry V's death in 1422 left this delicate relationship in the hands of his son, Henry VI, a baby king. Henry VI's reign was one of retrenchment and retreat in France, before the English were eventually expelled in the 1450s.

The period of the 1450s – 1480s was one in which England became divided during the Wars of the Roses; the French maintained an interest in English affairs, becoming involved on behalf of the Lancastrians to help Henry VI back on the throne for a brief stint in 1470–1. In the 1470s, the Yorkist Edward IV invaded France, although he was content to settle for a handsome pay-off to promptly return to England. As part of the deal, Edward renounced his claim to French soil; the French king bragged that while his father forced the English out through conflict, he was able to remove them through the use of good French wine.

However, 1483 changed the dynamic once again. The death of Edward IV destabilised the English kingdom, and Richard III's attempt to get his hands on Henry Tudor led to the challenger finding his way to the French royal court in 1484. The Tudor victory at Bosworth in 1485 was based on the generous support of France, and it would now appear that Henry VII was heavily in their debt. It may have been expected that a grateful Henry would become a strong ally of the French, and that he would be supportive in their ambitions to expand into Brittany, Flanders and possibly to the south in Italy. However, such assumptions were soon to be shattered.

The great inheritance left by Henry V may have collapsed into ruins, but Henry VII found that he was now in possession of scattered remnants of the old French-controlled lands. Although the Duchy of Normandy had been prised away – first in 1204, and then again in 1450 – the English retained control of the islands that are located in the Cotentin Peninsula off the coast of France. The continuing hold of the islands is something of a historical oddity, particularly when the shorter distance to the French mainland is considered; Jersey to the French coast is fourteen miles, while Jersey to the English coast is eighty-five miles. In 1259, Henry III signed the Treaty of Paris in which he renounced his claim to the Duchy of Normandy, although he maintained the Channel Islands; this placed the English monarch in the strange position of being a feudal vassal of the French king. This helps explain the political structures of the islands, with both Jersey and Guernsey operating their administrations (bailiwicks) and never being fully incorporated into England, remaining attached to the Crown. This anomalous situation has survived into the twenty-first century – Queen Elizabeth II was officially known as 'Duke of Normandy', with islanders toasting to 'The Queen, Our Duke'. Although ultimately, the islands themselves were not of great economic importance nor strategic value; the populations on the inhabited islands were small and they were not particularly useful in providing the setting of the launching of military attacks.

However, Calais was both of those things: economically important and of strategic value. This northern French town was captured in the early phase of the Hundred Years' War in 1347, and it became a valuable cog within the English domains due to the money generated from the wool trade, thereby being hailed by some as the brightest jewel in the English crown. This importance is reflected in Calais sending MPs to Parliament (from 1536), and the town remained a key part of the thinking of successive governments in the fifteenth and sixteenth centuries, particularly in the vast military expenditure in maintaining defences and an armed force. However, some believed that Calais was more trouble than it was worth; money was constantly ploughed into it and, perhaps more importantly, it provided an inviting base for English monarchs to launch an invasion into northern France. This was a particular temptation that Henry VII's son was unable to resist.

There were some who still coveted the return of other French lands to the English fold, particularly Aquitaine, which had been connected to the English Crown for three centuries in the medieval period. But the reality was that Henry VII's French possessions were miniscule in comparison to those held by Henry V earlier in the fifteenth century. However, this did not mean that the new Tudor monarch completely ruled out any intent on expanding these domains, even despite the help afforded him by the French in winning at Bosworth. What is incredibly telling is the signature that Henry VII used in official correspondence in 1487: he was both the King of England, as well as the King of France. The empire of Henry V may have been wiped out from history, but this did not mean that the Tudors could not consider their own attempts at resurrecting the English obsession. And one event would reignite the Anglo-French feud once more: the Breton Crisis.

The Breton Crisis

The French had long cast a covetous eye toward the Duchy of Brittany, which was a semi-autonomous region located in the north-west corner of France; they controlled their own affairs, but yet pledged fealty to the French monarch. It was the duchy in which Henry Tudor and Uncle Jasper had spent many years in exile, and during this period the Breton-French relationship began to deteriorate. In the 1480s Brittany went to war with France, ending in the defeat of the Breton forces at the Battle of St Aubin-due-Cormier in July 1488. Duke Francis II, the same man who had given shelter to Henry, was forced to acknowledge the overlordship of the French. Then, later that year, Francis died, leaving Brittany to his 12-year-old daughter Anne. Smelling weakness, the French monarchy sought to strike and to control Brittany once and for all.

In order to defend their duchy, the Bretons obtained allies; luckily, France had a catalogue of enemies who wished to see her weakened. In the autumn of 1488 embassies were sent to surrounding foreign courts, such as Emperor Maximilian of the Holy Roman Empire, King Ferdinand and Queen Isabella in Spain, as well as Henry VII in England. Henry was initially reluctant to interfere, particularly due to his own unstable position in England; however, by the end of the year he threw his hat into the ring to help Brittany.[1]

There are several reasons Henry changed his mind. First, England had long established ties with Brittany, stretching back more than a thousand years to when Britons left Britain to seek new pastures across the Channel, eventually leading to the formation of Brittany itself. As such, there were – and remain – cultural links between Brittany and other Celtic regions of Britain, particularly with the Breton and Cornish languages sharing many similarities. Second, there was a personal connection between the Tudors and Brittany, with Duke Francis having hosted Henry for more than a decade during his lowest ebb. Third, Brittany was an important location, particularly in preventing the French from controlling all the southern coast of the Channel; if France was to obtain the duchy then England would be further at the mercy of their rivals.

Some historians have claimed that there were additional – more proactive – reasons Henry became involved in the Breton-French struggle. Becoming involved in a grand alliance with other foreign monarchs would provide Henry with the opportunity to announce himself and flex his muscles on the international stage. Although he would jeopardise his relationship with France, potentially he would gain new, powerful friends in the form of the Habsburgs and the Spanish royal family. Furthermore, perhaps all of this would be a springboard for England once again making a declaration for their lost French possessions; a conflict with France could allow Henry the chance to dust off the old claims for the French throne. And this time, he could have influential friends to help him achieve the English obsession. This final reason is evidenced in an early agreement signed between Henry and Brittany, in which a clause compelled the Bretons to help with the recovery of the old French possessions.[2]

Henry spent the final months of 1488 calling a council to gain the backing of the chief lords of the country, while sending out diplomats to various royal courts in Europe. He was keen to beef up his naval presence, leading to the order to construct new 600-ton carracks, the *Sovereign* and the *Regent*. The early part of 1489 was spent negotiating with the Bretons, resulting in the Treaty of Redon. Henry agreed to provide 6,000 troops to serve in Brittany until November of 1489, with the Bretons reimbursing Henry and handing over two of their towns – Morlaix and Brest – 'as security for repayment'.[3] Furthermore, Henry followed up this treaty with other agreements; the Treaty of Dordrecht with Maximilian was confirmed in February, while the Treaty of Medina del Campo with the Spanish was signed in March. It seemed as if a firm alliance to strangle the French had been constructed.

While Henry was busy securing agreements, the French were active in taking Breton territory. In the final months of 1488 they gathered troops in Normandy to advance against Rennes, and in January they occupied key ports along the coast before seizing Brest in February 1489. Lower Brittany was now in French hands, with King Charles VIII leaving Paris 'so that he could personally command his army when it delivered the final blow to Breton resistance'.[4] This string of French victories intensified Henry's involvement, with plans to recruit a total of 10,000, split into three areas, now underway; the first, main bulk, would serve in Brittany as per the Redon treaty, the second would be based at sea, and the third would reinforce the Pale of Calais (with the possibility of getting involved in a campaign in Flanders). However, the costs associated with such a military presence were starting to rack up, and Henry had to foot the bill before waiting for an eventual reimbursement from the Bretons. The usual tax collection was not enough to cover such vast military ambitions, which led to Parliament voting in a subsidy in January 1489. Even this method of collecting money was time consuming, and so Henry resorted to the use of loans in the meantime. The higher level of taxation was a chief cause in the outbreak of the Yorkshire Rebellion in 1489, and although this revolt was eventually pacified, it exposed the weakness of the Tudor state in obtaining the funds to support such military adventures.[5] Furthermore, there were other issues that highlighted Henry's overstretch; there was a great difficulty in actually finding the ships required to sail across the men to Brittany, with the English army forced to rely on a 'motely fleet' of hired vessels from Brittany, the Netherlands and Spain.[6]

Despite these problems, when English soldiers landed in Brittany in March 1489 the whole 'political and military situation' was, in the words of historian John M. Currin, 'transformed', with the French advance halted.[7] Understandably, the Bretons celebrated the arrival of the English; in Morlaix, 'some Bretons greeted the English by placing in their windows a large red cross fashioned from paper, illuminated from behind a lantern'.[8] All of this led to the raising of morale and the ability for Brittany to become more proactive, leading to the recapture of Guingamp in April. Henry appears to have taken considerable satisfaction in the exploits of his soldiers, writing letters to the Earl of Oxford regarding English military success.

However, the French responded by putting more men into the field, leading to 1489 becoming a stalemate. Overall the year was something of a learning experience for Henry; he understood the joys of victories, but also realised the scale of the conflict in which he was now firmly entrenched. There were plenty of problems, including the fragility in retaining supply links, and issues of lack of pay and proper food for the soldiers. It became apparent that the Bretons simply did not have the money to maintain English troops, as had been previously agreed. As such, the financial burden fell on Henry. But perhaps the greater problem was in the Breton camp itself, which was deeply divided.

The Breton Divide

When Henry signed the Treaty of Redon he was pulled into the quagmire and confusion of internal Breton politics. The duchess, Anne, was the nominal head of Brittany; however, her young age was a debilitating factor in terms of providing strong leadership, as was her gender; the lack of a male heir caused much fear regarding the future of the duchy. Anne had plenty of potential suitors from all across Europe, including Maximilian, the future French king Louis XII, as well as even Henry Tudor himself back in his days of exile. Then there was Alain of Albret, who held a distant claim to the ducal throne; however, Anne refused to marry him due to her revulsion. Duke Francis had used his daughter as a means of obtaining friends, although his surrender to the French in 1488 stipulated that it was the French king who had the right to decide on whom Anne was to marry. Despite this, Francis – on his deathbed – obtained a promise from Anne that she would never bow down to the French.

In their correspondence, Henry and Anne referred to one another in warm terms; she called him 'bon pere', meaning 'good father', as well as 'mari' ('husband'). However, Henry felt more comfortable in doing business with the man trusted with protecting Anne, Jean IV de Rieux. This was due to Rieux's seasoned military experience, which gave the English greater confidence; however, Anne and Rieux continually clashed regarding strategy. The English military leaders – Lord Willoughby de Broke and Sir John Cheney – wanted to unite the Breton army with the English soldiers to bring about a clear, decisive campaign against the French. But the power politics within Brittany meant that this did not happen, due to the split of the pro-Anne side and the pro-Rieux side. Anne became suspicious of the English cosying up with Rieux, especially due to being left in the dark when a truce was agreed with France in the middle of 1489. She was especially on high alert when Henry suggested to her that the English army would come to guard her; she feared she would be kidnapped and held against her will, and so she reminded Henry that the English were in Brittany to help her, not others. Matters were not helped when Henry heard a rumour that Rieux himself was double-dealing with the French, but although Anne requested that Willoughby arrest Rieux for insubordination, the English captain realised that without Rieux the entire military operation would flounder. Both Anne and Rieux were reconciled in August 1490, but vital time was lost in dealing with internal division rather than uniting against the French.[9] This didn't stop all parties within the wider alliance continuing to double-deal: Maxmilian agreed a separate peace with France, the English continued to ignore Anne's requests, and the French put out the feelers to Anne, promising to restore Breton land when only the English had been expelled from the region.

By the autumn of 1489 the war was beginning to show on the coffers of both Henry and Charles VIII. A truce was agreed in November 1489 – at the end of the campaigning season – and over the winter around 2,000 English soldiers remained in Brittany. The winter months provided some breathing space to allow Henry to put together a second expedition in the new year; in 1490, however, the force was smaller, with estimates of men in Brittany and out at sea of up to 5,000.[10] Negotiations were held over the summer of 1490 to attempt a peace settlement, which was spearheaded by the Papacy due to a desire to unite the European monarchs to then launch a crusade against the infidel Turks. The Pope, no doubt, was calling in previous favours that he had provided Henry, such as his support in establishing the Tudor monarch on the throne and in granting favourable bulls. During the talks Henry played innocent, claiming that he had no real interest in a wider war against France and that his involvement in the Breton Crisis was due to his personal loyalty to the duchy.[11] The French delegation pointed out how the Tudors should have been more grateful to the help provided in 1485, but yet Henry was not swayed to agreeing to a permanent settlement. Although the truce was extended, Henry used the negotiating time to prepare for a fresh campaign in 1491.

The Collapse of the Bretons

Despite Henry's schemes – of bringing Maximilian back into the fold and in putting out more men into the field – the year 1491 saw the complete collapse of his Breton project. The internal divide between Anne and Rieux became toxic, while many in the duchy actively despised the encroachment of the English troops; the people of Moncontour and Saint-Brieuc dissented and planned to eject the English soldiers from their towns.[12] Furthermore, the Spanish withdrew most of their men from Brittany, leaving behind only a small garrison, thereby placing a heavier burden on Henry. Then, in March 1491, Alain of Albret – the man who Anne had snubbed – sniffed the winds of change and switched allegiance to the French. This decision gifted Nantes to the French, allowing Charles to enter the town as a triumphant hero. Momentum shifted to the French, who were able to take a swathe of towns, including Redon, Vannes and Guingamp. Brittany was cut in two, leaving English garrisons isolated from the Bretons. The pressure was too great in Morlaix, leading to the English decision to evacuate. All was looking lost.

On hearing of the fall of Nantes, Henry put together a third expedition. Anne pleaded for troops – at least 6,000 – however, the total amounted to less than 3,000, with many serving at sea. Henry's pockets simply were not big enough to assemble a larger force, and the number put together was no match for the impressive French force of 15,000. The English put forward a plan to evacuate Anne from Brittany to avoid the prospect of the French getting their hands on her; when the English ship arrived to escort her, however, Anne refused to leave. Lacking any other options, Anne accepted defeat and her fate, leading to Brittany reaching a peace settlement with France in November 1491; a week later, Anne married Charles VIII. Remaining obstinate to the end, Anne expressed her displeasure with her husband, leading to the order of two beds for the wedding entourage.

Henry didn't take the French victory very well. Two days after Charles and Anne's marriage ceremony, Henry wrote to the Pope in which he accused Charles of acting as a criminal in taking Brittany. This was followed with a flurry of letter writing in early 1492, in which the English monarch frantically attempted to resurrect an anti-French military alliance to get himself back into the game. A large amount of Henry's attention turned to a plot that intended on allies in Brittany surrendering towns into English hands, but the scheme fizzled out due to a feeling of Breton burnout at continuing the war. The French decided to fight fire with fire by developing a plot of their own. This led to the promotion of a new pretender that would cause Henry years of trouble: Perkin Warbeck.

Enter Perkin Warbeck

There are two origin stories of Perkin Warbeck. The first, outlined in his confession after he was eventually caught in 1497, suggests that he was from Tournai in Flanders and that his father was a municipal worker; Warbeck later found employment as a cloth merchant, before becoming involved in a plot to take the English throne. The second, as claimed by Warbeck from 1492, was that he was Richard, the younger son of Edward IV; Richard was one of the missing princes from the Tower, not seen since the frenzied days of 1483. But Warbeck asserted that the younger prince did not disappear or die, but rather that he escaped – 'rescued from murder by the will of God Almighty' – and found a new identity as a boy from Flanders to protect himself from a violent reprisal from Richard III.[13] In describing his escape in 1483, the contemporary historian Polydore Vergil has Warbeck explain the following:

> The man assigned the monstrous and horrible task of killing us poor innocents, the more he shuddered at this crime, the more he feared not to do it. Therefore, being of doubtful mind, so that he would both satisfy the tyrant and be free of guilt, at least in part, murdered my brother but spared me and gave me to a confederate to take to another country on the Continent and abandon in some far-flung land.[14]

After his escape, the young Prince Richard 'wandered through various nations' before being told of his 'true identity'. The sister of Edward IV, Margaret of Burgundy, helped the young boy find his feet, but what he needed was the support of other monarchs in Europe to help him recover his birth-right. Vergil writes of Warbeck giving the Scottish king, James IV, a speech, in which he pleads for help:

And so now I myself, an exile from my nation and my home, and lacking in all things, beg you, indeed I beg and beseech you with all my prayers, that you assist me, or at least give me a place to stay, so that I need not wander any more. For if by your help, your kindness, and your grace it shall have been permitted me to recover my ancestral throne, you will place not just myself, but all the kings born of my progeny who obtain it in later times, in your debt to the extent that they will never satisfy themselves in showing their gratitude.[15]

This, then, was the new threat to the still new and fragile Tudor dynasty: a pretender who now had the ear of the French. Yes, Henry had already dealt with one pretender in Lambert Simnel, but Simnel never had assistance from the powerful kingdom of France. What if France repeated the level of help that was provided to Henry himself back in 1485? Ships, men, money; Warbeck could soon be heading to England to rally the lingering Yorkist sympathies in the North. Henry was now playing a dangerous game.

The French Invasion of 1492

All of this was enough for Henry to up the ante during 1492. In the summer months, Henry's ships engaged with the French near the Breton and Norman coasts, and in June, the ever active and energetic Willoughby de Broke led a raid on the Norman coast. But Henry needed something more decisive than these skirmishes, and as such, he became resolved to invade the north of France to teach Charles a lesson. However, Henry would need to go it alone; the failure of the Breton plot showed that the duchy would not provide any support, and Henry was unable to convince Maximilian to agree to a joint invasion. Some historians, such as John M. Currin, believe that Henry was now out of options, and that he was involved so deep in the quagmire that only an invasion 'could salvage his honour and turn his loss into some kind of profit'.[16] Like a gambler too far in the red, Henry needed one final bet – placing everything on black – in a desperate attempt to reverse his fortunes.

An impressive 12,000 men were assembled for the invasion, which took place from Calais in October 1492. Highlighting the significance of this operation was Henry's personal involvement at the head of the army; this time, it was personal. The key aim was to take Boulogne on the northern coast, with the town becoming besieged over several weeks, during which time little of note occurred aside from the death of Sir John Savage, one of Henry's commanders at Bosworth. Savage was captured while out reconnoitring, fighting to the death rather than surrendering. The invasion, then, resulted in a stalemate. However, the incursion of the English army was enough to bring the French to the negotiation table to obtain a settlement, which led to the Peace of Etaples in November 1492.

The treaty was a favourable one for Henry. The French agreed to reimburse him for his vast military expenditure in Brittany, and also provided him with a healthy pension of 50,000 crowns per year (the equivalent of 5 per cent of Henry's total income). More importantly, the French renounced their support for Warbeck's claim to the English throne, thereby providing Henry with a layer of security from fear of a French-endorsed invasion. In return, Henry admitted that Brittany had been lost and was now firmly under the control of France. Furthermore, he also renounced any lingering claims that he may have harboured to the French crown. Both business partners were, on the whole, content, and Henry travelled back to England a satisfied man.

The French, having secured Brittany, were now free to shift their attention elsewhere, leading to the outbreak of the Italian Wars later in the 1490s. As for Charles himself, he suffered the ignominy of dying after hitting his head against the lintel of a door. His marriage to Anne had produced no heirs, and so the French crown passed to a second cousin once removed, Louis XII. Anne had desires to liberate her fallen duchy, but Louis acted fast; he had his two-decade-long marriage annulled and quickly married Anne. The couple had six children, but all died young.

What are we to make of the Tudor involvement in the Breton Crisis? And to what extent was Henry a perpetrator of war? The majority of historians view Henry VII as a man of peace who had limited intentions in terms of desiring further lands beyond his own kingdom. The Breton Crisis and French invasion could be seen, then, as the actions of a monarch who had no real desire for war, but who defended Brittany out of loyalty, as well as for the chance to secure a hefty pay-out if the French overwhelmed the Bretons. As historian P.S. Crowson claims,

Henry simply 'went through the motions' without fully committing.[17] However, the cost and energy spent in the period 1489–92 – to the tune of £124,000 – shows, in the words of John M. Currin, that Henry, 'who was never frivolous in expenditure, was engaged in a serious military undertaking'.[18] The debate continues regarding Henry's intentions: was he a man of peace – described by his poet laureate as '*Rex Pacificus*'[19] – or rather someone who ultimately desired the French throne?[20] If the cards had fallen differently and if Brittany had been defended, perhaps Henry would have used this as the first step in 'a future campaign for recovery of Normandy, and Guyenne, and perhaps even the French Crown itself'.[21]

But despite the claims of some historians, it is unrealistic to believe that Henry had such wide ambitious dreams. His involvement in the Breton Crisis highlighted the incapability of the English government to wage a full-scale war, with the majority of his military actions being defensive rather than offensive. When Henry put pen to paper on the peace treaty at the end of 1492 he did so in the belief that his honour had been safeguarded, and more importantly, that his kingdom was now secure from the threat of the French. In this view, and particularly regarding the context of the early part of the Tudor period – not yet on the throne for a decade – the entire Breton Crisis and French invasion was a success.

Chapter 4

The Disturbed Land

Henry VII's problems in Ireland in the 1490s

On the evening of 16 August 1487, Henry VII would have had cause for concern when looking at the aftermath on the battlefield at Stoke Field. The Tudors were victorious, but the confederacy that had formed against him demonstrated that all was not well within his imperial possessions, particularly the land across the Irish Sea.

Henry sent a diplomat, Sir Richard Edgcumbe, across to Ireland to obtain new oaths from the defeated Irish lords, in which they pledged the following:

> I become feithful and true ligeman unto kyng Henry the vijth kyng of England of Fraunce and lord of Irland of lif and lym and erthly worship and feyth and trouth. I shall beer unto hym as my soveraigne liege lord to lyve and dye agenst all maner creatours so god help me and his seyntes.[1]

Sir Richard left Ireland having consolidated Henry's authority, but the reality was that the Tudor hold of Ireland was precarious, ready to collapse at any moment.

The Disturbed Land

The Norman incursion into Ireland in the twelfth century had a profound impact on the island in the subsequent centuries. Ireland was treated as one of England's earliest colonies, with various monarchs interfering with the aim of obtaining control, with many English lords looking on the Irish as a savage people. By the fifteenth century the Lordship of Ireland had been established, with English authority acknowledged in principle; however, the reality meant that any English king needed the

37

support of the Irish lords to maintain peace and stability. Obtaining the support of the Anglo-Irish nobles was not a straightforward task, for they were continually in conflict with one another. The most serious factional rivalry in the late 1400s came in the form of the Geraldines (the earls of Kildare) and the Butlers (the earls of Ormond), with the period seeing a multitude of battles and skirmishes. Irish clans could put out significant armies in the field; in the 1480s, the Earl of Desmond was capable of putting out 400 horsemen and battalions of crossbowmen and gunners.[2] The various competing interests within Ireland – of the English administration in the Pale of Dublin, the Irish lords, and the native Irish – has led to the claim that Ireland was 'a disturbed land'.[3]

The task of obtaining acquiescence from the Irish lords was made even more difficult in the fourteenth century when the English Crown lunged from one crisis to another; particularly the defeat in the Hundred Years' War in the 1450s, the decades of instability caused by the Wars of the Roses, and after Bosworth, a new insecure dynasty on the throne. As a consequence, Henry VII had to tread carefully. He depended on the Irish lords to maintain enough law and order so that the island did not break out into open rebellion, and he did not have the time or space to concentrate on a different policy; and importantly, he did not have the money to support more ambitious plans. However, if he sided too heavily with one faction then the entire, fragile symbiosis could be destabilised. The same tactics that worked with the North of England, in which rebels could be reached and punished, would not work with Ireland: raising an army to cross a sea and then being stuck in a hostile land was filled with risks and problems.

As such, it was wise for English monarchs to heed the advice of the Irish lords; bestow titles and honours upon them, take a laissez-faire approach, and allow them to do their job. This was the approach taken by Yorkist monarchs in the second half of the 1400s. However, Henry could not undertake the policy of his kingly predecessors. For the key noble in all of Ireland – the Earl of Kildare – had been previously involved with the Lambert Simnel Rebellion.

The Uncrowned King of Ireland

Gerald Fitzgerald, the eighth Earl of Kildare, has had many nicknames bestowed upon him, including 'The Great Earl' and the 'Uncrowned

King of Ireland'. If the Stanleys had been the 'kingmakers' on the battlefield at Bosworth, then Kildare was the man who could potentially make or break the Tudor hold on Ireland. Kildare had obtained his title on his father's death in 1477, and he continued the ascendency of his bloodline as the preeminent family in Irish politics by serving in the role as Lord Deputy of Ireland. On coming to power in 1485, Henry VII retained Kildare in this position, but he had every cause to be concerned over the issue of loyalty.

The Fitzgeralds had more than their fair share of run-ins with Henry's forerunners. The government of Edward IV ordered for annual accounts to be submitted, but this was ignored, and when the Yorkist monarch decided to put an English lord in Kildare's place, the Irish lords created a breakaway parliament. Edward IV backtracked, restoring Kildare to his position, and nothing more was said on the matter. Yet despite these feuds, it was widely believed that the lords in Ireland were, on the whole, happy with the Yorkists. This placed Henry in a difficult position, as a Lancastrian claimant to the throne. His initial policy of attempting to establish a firm friendship by maintaining the status quo was reasonable, especially in the delicate early years when he faced rebellions in the North, a lack of funds, questions about his legitimacy, and potential banana-skins within his own royal court.

However, Henry's faith was soon dashed with the escalation of the Simnel rebellion in 1486–87. Although he was not the ring-leader of the rebellion, Kildare played a key role in welcoming – 'with open arms' – Simnel and Margaret of Burgundy's German mercenaries.[4] What is more, Kildare watched as Simnel was crowned as the 'rightful king' in a ceremony in Christ Church Cathedral, Dublin.[5] The Battle of Stoke Field in August 1487 was a disaster for Kildare; his brother, Thomas, was slain on the battlefield, and now the whole Fitzgerald powerbase was at threat of ruin.

However, Henry did not act in the same way as he had in the aftermath of Bosworth; Kildare was not attainted and was instead pardoned. But this speaks more of the lack of palatable options that Henry had available; punishing Kildare risked all of Ireland exploding, leading to further problems in attempting to keep it under control. But Henry was keen to flex his royal muscles; a year after Stoke Field, the Irish lords were invited to a banquet at Greenwich Palace. The waiter who attended Kildare's table was none other than Lambert Simnel himself. Kildare's 'king' had been reduced to the status of a servant, and this was a clear reminder as to the fate that could befall the Irish lords if they chose to step out of line in the future.

Warbeck's Arrival

In 1492, fresh rumours spread across Ireland. Perkin Warbeck, the new pretender who had caused Henry anxiety with the French, landed in Cork. As had happened with Lambert Simnel, the Irish lords were amenable to what Warbeck could offer and how they could turn the situation to their advantage. As had happened during the Wars of the Roses, a weak and destabilised Crown provided opportunities for greater autonomy and sway for the lords.

Furthermore, other problems were brewing in Ireland in the early 1490s, with the Fitzgeralds and Butlers once again rubbing against one another. In 1492, a deputy to the Earl of Ormond ran in fear of his life through the streets of Dublin, finding safety in St Patrick's Cathedral. Kildare himself followed him into the building and spoke to him through the door behind which the deputy was secured; a hole was cut in the door to allow both men to shake hands to assure the deputy of Kildare's goodwill. The deputy, however, feared that if he placed his hand through the hole then it would be 'hacked off', and so, Kildare himself was said to have:

> stretcht in his hand to him, and so the dore was opened, they
> both embraced, the storme appeased, and all their quarrels
> fro that presente, rather discountinued than ended.[6]

However, the quarrel itself was not resolved with this one incident.

The factional divides created a prospect for Warbeck to find support and use Ireland as a base; if this happened, Henry could expect a fresh invasion from the island. Plots were developing, with Warbeck writing in a letter dated September 1493 that he was 'joyfully welcomed' by both Kildare and Ormond. Consequently, in November 1493, Henry summoned Kildare and Ormond, along with other leading magnates, to England. This was, no doubt, Henry's attempt to gather them together to talk some sense into them, and to impress upon them their loyalty to the

English crown. The instability led to Henry forging ahead with a new policy to disregard the long-established laissez faire approach; he would become more hands-on in creating his youngest son, Prince Henry, as Lord of Ireland, and in sending across a new lieutenant to firmly state his control. When Kildare and Ormond returned to Ireland, they did so in the company of Sir Edward Poynings, the man given the unenviable task of cementing Tudor rule.

The Diplomatic Trouble-Shooter

Edward Poynings was an early convert to the Tudor cause, having attempted an uprising against Richard III back in 1483 within the wider, failed, Buckingham Rebellion. He evaded capture by escaping abroad, before ending up in the company of Henry Tudor in Brittany. From that point onward, Poynings was right by Henry's side: as they moved into France, there on the fateful landing at Milford Haven in early August 1485, as well as at Bosworth. Poynings developed a reputation as a diplomatic trouble shooter, as shown in his various travels in the years after Bosworth; in 1488 he was part of a commission that inspected the Pale of Calais, before serving as governor in 1493, and in 1492 he was part of the negotiations of the Treaty of Etaples with the French. Furthermore, he also had extensive dealings in Burgundy: in 1492, he commanded 1,500 men to aid Emperor Maximilian against a rebellion, laying siege to Sluys and being a principal part of negotiations that ended the rising. Then, in 1493, he was sent on a diplomatic mission to Archduke Philip to obtain agreement on the expulsion of Warbeck from the lands of Burgundy. Unfortunately, Philip was unable to agree, due to the powerbase of Henry's continual arch-enemy, Margaret of Burgundy. Such a long list of achievements meant that Poynings was exactly the type of man that Henry needed to place in Ireland to make sense of the mess that was unravelling there.

Some historians believe that Poynings was sent across to Ireland with the objective of conquering it. The reason, argued G.O. Sayles, was that if it remained only partly controlled then it would remain 'a continual menace to the stability of the new and still precarious Tudor dynasty'.[7] However, such an ambition was not realistic nor likely; Poynings was only sent across with a mere 400 men, which could not rival the armies that the Irish lords could put into the field. As such, Henry's immediate aim appears to have been to beef up the Pale and to achieve stability, before then setting out to punish the Warbeck-supporting rebels. A final aim was to attempt to make Ireland profitable with the hope of it paying its way.

Poynings was assisted with a few of Henry's trusted advisors, including Henry Deane (recently appointed Bishop of Bangor, and a future archbishop of Canterbury) as chancellor, as well as another one of Henry's long-term supporters, Hugh Conway, as treasurer. But Poynings faced a veritable hornet's nest; he had the two quarrelling rivals – Kildare and Ormond – by his side, both of whom were tasked with assisting him in bringing the rebels to heel. His first action was to head north into Ulster to find and punish O'Donnell, O'Hanlon and Magennis, all of whom had supported Warbeck in his bid for the crown. However, the expedition was stunted when rumour spread that Kildare was in cahoots with O'Hanlon and Magennis. Poynings and Kildare had a 'bitter quarrel', which culminated in Kildare being arrested.[8] The Great Earl was charged with plotting the ruin of Poynings' enterprise and with communicating with England's enemies; his reputation was further tarnished when his brother James seized Carlow Castle in the south. Poynings was forced to abandon his initial mission into Ulster, turning south to retake Carlow Castle.

These first few weeks would have been enough to provide Poynings – and Henry – a taste of what it was like to meddle with Irish affairs. Poynings took stock of the situation and went to Drogheda to summon the Irish parliament. This parliament was created in the 1200s and was used by the English Crown to obtain support and cooperation from the Irish lords for the various taxes levied by the English administration. It had played a vital role in the Simnel affair, with the Irish lords agreeing to bestow the crown on the young pretender in 1487; understandably, the English were keen to control it to avoid any other mishaps. Poynings' Parliament opened in early December 1494 and lasted until April 1495; in that time, a series of laws were enacted, including punishment of Kildare's supposed treachery (he was attainted and packed off to the Tower in England), as well as passing a series of acts that are known to history as Poynings' Law. This was a significant change, thereby highlighting the Tudor thirst for control of Ireland.

All Irish parliamentary bills were to be sent to the English governor, and also the English monarch, to be scrutinised, amended or potentially rejected. This provided Henry with the power of veto, and as such, it limited the power of the Irish lords. As historian Patrick Weston Joyce noted, this made the Irish parliament 'a mere shadow, entirely dependent on the English king and council'.[9] It would not be until centuries later, in 1782, that Ireland freed itself of Poynings' Law. Other notable developments involved the consolidation of English rule in Ireland, with chief castles to be placed in English hands, and it was to be illegal to carry weapons and make private wars without licence from the English administration. In addition to this, the 1366 Statutes of Kilkenny were re-enacted, in an attempt to once again prevent the English colonists adopting Irish customs.

After the passing of these acts, Poynings then continued his attempts to punish the rebels in Ulster, although this proved inconclusive. More pressing matters were at hand when, in July 1495, Perkin Warbeck himself was back on Irish shores. With eleven ships, Warbeck blockaded the port of Waterford in the south of Ireland, while his ally the Earl of Desmond laid siege to the town. Waterford held out long enough for Poynings to arrive with support, at which point Warbeck scarpered to the sea. All of these events emphasised to Henry the instability of the disturbed land; there were to be no easy solutions to achieve his aims.

The Kildare Supremacy

In January 1486, after more than twelve energetic and stressful months in the snake pit of Irish politics, Poynings was recalled back to England. His attempts to improve the overall administration of the Pale was beset with difficulties, due largely to subordinate officials who impaired his success. However, some contemporaries, such as the under-treasurer, declared that the things were 'in moche bettir odir than hath ben in tyme past',[10] which is demonstrated with the improvement in customs revenue. After his Irish commission, Poynings remained busy as a diplomatic problem solver for Henry; he was appointed to conduct Catherine of Aragon to London, in preparation for her marriage to Prince Arthur, and in 1508 he conducted negotiations for the marriage of Henry's sister, Princess Mary, to Prince Charles of Castile (although the marriage did not go ahead). Then, during Henry VIII's reign, he continued this good service, notably assisting during the French War of 1513, and then at the summit of the Field of Cloth of Gold in 1520, before passing away at his manor in Kent in 1521.

In a volte-face, Henry restored the Great Earl to his position as his lieutenant in Ireland in August 1496. Kildare had suffered greatly over the past eighteen months: he had lost his land and powerbase, while his wife – Alison – died soon after his arrest, reportedly due to grief. But Kildare, ever the great political survivor, endured a trial and managed to convince Henry that it was actually the other lords in Ireland who were the real problem. However, the reappointment was a risky one; Kildare's previous actions suggested that he could be interested in future plots, and his reappearance in Ireland could render the land back into factional mire. But Henry realised the sobering truth: Ireland was virtually ungovernable, and it was better to make a deal with the only person who could potentially restore a balance of power, even if it came at a cost. As the king himself reputedly declared: 'All Ireland cannot govern this Earl; then let this Earl govern all Ireland'.[11]

So, Kildare triumphantly returned to Ireland, with his second wife, Elizabeth St John, a distant cousin of Henry, in tow. He sought to build bridges with his former enemies, specifically the Butlers, and a pact was drawn up and agreed, with the two earls promising to be 'loving, amiable, friendly and concordable'.[12] Clear problems remained and the faction-fighting didn't stop with the peace pact, but most importantly, Kildare stuck to his word in remaining loyal to the Tudors. In a letter to Kildare from June 1498, Henry called him 'our right trusty and right well-beloved cousin, the earl of Kildare', which suggests that faith between the two had been restored.[13] In the years until the end of his life, Kildare served as Henry's representative in Ireland with a stern, temperamental, tough approach. This is seen in his dealing with a rebellion in Cork in 1500, in which he ordered the hanging of the city's mayor, and in fighting against rebels at the Battle of Knockroe in 1504, in which his men engaged in looting on their victorious march home.

In 1513, while on a military expedition against another Irish clan, Kildare was shot while watering his horse. Although injured, he moved onward to Kildare town, before dying on the third day in September at the age of 57. Such was the level of Kildare's fame that a legend developed regarding his life and death; he was supposedly a master in the black arts and had the ability to shapeshift; however, having transformed into a goldfinch he was whisked away by a sparrowhawk and never heard from again. Another tale suggests that Kildare sleeps beneath the Curragh of Kildare and is awaiting the right moment to return to drive out the English from Ireland. All of these fictional stories attest to Kildare's political power during this period, and although his death was momentous, it did not result in the end of the Kildare supremacy; his son continued in his father's footsteps until the religious and political upheavals of the 1530s during the reign of Henry VIII.

Ultimately, Henry VII was never able to bring the entire island to heel, although it is unlikely that he realistically ever expected to do so. His return to reliance on Kildare suggests that he realised his attempts to rule Ireland in a similar manner to other regions of his empire – such as the North – was an impossibility. But in reaching this conclusion, Henry tried a variety of policies: maintenance of the status quo, to taking a more proactive approach, before then reverting back to the status quo with Kildare. These continuing shifts did result in a key accomplishment, however: the veto over the Irish parliament and the removal of any further threats to the English throne. As such, Henry was ever the pragmatist, seeking workable solutions to his problems, and in the post-1496 re-establishment of Kildare he found a solution that meant that Ireland would not be as likely to pose any further problems during his reign.

Chapter 5

The Wild West

The Cornish rebellions of 1497

The key actions of the Wars of the Roses took place hundreds of miles away from the distant land of Cornwall; however, a notable side-drama happened that reflects the changing pendulum of the fortunes of the Lancastrian and Yorkist houses. In 1483, Richard Edgcumbe of Cotehele estate decided to throw his support behind a rebellion to replace Richard III with the unknown Henry Tudor. The rebellion collapsed, and soldiers were sent to Cotehele to arrest Edgcumbe:

> Edgcumbe knew what would happen now that suspicion was aroused. He would be seized by a party of soldiers, taken to the Tower, and beheaded. He thought there was time to prepare for flight, but he was wrong, for a servant ran in to say that there were soldiers in the garden. Sir Richard had no wish to be dragged out of hiding in cellar or attic. He leapt through the window and ran to the woods, but a solider saw him and the hunt began.
>
> Sir Richard ran through the woods to the river with a wild hope of finding a boat; but no boat was there. Wondering whether he might swim to the other side and escape, he panted on, and a prayer rose to his lips. As if from Heaven, an idea came to him. Making a desperate effort, he rounded a wood-covered cape. There he stopped a moment, hurled a great stone into the water, threw his cap after it, and plunged once more into the woods. The next moment the foremost soldiers rounded the cape. They had heard the splash and saw the floating cap. After watching in vain for some time they concluded that the exhausted Edgcumbe had been swept away by the current; they returned to London and reported one more traitor dead.[1]

Edgcumbe was able to escape the kingdom to reach Brittany, where he joined Henry Tudor's growing forces. Two years later, he returned with the Tudor army, and fought at Bosworth to help Henry topple Richard. For his efforts Edgcumbe was rewarded and became a key cog in the Tudor state machinery in the 1480s. However, Edgcumbe had a personal quest: to make a triumphant return to Cornwall to obtain his revenge against the man who had chased him and displaced him in 1483: Henry Bodrugan.

Bodrugan had developed an undesirable reputation as a lawless and violent menace, and the new Tudor regime called for his arrest. Edgcumbe played cat-and-mouse, with Bodrugan on the run; the climax of which was a daring leap from a cliff to escape. Bodrugan appears to have survived, although both he and his family name faded into obscurity, thereby demonstrating the power of the rise of the Tudor supporters. But despite such positive beginnings, the Cornish and the Tudors would go head-to-head, leading to a year of uprisings in which 'the whole kingdom was in chaos',[2] culminating – for Henry – in 'the most dangerous day of his reign'.[3]

Cornwall's Odd Constitutional Status

> Britain is divided into four parts; whereof the one is inhabited of Englishmen, the other of Scots, the third of Welshmen, and the fourth of Cornish people, which all differ among themselves, either in tongue, either in manners, or else in laws and ordinances.[4]

So wrote Polydore Vergil, an historian from the start of the sixteenth century. It outlines how the island of Britain contained separate identities, highlighting how the Cornish were considered at that time as distinct as a Scotsman from a Welsh person. Today the Cornish are confined to one county of the English state, but there were clear cultural differences between the English and the Cornish that stretched back centuries. This is illustrated with the foundation myths of the early British tribes; while Brutus named Britain after himself, it was Cornieus – having fought the giant Gogmagog – who established Cornwall. As Mark Stoyle notes: 'Cornishmen and women continued to regard themselves as the descendants of Cornieus until well into the early modern period. They spoke of him with pride, alleging him to have been the first Duke of

Cornwall.'[5] The arrival of the Anglo-Saxon tribes led to the gradual removal of the Celtic peoples, leading to the reduction of influence and political autonomy of the Cornish. During the medieval period, Cornwall was brought more firmly into the English state; first by the development of the Earldom – a title that many close to the English royal family held – and then in the creation of the Duchy in the 1300s. The Duchy put Cornwall in an odd position: it became welded to the English royal family – with the eldest son of the monarch automatically becoming Duke of Cornwall – but yet it retained a level of autonomy that made it distinct to other English regions.

This constitutional anomaly is seen nowhere more clearly than in the Cornish Stannary Parliament. Initially established in the thirteenth century, this parliament had power and protection over those involved in tin mining; and because so many in Cornwall were involved in tin, this meant the parliament had large powers and influence. This can be seen with its own tax system, which exempted tinners from other taxes and obligations initiated by Westminster; as such, the Stannaries seemed to confirm Cornwall's odd 'quasi-autonomous status'.[6] Furthermore, the Cornish remained distinct from the English through its culture and customs, principally the use of a separate language. Although English was the preferred tongue of the ruling gentry, Cornish remained the language of the majority of the population, particularly in west Cornwall.[7]

Contemporary accounts highlight the difference between the Cornish and the English. Writing in the early seventeenth century, Francis Bacon outlined the harsh environment of Cornwall:

> the people there grew to grudge and murmur, the Cornish being a race of men stout of stomach, mighty of body and limb, and that lived hardly in a barren country, and many of them could for a need live underground, that were tinners.[8]

Vergil similarly stresses how Cornwall was the 'least fruitful of regions' and 'most barren part of the island'.[9] The words of a Venetian ambassador, who spent a week in Cornwall in 1506, supports such words:

> We are in a very wild place which no human being ever visits, in the midst of a most barbarous race, so different

in language and custom from Londoners and the rest of England that they are as unintelligible to these last as to the Venetians.[10]

Cornwall, then, was different and distinct to England. To paraphrase L.P. Hartley: Cornwall was a foreign country; they did things differently there.

The Cornish Wild West

After the drama of his flight and return to Cornwall, Sir Richard Edgcumbe proved himself as one of Henry VII's most trusted diplomatic trouble-shooters. He negotiated peace with Scotland, dealt with the Earl of Kildare, and was involved in the discussions with Brittany, before dying across the sea at Morlaix in September 1489. However, unfortunately for Henry, not every Cornishmen was as useful and loyal as Edgcumbe. The Tudor regime rewarded the Cornish who supported him, using the Duchy of Cornwall to dish out patronage.[11] However, Cornwall proved to be – in many ways – ungovernable and lawless.

During the 1490s, 'disturbances in Cornwall were commonplace', including piracy and smuggling – old traits of Cornish life – along with burglaries and robberies.[12] There were numerous incidents, including one from July 1492 in which 200 men attacked the Franciscan friary at Bodmin 'apparently in a dispute over tin rights'.[13] The misadventures of rabble-rouser Roger Whalley demonstrates the volatility of the region; he racked up twenty-six complaints from neighbours – the Tudor equivalent of antisocial behaviour orders – which included 'driving off their cattle, killing their sheep, refusing to pay tithes, and assaulting John Trenowith' and his wife, before shooting at Trenowith's windows.[14]

A key reason for this instability was the lack of engagement of the bulk of the Cornish population with the Tudor regime. Although Henry had drawn in many notable members of the gentry – such as Richard Edgcumbe and Richard Nanfan – there remained a disconnect with the remainder of the Cornish-speaking population; a detachment that grew only wider during the period.[15] The political instability of the Wars of the Roses had led to a merry-go-round of control, as illustrated with the example of Edgcumbe and his rival Bodrugan. As such, the gentry did not have as strong a hold on the region as in earlier and later times, thereby providing weight behind historian Philip Payton's remark that Cornwall experienced a 'lawless independence' during the late 1400s.[16] Also, tin-mining – which was so crucial to the local economy – had suffered during the fifteenth century. The annual yield had fallen from 1,600 thousand-weight in 1400, to 800 thousand-weight in 1455, not rising above 1,000 until 1496.[17] This decline can be contributed, in part, to the political upheaval of the period, but also due to the inability to extract the 'more difficult deposits'.[18]

Despite the depression in the tin industry, the Duchy of Cornwall introduced new rules of regulation, thereby attempting – in a similar manner to other centralising aspects of the new Tudor state – to provide a greater degree of control. However, these new rules were ignored by the Cornish, due to appealing 'little to the conservative and independent Cornish spirit'.[19] It was just another in a long-list of examples of those in the region choosing to avoid the wishes of their new Tudor masters. This led Henry VII to take a decision: he suspended the Stannary Parliament. As with the other corners of his kingdom – the North and Ireland – Cornwall would be brought to heel, thereby confirming Payton's assessment: 'Cornwall and the Tudors were on an inevitable collision course'.[20]

The First Rebellion: The Rise of An Gof

The hard-line approach of the Tudor government did not win over hearts and minds in Cornwall. The removal of the proud, historic institution of the Stannary Parliament was an insult, but worse was to come. In January 1497 the Westminster Parliament voted for new taxes to pay for the resources to prosecute the looming war with Scotland. Four commissioners were appointed to oversee the collection of this tax in Cornwall, but it was argued by the Cornish that the payment for the defence of the Scottish border should come from those who lived in that region, as had happened in the past. The attempt at collecting this tax was the straw that broke the camel's back.

Resistance to the tax first appeared in the west of Cornwall; the area was already strained due to the previous actions of Sir John Oby, the Provost of Glasney College, 'who was notorious for his zealous behaviour as a tax collector and could be expected to enforce the new tax levy with enthusiasm'.[21]

A leader from the people rose up: Michael Joseph, now known to history as *An Gof* (the Smith),[22] and support came from other areas of Cornwall, including members of the local gentry, as well as the rabble-rousing Roger Whalley. Joseph has been portrayed as providing the protest with its heart, and in Thomas Flamank the revolt found its brain. Flamank was 'a clever and persuasive lawyer', a former MP, who 'emerged as the intellectual leader of the rebellion'.[23] Flamank clearly found this new taxation one step too far and his decision to involve himself in the movement was in opposition to those in his family; his father was one of the appointed tax commissioners for Cornwall, and his father-in-law was a justice of the peace.

There was a long list of problems: of over-taxation and the reduction of the status of the Cornish. However, despite momentum there was the lack of a clear plan. The choices were to maintain peace and order and 'humbly ... petition the king', or to take their grievances directly to Henry himself.[24] It was agreed that the Tudor king was not at fault for the problems, but rather it was 'the cruelty of his counsellors' who were 'the cause of this evil'.[25] A direct demonstration was required; the leaders would gather their men and head to Henry in London. If Henry listened, then their efforts would be rewarded. And if he didn't? Then war would be waged.

Strikingly, the rebels marched across the south of England 'with frightening speed', from Cornwall to Devon, then into Somerset.[26] In the town of Wells they met James Tuchet, Lord Audley, 'a nobleman of an ancient family' who had favoured the Yorkists, leading to him missing out on the spoils of Tudor patronage. The Cornish now had a peer within their number, and Audley was with 'great gladness and cries of joy accepted as their general'.[27] The rebels then moved on to Salisbury, to Winchester, and then into Kent. Due to Kent's history of revolts – notably that of Jack Cade's Rebellion from 1450 – it was hoped that the Cornish would find further support. However, no help was forthcoming, and in fact they experienced the reverse; the Earl of Kent gathered men to resist the Cornish.

By this point they had grown to 15,000 strong. The rebels camped on Blackheath; in the near distance lay Greenwich and the City of London. Historian Thomas Penn describes the scene:

> London, terrified by reports of the ravaging Cornishmen, bolstered its defences; Queen Elizabeth, Lady Margaret and the royal children were moved into the Tower.[28]

Polydore Vergil expands on the chaos and confusion:

> fear mounted hourly within the city, the alarm was sounded
> in every ward, men came running to the gates, and likewise
> the watch and was wonderfully maintained lest by chance
> that mob of paupers might suddenly descend on them to get
> within the walls and steal the townsmen's wealth.[29]

How true was this fear of 'ravaging' rebels? Accounts from historians are divided on their portrayals of the behaviour of the Cornish. Polydore Vergil – writing twenty years after the rebellion – is dismissive of the Cornish, calling them 'madmen', 'the rabble', a 'mob of paupers', a 'band of roiling dregs', and deeming them 'wretched Cornishmen'.[30] However, other accounts clearly state that the Cornish acted 'without any slaughter, violence, or spoil of the country'.[31] Furthermore, in the early seventeenth century Francis Bacon noted that the rebels 'behaved themselves quietly and modestly by the way as they went' through the country.[32] This is supported by modern historians such as Payton, who stresses that the rebels were able to resist 'the temptation to loot and slaughter'.[33] However, past rebellions had shown that things could turn nasty quite quickly whenever an angry mob was involved.

As such, Henry and the people of London were correct to be concerned. Henry was facing considerable pressure in 1497: the Scottish army was threatening north of the border, and now he had to deal with a second threat from the West. The Cornish rebelled just as he was planning on sending men north to deal with James IV, thereby leading to a change in the scheme with soldiers being kept behind near the capital. The king's army eventually swelled to 25,000 men, principally consisting of those who had originally been 'earmarked for action against the Scots'.[34] Lord Giles Daubeney was placed in command, a man Henry trusted deeply; Daubeney had fled to Brittany to help support his rebellion and was there at Bosworth, as well as being present during the invasion of northern France in 1492, and who was made Lord Chamberlain after the execution of Sir William Stanley.

In comparison, the Cornish rebels were shrinking in size. The lack of further support from Kent had knocked their confidence, and the growth of Henry's forces made many rethink their part in the cause. Vergil notes how 'no small number of them lost their enthusiasm and, furtively stealing away by night, went home'.[35] Estimates place the strength of An Gof's men at 10,000 or under on the day of the fateful Battle of Blackheath. Of course, there remained the element of pure chance. What if the king's army failed him? What if the rebels got the better of their opponents? Furthermore, there was also the reputation of Cornish archers; their fame stretched back to the epic English victory at Agincourt in 1415. However, the reality was that the Cornish rebels were out-matched and out-gunned; they did not have the resources – such as artillery and cavalry – to match the royal army, and they did not have the experience to plan a successful battle.

Lord Daubeney took the initiative by leading a charge against the rebels, and although he was briefly captured, he was able to regain his freedom and pushed forward.[36] Francis Bacon describes the scene:

> The rebels maintained the fight for a small time, and for their persons showed no want of courage. But being ill armed and ill fed, and without horse or artillery, they were with no great difficulty cut in pieces and put to flight.[37]

The outcome, then, was predictable. The royal army were victorious, and slayed the rebels; some estimates – such as that of Polydore Vergil and Francis Bacon – predicts that 2,000 were slaughtered, although other estimates – such as Rowse – note that 200 were killed. There remains significant differences in terms of what historians can agree; with Mark Stoyle noting how 'many hundred Cornishmen' were killed at Blackheath.[38] Contemporary accounts note that 300 of the king's men perished; Bacon notes that 'most of them [were] shot with arrows, which were reported to be of length of a tailor's yard, so strong and mighty a bow the Cornishmen were said to draw'.[39] However, a more modern study – from A.L. Rowse – puts the figure far below 300, at a mere eight. Once the dust had settled, Henry rode out to Blackheath and rewarded those who had defended him; several were knighted, in a similar manner to what had happened after the victories at Bosworth in 1485 and Stoke Field in 1487. Then after doing so, he moved back to the relieved and rejoicing people of London, attending a thanksgiving service at St Paul's Cathedral.

The rebels were treated lightly: they were pardoned and were free to return to their homes. Both Vergil and Bacon believe that this was because Henry felt pity, although it is more likely that he decided to use the occasion to build bridges with the Cornish, rather than to create future enemies. However, the fate of the leaders was far more gruesome. Two of them – Flamank and Audley – were caught on the field of battle, while Joseph attempted to flee for sanctuary and was caught before he could enter the church. After their sentences, Lord Audley was 'led from Newgate to Tower Hill in a paper coat painted with his own arms, the arms reversed, the coat torn'; [40] due to being a peer of the realm, he was reserved the honour of being beheaded at Tower Hill.

Such a refined death was not reserved for Joseph or Flamank. A day earlier – on 26 June 1497 – they were condemned to be hanged, drawn and quartered at Tyburn. Again, Henry demonstrated compassion by sparing them the pain of the second and third steps in the punishment; instead, they both were hanged to death, before their corpses were decapitated and quartered. Furthermore, he also reconsidered the initial idea of having the body parts sent to Cornwall as a warning to other would-be rebels; he felt it best to avoid inflaming further passions in the region.[41] The body parts, though, were still used to demonstrate Henry's authority:

> Their heads, boiled and tarred, were jammed on spikes on London Bridge; their body parts were dismembered, some nailed to the city gates.[42]

Before their executions, some believe that Flamank spoke to the crowd, telling them: 'Speak the Truth and only then you can be free of your chains.' The reputed final words of Michael Joseph are more widely recognised, when he proclaimed that he 'should have a name perpetual and immortal'. However, the baying crowd did not reflect on such words at the time, instead revelling in the spectacle of the utter defeat of the Cornish and their rebellion.

The Second Rebellion: The Fall of Warbeck

Despite Henry's careful and considered approach to treating the Cornish rebels, he was unable to avoid his fear of a reaction to the events at Blackheath. A handful of months later in early September, one of his enemies arrived on the coast of Cornwall, thereby provoking a second rebellion in 1497 in the Cornish land.

The arrival was none other than Perkin Warbeck himself. The infamous pretender who had kept Henry on his feet throughout the decade of the 1490s, from France to Flanders, from Ireland to Scotland, he had been on the run causing Henry repeated headaches. Warbeck's Scottish adventure had not gone entirely to plan and James IV had come to terms with Henry, thereby leading to the pretender being off-loaded from the Scottish realm. He was running out of options; after leaving Scotland, he failed to raise an army in Ireland, and all seemed lost. However, the defeated, bruised, angry Cornish offered him salvation.

The alliance of Warbeck and the Cornish is best seen as a marriage of convenience; it was a union of desperados with nothing left to lose who were united by a common enemy. Vergil notes how the Cornish were 'ready to take up arms once more to avenge' the defeat at Blackheath, and Warbeck was able to take full advantage of their pain. 'He solicited them, he incited them,' writes Vergil, 'he promised them such great things that at a stroke he was hailed as their leader, with all men shouting they would obey his commands.'[43] Writing a century after the rebellion, Francis Bacon suggested that it was the Cornish who made contact with Warbeck, thereby letting 'him know that if he would come over to them they would serve him'.[44] This led to Warbeck being declared Richard IV at Bodmin; the Cornish placed their faith and support behind the pretender. The scene was set for the second Cornish uprising of 1497.

However, despite the union, there was an issue of manpower. Warbeck arrived with 'some sixscore or sevenscore fighting men', putting the estimate between 120 and 140.[45] Support for this second rebellion was more difficult to find, no doubt in light of what had happened earlier in 1497. The 'grander families steered clear of Warbeck', wisely realising that he had failed in all of his previous attempts to take the crown.[46] However, there were others who were eager to settle scores; John Tresynny – one of An Gof's captains at Blackheath – and Roger Whalley had both flocked to Warbeck.[47] There were many other members of the gentry who still smarted at the defeat at Blackheath, and so they, too, supported the uprising. The reasons for this are varied, with Philip Payton stating that it was out of opposition to Henry VII rather than due to lingering Yorkist sympathies:

they used Warbeck as a focus and as a catalyst in their desire to regroup after the disaster of Blackheath. To that extent, the Warbeck rising was really the second act of the An Gof rebellion.[48]

It could be argued that the second uprising should not be compared on the same level as other Yorkist threats of the period, particularly Warbeck's earlier attempts, such as in Kent in 1495, or more notably with Lambert Simnel in 1486–7. However, the two rebellions are clearly different in their aim and purpose; the first rebellion was about highlighting the grievances in Cornwall regarding economic factors – such as unfair taxation – and issues relating to their identity and political status within the Tudor state. As such, it was about addressing their problems to find solutions. Whereas the Warbeck uprising was no longer about finding accommodation with the Tudor dynasty, but rather in destroying it. The Cornish would help Warbeck to the throne, and in turn he would compensate them handsomely in terms of restoring their old position – particularly with the Stannary Parliament – before the rise of the Tudors. Bacon suggests as much, noting how Warbeck was able to set about 'stroking the people with fair promises and humouring them with invectives against the King and his government'.[49]

Estimates of the number of supporters range between 3,000 and 6,000; even the larger figure is smaller than the 10,000 plus who marched to Blackheath, but yet it remained a sizeable enough number to cause a disturbance in the region.[50] From Cornwall, the rebellion moved into Devon with the aim of taking Exeter, the principal town in the West Country; initially Warbeck attempted to convince Exeter to join him, but they remained defiant to his words and then his demands to open the city gates.[51] This led Warbeck to:

> smash its gates opens, and with great vigour he began to pound them with stones, pry at them with steel, heap them with wood, and set them afire.[52]

The fighting was fierce, with hundreds of lives lost. The Cornish archers were even able to send an arrow into the arm of 'Exeter's chief defender', the Earl of Devon. However, the Cornish lacked resources, particularly artillery, and the people of Exeter defended their city with the digging of ditches and making of earthworks. Vergil describes the scene:

> Then they courageously decided to fight fire with fire and, since the bars of the gates were already shattered, they added their own wood to the fire, so that the flames raging on either side would both prevent the enemy from coming within and their own citizens from leaving.[53]

The siege of Exeter was costly, both in terms of wasting time, resources and men (estimates ranging between 200 and 400).[54] However, this valiant defence bought Henry the time required for him to gather a force to send into the West. Lord Daubeney – the hero of Blackheath – was tasked for the second time in a handful of months with taking down a Cornish rebellion. When hearing news of the advancing army, Warbeck took the decision to abandon the siege and to move to Taunton. Taunton was the location of a brutal incident in which the rebels took hold of John Oby, the infamous tax collector who had infuriated the people of west Cornwall. The sixteenth-century *Chronicles of London* records how in the marketplace the rebels 'slew him piteously, in such a wise that he was dismembered and cut in many sundry pieces'.[55]

At this juncture it appears that Warbeck recognised that he was once again in a no-win situation. The Cornish were not prepared for battle, with only a few being armed with swords and others 'ignorant of how to fight',[56] all of which led Warbeck to realise that 'he had no great trust in that army'.[57] As such, Warbeck reverted to his old tactic of slipping away to fight another day, abandoning the Cornish to head to the New Forest; Vergil writes as how the leader 'furtively slipped away in the night and quickly fled'.[58] The Cornish soldiers were left stranded, leaderless and with yet another crushing military defeat awaiting them. Historians' accounts from the sixteenth and seventeenth centuries highlight how the Cornish were ready to fight until the bitter end, with Vergil noting how 'that they had all determined on conquering or dying to the last man in that battle',[59] and Bacon writing:

> the Cornishmen were become like metal often fired and quenched, churlish, and that would sooner break than bow, swearing and vowing not to leave him till the uttermost drop of their blood was spilt.[60]

However, battle – and a second crushing defeat – was averted. As at Blackheath, Henry offered a general pardon, which was wisely accepted, and with their surrender came the end of the second Cornish rebellion of 1497.

However, the Warbeck saga was not yet over. He sought sanctuary in Beaulieu Abbey but found the location surrounded by Henry's men. Henry had several options: to march into the abbey and take Warbeck by force, or to offer a deal. Clearly Henry was adverse to the first option due to the scandal that it would cause, particularly in terms of angering the Papacy. However, he needed to get his hands on Warbeck once and for all to ring out a confession to declare the truth to the people. Ultimately, Warbeck realised that there was no escape from this entangled web, and so he decided to throw himself upon Henry's mercy.

Warbeck was transported to London, as was his wife – Lady Katherine Gordon – who had been living at St Michael's Mount after their arrival in Cornwall. Vergil writes how Henry was struck by Katherine's beauty, and so sent her to the queen in London 'with an escort of honourable matrons'.[61] Warbeck confessed to having been born in Flanders, not the son of Edward IV, but rather the son of the unknown John Osbeck. His confession describes how he became involved in the conspiracy while in Ireland:

> For they forced not what they took, so that they might be revenged on the King of England, and so against my will made me learn English and taught me what I should do and say. And after this they called me the Duke of York, second son to King Edward the fourth, because King Richard's bastard son was in the hands of the King of England.[62]

From here, Warbeck then outlines how he then moved on to France, and 'from thence into Flanders, and from Flanders into Ireland, and from Ireland into Scotland, and so into England'.[63] Finally, after a decade of worries and troubles, Henry had his man. After this point, Warbeck existed in an odd state of limbo, 'in show at liberty, but guarded with all care and watch that was possible' and seen with 'scorn and contempt'.[64] Bacon writes as to how he was:

exposed to derision not only of the courtiers but also the people, who flocked about him as he went along, that one might know afar off where the owl was by the flight of birds, some mocking, some wondering, some cursing, some prying and picking matter out of his countenance and gesture to talk of.[65]

It seemed as if Warbeck would follow the same path as Lambert Simnel; reduced to a mere curiosity. However, in 1499 he was alleged to have conspired with the Earl of Warwick to escape from the Tower and to plan another uprising; the result of this was Henry's decision to have both executed. The Warbeck story was finally resolved.

The Uneasy Tudor-Cornish Relationship

Henry reached Taunton on 4 October 1497, where he was personally able to receive the surrender of the Cornish. After doing so, he continued into Exeter to 'a joyful entrance',[66] where:

a host of Cornish prisoners with halters around their necks were brought before him. He spoke to the crowd, pardoning the rebels for their actions, at which point the prisoners threw their halters in the air and cheered 'God save the King!'[67]

As with the aftermath of Blackheath, Henry preferred to avoid widespread bloodshed; the chief ringleaders were executed, and the remaining rebels were spared. However, the Cornish did not escape punishment, with Henry preferring to implement 'a rigorous programme of fines'.[68] Vergil writes as to how 'no man implicated in that capital affair could evade his deserved punishment', and this is evidenced in the cost of the penalty: £13,000.

Some have deemed the aftermath of 1497 – a Cornish *annus horribilis* – as one of defeat and humiliation. Philip Payton notes how it is therefore 'tempting to see Cornwall ... as both broke and broken, overtaken by poverty and cowed-down in the face of the Tudor regime'.[69] After all, the Cornish were not to stir again for five decades, and this interpretation would provide further evidence of the consolidation and enhancement of the Tudor empire in the West.

However, Henry did not press his advantage on the beaten Cornish in the remainder of his reign. A decade after the initial shock of fines were implemented, he restored the Stannary Parliament in the Charter of Pardon of 1508; furthermore, the parliament now had a veto that could overrule any legislation made by the monarch or by the Duke of Cornwall. As such, the Pardon of 1508 could be seen as 'a powerful reaffirmation of Cornwall's distinctive place within the state'.[70] This approach is an intriguing one; had Henry grown soft in his advancing age?

The Tudor-Cornish relationship in the early 1500s does not fit in with the accepted argument of centralisation of the Anglo state. However, the example of Cornwall does conform with the wider pattern of Henry VII's wheeling and dealing to obtain obedience from his imperial subjects. The situation in Cornwall, then, is similar to what had happened in Ireland: initial problems were resolved with negotiation, due to Henry accepting the reality of the situation. The Cornish deal was preferable to having to put down another rebellion, especially when this deal was sweetened by the payment of fines.

1497 remains a special year for the Cornish. They rose twice and were defeated twice, and it would be easy for it to be portrayed as a year to forget. However, these rebellions highlighted the distinct identity of the Cornish; they rebelled because they wanted to fight for the preservation of their way of life.[71] The rebellions are seen as a time of heroes, particularly the efforts of Joseph and Flamank in the first uprising; this is seen clearly in the celebration of the 500th anniversary in 1997 when a statue was revealed in St Keverne, Cornwall. The inscription echoes An Gof's famous final words, declaring that these leaders will have: 'A NAME PERPETUAL AND A FAME PERMANENT AND IMMORTAL.'

Chapter 6

Brave New World

John Cabot and the early voyages to North America

In the summer of 2020 – in the heat of the Black Lives Matters protests – the statue of former prominent son of Bristol, Edward Colston, was unceremoniously torn down. The statue, which had been in place since 1895, was decoupled from the plinth and dragged through the streets of Bristol before being thrown into the harbour to the cheers of the celebrating crowd. Colston was being punished – three centuries after his death – for his involvement in the slave trade, and the statue had been a source of controversy in the city in preceding years. A few days later, the statue was retrieved from the water, and it is now positioned in its damaged state in a local museum.

A short walk from the statue's former resting place is a more modest figure; that of famed explorer John Cabot, sited on the cobblestones beside the water. Cabot is portrayed sitting on a beam, with a pensive expression on his face, slightly restless in lurching toward the harbour. The statue was a later construction – from the 1980s – but it links Bristol with its participation in the historical voyages that linked it to the wider, unknown world. Whereas other statues continue to fall, Cabot's association with Bristol remains strong, with him being proudly claimed as one of the city's cherished adopted sons.

However, for hundreds of years, John Cabot was a forgotten man and his exploits had become suppressed by the weight of history. Yet it is Cabot's voyages in the 1490s – his sticking of Henry VII's flag into the ground of the New World – in which the later British Empire arguably finds its origin.

The Exploration 'Space-Race'

John Cabot was not to be the first to place a European monarch's flag into the turf of the New World. The Age of Discovery did not begin with initiation from Henry VII and England, but from further south in Europe in the Iberian peninsula. In 1492 – a handful of years before Cabot arrived at the court of Henry VII – the Spanish monarchy funded Christopher Columbus to sail west into the Atlantic, with the hope of establishing a direct trade route to the riches of the Asian kingdoms, notably China. Columbus was disappointed that islands and land stood in his way, and although he protested otherwise, he had discovered a new giant landmass that later became known as America. This established a Spanish presence in the New World, which would eventually lead to their domination of the Caribbean islands in the early 1500s, the conquest of the Aztec Empire in the 1520s, and then in the 1530s the downfall of the Incan Empire in Peru. Such actions transformed Spain into a world power.

In an alternate history, it is England who were transformed. After all, Columbus initially had the idea to come calling at Henry VII's court before obtaining the support from Spain. In this 'what if' scenario, it is the Tudors who surge full-speed ahead in their conquests of these strange new lands, leading to a confident and financially muscular Henry VIII – his coffers brimming with gold and silver – realising his dream of launching an unstoppable invasion of France. The two crowns – of England and France – would be united, as they had once briefly been under Henry V, but the Tudors would not simply stop there. They would become the European juggernaut, crushing any opposition or dissent, becoming the dominant rulers of all worlds. However, real history did not play out that way, for in a 'sliding doors' moment, Henry did not endorse Christopher Columbus' plans to sail out into the Atlantic. Instead, he passed on the offer. This refusal was to cost Henry VII and the English kingdom very dear.[1]

This counterfactual history is not entirely fanciful; Bartholomew Columbus – brother of Christopher – was dispatched to England with the aim of obtaining funding for a transatlantic enterprise. Bartholomew was armed with several maps of enticing legendary far-away lands to win the interest of Henry; however, the younger Columbus brother's travel plans turned to disaster: he suffered shipwreck, illness and – if the legend is true – capture by pirates.[2] However, he finally managed to arrive in England, at which point his plans were examined by Henry and his council. Henry rejected the proposal, which led Bartholomew to move on to France in the hope of securing patronage. But such attempts were, by this point, entirely moot: his older brother had already obtained funding from the Spanish and had completed his first historic transatlantic mission. Without the use of records, we can only surmise Bartholomew's feelings on being left out of history being made, especially having suffered such hardship; however, he would get to taste voyages to the New World in later years.

Columbus' discovery of the New World – although he himself continued to insist that he had found Asia – gave rise to Henry entertaining ideas of how to mimic the Spanish success.[3] But following the path of the early exploration trend-setters could potentially lead to upset; in 1494 both Spain and Portugal agreed the Treaty of Tordesillas, which divided the new lands between these respective crowns. Land to the west of the line – centring on the Cape Verde islands – went to Spain, whereas land to the east was for the ownership of Portugal. This essentially provided carte blanche for Spain and their newly claimed territories in the Caribbean, leading to their vast expansion on the mainland in Central and South America. As for Portugal, they held the keys to the east, which included African lands to be exploited and the prize assets of links to India. And as for the Tudors? There was no mention of England in this treaty, thereby confirming that Henry and his family remained the unestablished upstart rulers of a second-rate power. As such, Henry would need to plan carefully if he intended on emulating the success of Columbus in this exploration 'space-race'.

Legends of the Atlantic

As far back as the first century, writers speculated about the existence of a New World. 1,400 years before Columbus' voyage, the Roman philosopher Seneca prophesied:

> The time will come in later years when oceans may relax
> the chain of things, and a vast continent may open; the sea
> may uncover new worlds, and Thule cease to be the last of
> lands.[4]

Since that time, many sailed off in search of adventure and glory to find what lay beyond the horizon in the Atlantic. So, what was actually 'out there'?

A long list of speculated legendary islands were said to have been located west in the ocean. Atlantis was established in the popular imagination, with the origin of this fictional island rooted in the era of ancient Greece and the works of Plato. There were rumours of a great lost civilization somewhere in the Atlantic, and this speculation led to the rise of a variety of other islands that reputedly had actual historical origins. The island of Antillia – which appeared on maps from as early as 1424 as an oddly shaped rectangle – was also known as the Island of the Seven Cities. This claim was based on an old Portuguese legend, of seven bishops who fled Iberia in fear of the Moorish invasion of 734, thereby leading to the supposed colonisation of this Atlantic territory.[5] The island was a serious consideration into the late 1400s, with Portuguese kings authorising explorers to search and claim it, particularly due to the rumour that silver would be uncovered. Similarly, the island of Brasil was indicated on maps of the period, positioning it nearby the coast of south-west Ireland.[6] This was based on an old Irish myth – 'Breasil' meaning 'Blessed' in Irish – and a series of other myths became attached to it; it was even mooted as a suggested burial place for King Arthur.[7] Further north was Great Ireland – otherwise known as White People Land – in which the natives were said to have 'hair and skin as white as snow'.[8] Such places were difficult to find, it was believed, due to the distance involved, as well as other folklore superstitions; the island of Brasil was apparently covered in mist and would only become visible once every seven years.[9] However, these maps were based on phantom islands: they did not exist. The belief in these legends, which had circulated for centuries, was to be eradicated at the end of the 1400s, which leads to a big question: why was it only at that point in history when European sailors became ambitious enough to set out across the Atlantic to find the truth?

There were several important factors in play: first, there was a growth of connections between explorers of various states during the 1400s, thereby encouraging the sharing of information and the further stimulation of attempts through curiosity and competition. In the 1400s, England reconnected with Iceland for trade, which led to the circulation of old stories of lost Atlantic islands, no doubt based on the actual exploits of earlier Viking explorers. There was mention of a Greenland colony and how a distant territory – North America – had been reached under the leadership of Vikings hundreds of years previously.[10] Other huge influences on English sailors was the connection with Portugal, which at that time was expanding into the Atlantic – in the form of the Azores – and Africa. Edward IV – interested by reports of Portuguese expansion into Africa – appealed to the Pope to authorise English trade along the Guinea coast; such requests were rebuffed, however.[11] Second, England faced competition in its trade links and foreign markets; during the reign of Edward IV the monopoly of trade with Iceland was diminished due to the rise of the Hanseatic League.[12] The Danish king – who controlled Iceland – signed an exclusive trade deal with the Hanse, leading to merchants seeking out new markets.[13]

Third, the period saw notable advancements in shipbuilding. The largest hurdle for transatlantic voyages was the distance, rather than the psychological barrier of fear of ghouls and monsters. No rational explorer of the period believed that the world was flat and that their adventure would culminate in a ship falling off into a dark void; however, there was the real danger that a ship would simply become stranded in the blue of the ocean. The development in ships – particularly their size – meant that they were more suitable for traversing ocean distances, as demonstrated by the development and popularisation of the carrack and caravel. These developments were further aided by progress in navigation techniques and cartography, thereby arming explorers with the needed tools to make a success of delving into the Atlantic.

These factors helped to stimulate exploration attempts, as was evidenced in Bristol in the early 1480s. Local merchants were given licence to explore the island of Brasil and find trade – including a 'special licence' to find new fishing grounds – but the two voyages in 1480 and 1481 did not uncover anything of note.[14] However, some have speculated that these Bristolian attempts may have been more successful; not with the impossible task of locating the island of Brasil but in discovering North America.[15] The claim suggests that this discovery was not widely announced because the explorers cunningly realised that they could keep it a secret to fully exploit the fishing grounds in Newfoundland. However, such claims appear to be fanciful for several reasons: a lack of evidence and the consideration as to how such a great discovery could be kept secret from sailors returning home.

Despite these setbacks, it appears that Henry was curious about Bristol's links into the unknown ocean; as early as 1486, he visited Bristol and learned of their trade links and shipping prowess. Although he did not commit with financial support at this stage, the mayor remarked that he 'hadn't heard such good comfort from a king in a hundred years'.[16] Despite this growth of activity, Henry remained reluctant to financially and politically support such a large undertaking as a transatlantic voyage. It was a risky strategy for a monarch who was still dealing with threats and rebellions on his own doorstep. As such, the Columbus enterprise was rebuffed, leading to feelings of regret after Spain were able to hail their achievements. But he was soon to be given a second bite of the cherry when another Italian explorer arrived on his shores.

The Arrival of John Cabot

English history has cemented his name as John Cabot; however, during his life-time he went under other spellings and pronunciations: Giovanni Caboto in Italian, and Zuan Chabotto in Venice. As Margaret Condon and Evans Jones note, Cabot is 'the most enigmatic explorer of the Age of Discovery, so little being known about his birth, life, or even death'.[17] The scant sources indicate that he was born in Genoa before becoming a citizen of the Venetian Republic where he was involved in Mediterranean trade.[18] But a series of financial difficulties in the 1480s led to him leaving Venice, whereby he became involved in an aborted project of building a stone-bridge in Spain. Such a backstory doesn't provide a confident basis for England's first transatlantic hero, but there was more to come from John Cabot.

Cabot's own interest in the Atlantic may have been sparked from his time in Spain. In 1493, while he was attempting to construct the stone-bridge, he would have heard of the launch of Columbus' second expedition; although he was perhaps envious of Columbus striking out into the deep blue, it also offered the possibilities of further voyages. Cabot initially sought the patronage of others in Spain and Portugal; however, the Spanish monarchs had already granted a monopoly to Columbus, whereas Portugal had their own plans in place to reach India by sailing around Africa (as happened under Vasco da Gama in 1497).[19] England, then, was another option on a list that was being whittled down; the choice of Bristol appears due to that city's trading connection with Iberia.[20]

The exact date of Cabot's arrival in England is unknown, but it is likely that he had set up a household in Bristol by 1495, along with his wife and his three sons (Ludovico, Sebastiano and Sancio).[21] As with Bartholomew Columbus before him, Cabot arrived in England with the intention of securing funding from the English Crown for a voyage into the Atlantic, with the aim to reach Asia to establish a direct trade link. However, Cabot had an interesting variation of this plan; because he would travel further north, the actual distance to reach Asia would be smaller. As such, travel-times could be reduced, and while the Spanish were stuck attempting to find passage through the Americas, Cabot – and by extension the Tudors – would simply bypass them all.

The backing of the Crown was instrumental if Cabot hoped to obtain funding from the Italian banks to push forward his project.[22] Luckily for Cabot, Henry was still smarting over his earlier rejection of the Columbus brothers, and the scheme was enough to entice him to provide his support. On 5 March 1496 he issued Cabot letters patent with the following authorisation:

> Be it known, that we have given and granted ... to our well beloved John Cabot, citizen of Venice, full and free authority, leave and power to sail to all parts, countries, and seas of the East, of the West, and of the North under our banners and ensigns.

The aim would be to:

> seek out, discover and find whatsoever isles, countries, regions or provinces of the heathen and infidels whatsoever they be, and in what part of the world soever they be which before this time have been unknown to all Christians.

Henry provided licence for Cabot to:

> set up our banner and ensigns in every village, town, castle, isle or mainland newly found by them which they can subdue, occupy, and possess as our vassals and lieutenants, getting unto us the rule, title and jurisdiction of the same villages, towns, castles and firm land so found.[23]

The wording has shades of Captain Kirk's opening to the TV show *Star Trek*: 'to explore strange new worlds. To seek out new life and new civilizations. To boldly go where no man has gone before.' It is clear that Henry's intention was to strike out and discover new land, with the possibility of it becoming annexed to his empire. But of course, Henry did not know what to expect, and as such the letters patent provides Cabot with wide room to manoeuvre: to discover, to trade, to enter agreements and alliances, or to pillage and plunder. If successful, Cabot and his heirs would obtain never-ending profit, and Henry himself would obtain one-fifth of all profits; a good deal for simply endorsing the project.[24] Furthermore, it was also a good deal for the city of Bristol: it was to be used as the principal port for England's exploration, leading to further investment; thereby operating in a similar manner as Seville to the Spanish, and Lisbon to the Portuguese.[25] As such, it was a win-win deal for all parties. However, Henry's approach to the entire venture is revealing of his usual cautious approach; although he provided political protection to Cabot, he only coughed up £50.[26] By comparison, the Spanish Crown paid for more than half the cost of Columbus' 1492 voyage, paying for more men and ships than Cabot's initial voyages. The Anglo effort was empire-building on the cheap.

The key aims of Cabot's voyage can be outlined as follows: first, to resolve the question whether land could be reached. Second, to establish a direct trade connection with Asia, and other suggested islands, such as Brasil. This would enable England to obtain luxury goods, such as spices and silks, by cutting out the middle-men of the Mediterranean and Middle East. Third, to find new fishing grounds to exploit, especially needed due to the reduction in Icelandic trade. Fourth, to expand the Tudor empire by claiming land. Out of all of these aims, the most crucial was the ability to trade directly with Asia; this would lead to an increase of commerce and ultimately put more money into the pockets of the Tudors.

Despite such optimistic beginnings, the first voyage in the summer of 1496 was a failure. There were several problems, primarily in payments and organisation. Bristol merchant John Day – writing two years later in 1498 – sent a letter to Columbus outlining the problems:

> Concerning the first voyage which your lordship wants to
> know about, what happened was that they took one ship,

and he [Cabot] was unhappy with the crew and he was badly provisioned and he found the weather to be unfavourable, so he made the choice to come back.[27]

Such beginnings did not appear auspicious, but Cabot was able to use the winter months to start plotting and planning a fresh voyage in 1497.

The 1497 Voyage

The second voyage began on 2 May 1497 from Bristol. The preparation time – although no doubt initially undesired – helped Cabot to form a willing crew that were prepared to risk their lives in the unknown Atlantic ocean.[28] The crew amounted to no more than twenty men, including what appears at first sight to be an odd addition: a barber from Genoa. However, barbers in this era would perform a range of other tasks – such as emergency dentistry – which leads to the suggestion that this Genoese man acted as the ship's surgeon.[29] A ship was readied – the fifty-ton *Matthew* of Bristol – and supplies were collected that provided them with enough rations for seven to eight months. Cabot initially passed Ireland before heading out into the empty horizon, spending thirty-five days on the ocean before sighting land on 24 June. He made landfall and placed the banners of Henry VII, Pope Alexander VI and St Mark of Venice into the turf of the New World. The Tudor empire had reached America.

But a lingering question continues to remain unanswered: where exactly did Cabot land? As with Columbus, Cabot was confident that the land he had discovered was a part of the larger Asian landmass. He believed that this land was the far reaches of those belonging to the Emperor of China.[30] John Day – later writing of Cabot's 1497 voyage – noted how those in Bristol initially believed the island of Brasil had finally been located.[31] Other letters written during this period – such as the merchant Raimondo de Soncino's letter to the Duke of Milan – suggest that Cabot had discovered the Island of Seven Cities, Antillia itself.

Of course, Cabot and his contemporaries were very much mistaken, as he made landfall on the North American continent, not Asia; but it is difficult to state firmly where on this continent he landed. A variety of locations have been suggested over the years, ranging from the likeliest at Newfoundland, but also including areas further afield, such as Nova Scotia, Labrador, or even as far south as New England. John Day's letter provides an indication of the latitude, which Jones and Condon believe 'suggests an initial landing' on Newfoundland in the Avalon Peninsula.[32] For the 500th anniversary celebrations, the Canadian and British governments became resolved to settle on Cape Bonavista in Newfoundland as the official landing place.[33]

John Day's letter states that the crew only disembarked once from their ship, principally to assert the possession of the land for the control of England, and to exert the Catholic faith's religious hold.[34] It seems peculiar as to why Cabot did not attempt to penetrate further, such as to find a settlement in which to establish exchange of information or a trade connection, particularly in terms of verifying whether they had landed in Asia. However, Day later noted the reason for this caution: 'since he was there only with a few men, he did not dare to penetrate into the land any further than a crossbow's shot'.[35] Therefore, any reconnaissance was brief, consisting of the discovery of the remains of a fire and some basic tools; these were likely left behind by the native Beothuk people.[36] Such 'primitive artefacts' were gathered to bring back to England as evidence that this new land was inhabited.[37]

Satisfied that one of their central aims – of reaching land – was achieved, Cabot then turned back and headed home for Europe. It took fifteen days to sail 2,200 miles, before arriving back in Bristol on 6 August 1497.[38] Cabot then headed to the manor of Woodstock to inform Henry in person of the success of his mission, no doubt preparing himself for the rewards that would come his way. Some historians note that Cabot was paid a 'substantial pension' from the king, but the amount itself – £10 – hardly inspires jaw-dropping awe, even if we do adjust the price according to the value of the period.[39] £10 was double the amount a labourer could be expected to earn in a year, while key members of Henry's government – such as John Heron – would obtain a salary of around £13. But yet, wasn't Cabot's achievement – of discovering new land – of such value that it would rank higher? Perhaps we could forgive Henry for being preoccupied with other matters; he was in the throes of the final Warbeck threat, in which he was based in the West Country for several weeks dealing with the aftermath of the rebellion. Later in December, when stability was resumed, Henry provided additional financial gifts, including a pension of £20 per year.

It is reasonable to assume that Henry was cautious on whether to bestow higher rewards on Cabot. After all, what had been accomplished in the 1497 voyage? Yes, land had been reached, but for what purpose? Even if Cabot was under the illusion that he had reached Asia, he hadn't made firm contact on which to establish a direct trade connection. As such, more work was needed to cut out the middle-man and reach huge profits. Furthermore, despite the planting of Henry's flag, the idea of conquest and colonisation was a far-off pipe-dream, especially considering the large effort and expense that would be required to secure this land. Perhaps the more immediate gain was the discovery of fresh fishing grounds, with the Newfoundland coast becoming an important cod fishery; but even this was beset with difficulties due the vast distance involved.[40]

Of course, both Henry and Cabot could claim bragging rights in terms of pulling off the feat of the transatlantic voyage. Henry was no longer watching on with envious eyes at the Spanish voyages; even if his own success paled in comparison to what the Spanish had achieved, he himself could puff out his chest alongside other European monarchs, such as Ferdinand and Isabella. Furthermore, Cabot appears to have revelled in his new-found fame, which enabled to him to become the talk-of-the-town both in England and in royal courts across Europe. The Venetian merchant Lorenzo Pasqualgio wrote to his brother, noting how Cabot 'is called the Great Admiral, and vast honour is paid to him', and that 'he goes dressed in silk, and these English run after him like mad'.[41] Cabot had established himself as a hero. But he wanted more.

Cabot's Disappearance from History

The 1497 voyage unsettled Henry's fellow monarchs in Europe. As early as 1496, Ferdinand and Isabella had learned of Cabot's arrival in England, with the explorer being described to them as 'one like Columbus'.[42] The historian Lorraine Attreed argues that the Spanish monarchs took Henry's plans for further exploration very seriously, stating that the more expansive plans for 1498 'deeply upset the Catholic monarchs'.[43] In a letter dated 18 December 1497, Raimondo de Soncino wrote to the

Duke of Milan about how Cabot intended to head back to Newfoundland to 'plant a colony there', to be populated with 'criminals' if needed. There was a suggestion that the Northwest Passage would be discovered, thereby making 'London a greater place for spices than Alexandria'.[44] These rumours highlight the buzz of excitement in Europe's royal courts, with the high hopes for Cabot's third voyage illustrated by a greater ambition of a fleet of five ships, including one personally financed by Henry himself to the tune of £113.[45] Establishing a trade connection was of high priority, as shown with the cargo carried in some of the ships (such as English cloth), while there was also the suggestion of establishing a Christian mission in the New World.[46]

Cabot's fleet set off in May 1498 with an estimated return in the autumn. However, beyond this point the records become bare and there is no evidence of what became of Cabot's third voyage, or of his return to England. The earliest historian of this period – Polydore Vergil – wrote how Cabot sailed into the 'British ocean', describing how:

> nowhere but on the very bottom of the ocean, to which he is thought to have descended together with his boat, the victim himself of that self-same ocean; since after that voyage he was never seen again anywhere.[47]

Despite Vergil writing years after 1498 and being reliant on second-hand information, his version of events established the belief that the third voyage was ruined, thereby leading to Cabot's untimely watery death. This was followed by other historians and within a couple of centuries the entirety of John Cabot's contribution to the Age of Discovery became completely obscured from the record. A key reason for this erasure of history is the scant records relating to the voyages of Henry VII's reign; the evidence exists in the form of a handful of letters – none from Cabot himself – and as Jones and Condon note, even the revealing John Day letter was only uncovered in the 1950s.[48]

This, then, provides the opportunity for speculation and a variety of claims as to what actually became of Cabot. Historian Alwyn Ruddock made a series of claims, stating that Cabot did not die at sea in 1498, but instead enjoyed a two-year voyage of exploration that possibly stretched as far as the Caribbean.[49] This claim rests on the chart of Spanish cartographer Juan de la Cosa, who noted a series of English discoveries stretching along the North American coast. Unfortunately, Ruddock was never able to provide evidence, and even ordered her research papers to be destroyed after her death.[50] However, all may not be fully lost; since the 2010s, the Cabot Project – under the direction of Evan Jones and Margaret Condon – have started to uncover some of the evidence that Ruddock alluded to, leading to the suggestion that Cabot may have returned home by 1500. But Jones and Condon are not entirely convincing in their explanation:

> But by the standards of the time, even a voyage right down the eastern seaboard as far as Florida might not have been regarded as a great success. Such a voyage would merely have demonstrated that the land was not inhabited by rich and civilised peoples with whom the explorers could trade.[51]

Could it be true that such a voyage – especially one as far as Florida – would have been unheralded by Henry and the English? After all, the voyage to the backwater of Newfoundland increased Cabot's fame in England, leading to him becoming spoken of by a variety of ambassadors across Europe. There is a further claim by Jones and Condon that the inability to reach and directly trade with Asia 'would have been a sore point' with Henry VII; however, this again is at odds with the experience of 1497.[52] How could such a celebrity become forgotten so quickly? Centuries later Andy Warhol would claim: 'In the future, everyone will be world-famous for fifteen minutes'; perhaps 1497 was Cabot's very own fifteen minutes of fame. It was only in the nineteenth century that his involvement in the voyages of the 1490s became uncovered. And so, the mystery of Cabot's fate remains unknown; we are unsure if he died, returned to safety, or even made it to America and decided to remain there.

Cabot's Successors

Cabot's voyages helped spur on further voyages in the remaining decade of Henry VII's reign; however, the vast majority of these voyages became obscured to history for centuries, due to the lack of recorded evidence. On 12 March 1499, a letter was sent by Henry to John Morton, his Lord

Chancellor, which makes mention of a voyage by William Weston, but this letter was filed away and forgotten before being discovered hundreds of years later at the end of the twentieth century.[53] As such, the history books have literally been rewritten over the past decade, due to the expansion of our knowledge of this era.

The aforementioned William Weston occupies little space in student textbooks, and yet he is the first Englishman to lead a transatlantic voyage. Weston was involved in the expansion of Bristol commerce in the 1480s and 1490s, with visits made to places in the known Atlantic world, such as Madeira. His own reputation was rocked in 1488 when the largest ship in the Bristol fleet – the *Anthony* – sunk on its return from Lisbon. The ship belonged to local merchant John Foster, and it appears that Foster held a lingering grudge in not approving of the marriage of Weston to his daughter Agnes. Foster's wrath can be evidenced in his refusal to leave nothing in his will to his son-in-law, and much little else to his daughter.[54] However, Weston became acquainted within dynamic circles, particularly in his friendship with Cabot. In 1498, Henry rewarded Weston, along with Cabot, for their exploration efforts, which suggests that Weston was involved in some, if not all, of Cabot's voyages in 1496 and 1497.

Due to the lack of recorded evidence it is difficult to ascertain when Weston's voyage – or voyages – took place. Ruddock claimed that the expedition took place in 1499, with Weston sailing up the Hudson Strait, which presumably was an attempt to find the Northwest Passage to Asia. These claims also suggest that Weston founded the first Christian settlement in the New World, at Carbonear in Newfoundland. However, as noted earlier in this chapter, caution must be used when considering Ruddock's claims. In 1500, Henry rewarded Weston once more, with £30 being paid to him 'for his expenses about the finding of the new land'.[55] By 1504, Weston was dead, and after this point his 'contribution to England's first attempts to explore the New World was forgotten', which led to 'five hundred years of silence'.[56]

Letters patent were issued to a group of Bristol and Azorean merchants, in what has been labelled an 'Anglo-Azorean syndicate',[57] which provided them 'vice-regal powers' in claiming undiscovered lands.[58] This group conducted transatlantic voyages in the first decade of the sixteenth century and eventually established the Company Adventurers to the New Found Land. This provided them with extensive rights to explore and colonise, although the chief focus continued to be the discovery of the Northwest Passage to Asia.[59] Henry authorised them to:

> chastise and punish according to the laws and statues set up by them in that region all and singular those whom they may find there hostile and rebellious and disobedient to the laws, statues and ordinances aforesaid, and all who shall commit and perpetuate theft, homicide or robberies or who shall rape and violate against their will or otherwise any women of the islands or countries aforesaid.[60]

It could be suggested that this language demonstrates Henry's moral compass; however, such a document is not focused on the welfare or rights of those that the English would find and subjugate, but rather in reaffirming the need to regulate and discipline the Englishmen that would colonise these new lands. The idea of a colony run exclusively by English males, without female companionship, was of clear concern; a feature that would become prevalent a hundred years later when Jamestown was established during the reign of James I. As such, this provides light on the motivations of Henry; perhaps his empire could be extended further in the New World.

The first decade of the sixteenth century saw a notable level of activity; the *Gabriel* sailed to North America, under the direction of Robert Thorne and Hugh Eliot (who may have been involved in Cabot's earlier voyages),[61] while a voyage in 1503 introduced 'birds and bobcats' from the North American continent to the royal court.[62] Henry may have been pleased by such presents, and he was also able to entertain a trio of native Americans attending his court, thereby providing further confidence in his New World project.[63] Furthermore, the syndicate were able to expand their operations further afield of Newfoundland, when in 1501 the Azorean Joao Fernandes attempted to head toward Greenland.[64] However, his second voyage in 1502 'ended in disaster', and after that, Fernandes – like many other explorers during this period – is not heard from again.[65]

Despite the growth of this confidence, the attempt at establishing a long-lasting settlement appeared to be beyond the means of the explorers and Henry's pockets. Furthermore, the failure to find the Northwest

Passage, and the lack of a developed civilization in the Newfoundland region – comparable to what the Spanish found in Central America – meant that trade links could not be established. This disillusionment and lack of profits appears to have led to the collapse of the Company Adventurers, with the group falling out with one another due to debts and unpaid bills.[66]

Henry shifted focus from the group toward another explorer: Sebastian, the son of John Cabot. Interestingly, Sebastian Cabot occupies a more prominent place in the history books; whereas John Cabot and William Weston were hidden for centuries, Sebastian was trumpeted by early modern historians, such as Sir Francis Bacon, as 'a man expert in cosmography and navigation'.[67] This is partly due to a mistake: for hundreds of years, historians confused Sebastian with his father, therefore leading to the son to be awarded the credit for the voyages in the 1490s. Furthermore, Sebastian was a shameless self-publicist – being deemed 'not an entirely reliable witness', thereby claiming much of what happened during the period.[68] As such, these boastful claims eclipsed what his father had achieved.

Sebastian became involved with his father's exploration attempts from an early age, with many speculating that he was part of his father's expeditions in the late 1490s. By 1504, he appears to have led his first expedition to the New World, seemingly funded by the Company Adventurers. Henry appears to have been pleased with these efforts, bestowing upon Sebastian the usual reward of £10. Sebastian Cabot's largest voyage was the one launched in the summer of 1508, in which he had two ships at his disposal, as well as 300 men.[69] There is much speculation as to the success of this expedition; it is claimed by some that he went as far as the Hudson Bay, clearly with the intention of establishing the Northwest Passage, before the danger of ice forced him to turn back. Frustratingly, the path that Sebastian believed would take him to Asia was not a new ocean, but more than likely Hudson Bay. Peter Martyr's 1516 account claims that Cabot then turned south and headed toward New England and the Chesapeake Bay, before sailing back to England.[70]

However, despite such heroics, Sebastian Cabot returned to an England that was under new management; Henry VII had passed away and his son – Henry VIII – was now the new king. Henry VIII's interests were not focused on the exploration of the unprofitable backwater of the New

World, but rather with more pressing concerns in Europe, particularly France. This led to a dejected Sebastian Cabot leaving England in search of new, gainful employment in Spain, and the hive of activity of these decades in Bristol declined.

A Missed Opportunity?

The exploration efforts during the reign of Henry VII can be viewed as a moment of lost opportunity; a time in which England could have developed its empire, but ultimately did not. The policy of Henry VIII in the first half of the sixteenth century – to turn inward to Europe – meant that further voyages were 'modest affairs'.[71] The British Empire was stunted by at least half a century; it would not be until the Elizabethan era when others would follow in the footsteps of those in the early 1500s.

The La Cosa map from 1500 provides an overview of the English claims on the North American coast, including places such as Cape of England (*Cavo de yngaterra*), Cape of St George (*Cavo de S. Jorge*) and Cape of the Lizard (*Cavo de lisarte*).[72] These claims may have come from either Cabot's voyages or Weston's, and this map suggests that these English dots on the map were common – if not fully accepted – knowledge among other cartographers and monarchies. As such, they represent the first steps of imperial expansion from the English Crown into the New World. Yet despite this, the maps remained drawings and therefore did not reflect the reality of England's nascent empire during that period. The truth was that England held no colonies in the New World and could be easily out-muscled by fellow European nations. Trade had not been established and the key aim of connecting directly with Asian markets proved impossible. As such, these early ventures floundered and proved unprofitable.

By missing the boat – literally – these English attempts were completely eclipsed by other nations. The English were already at a disadvantage in the race for the New World, as shown with Spain's penetration into America and the Portuguese discovery of the coast of the *actual* Brazil. Furthermore, the English claims to ownership of Newfoundland wasn't a settled fact, with Portuguese explorers charting the coast in the early 1500s, with their own – failed – attempts to find the Northwest Passage. The gap grew larger during the subsequent decades due to a lack of English activity; while Henry VIII focused on raiding northern French territory, which achieved limited success, Spain was busy conquering the Aztec and Incan empires. As such, the gulf between these two nations with their imperial projects became even greater, and it would be Spain who would reap the rewards in becoming the powerhouse of Europe during the century. Furthermore, while John Cabot and William Weston became forgotten figures due to a lack of published and circulated evidence, other explorers from Europe became celebrated and involved in the labelling and shaping of the New World; the name of Amerigo Vespucci was used for the name of these American continents, and Christopher Columbus had nations and locations dubbed in his honour.

Who is to blame for the lack of imperial growth? Henry VIII is the often-cited culprit; his French obsession led to a lack of further progress in the New World, as illustrated by Sebastian Cabot leaving the employ of England in preference of the Spanish Crown. But it is difficult to blame Henry VIII for choosing the Old World over the New World. After all, the grandiose project of achieving glory in fighting for the French throne was clearly a far more desirable ambition than pumping more money and energy into seemingly improbable progress in the far-flung North American backwater. With no direct connection with the Asian markets, the English were left with relative obscurity when compared to the Aztec and Incan civilizations.

Perhaps then we should point the finger at Henry VII himself? Yes, he sponsored and supported exploration efforts, but this was on a low-cost and low-risk basis. Such an approach is in line with Henry VII's reluctance to gamble with stability, but a firmer hand – and cash injection – may have led to greater gains. Of course, no amount of money was going to create a Northwest Passage, as ultimately such a route was physically unachievable, and no amount of greater interest from the Crown would magically conjure an advanced North American civilization to appear – something on the level of the Aztecs – with which the English could create a booming trade, or dominate. But it could be argued that more money could have stimulated the effort to establish a permanent colony, thereby trumping the later efforts – of Roanoke in the 1580s and of Jamestown in the 1600s – by almost a century.

However, this interpretation – of a missed opportunity – is too harsh an assessment, due to it not fully acknowledging the context of the period.

A key question must be asked: was the aim of a New World colony a serious consideration? The letters patent issued during Henry VII's reign provide instructions to 'subdue, occupy, and possess' those that lived in these far-away lands, and there were also instructions on how English colonists should behave.[73] As noted earlier, there was talk in Europe of how the 1498 Cabot voyage intended to 'plant a colony' in the New World. Some have claimed that a settlement was established, with one possible location cited as Carbonear. The Augustine friar Giovanni Antonio de Carbonariis may have accompanied the 1498 expedition and may have remained in Newfoundland to establish the very first Christian church on the North American continent. However, perhaps the word 'may' has been overused; there is no evidence to confirm any of this speculation. The reality was that building a permanent colony was an incredibly detailed and financial undertaking, an 'enterprise equivalent to exploring the moon today'.[74] Henry VII may have become known to history as a penny-pinching king but his pockets were not deep enough to establish and sustain such a venture.

Furthermore, there were other contextual factors in England at this time: the population had not fully recovered from the Black Death some 150 years previously, and as such, there was no issue with over-population that would later lead English people – as in other nations – to choose emigration over remaining in a competitive, destitute position. The sparse population also meant that there was plenty of cheaper land, with the politically toxic issue of enclosure only becoming more prevalent later in the sixteenth century. As such, colonisation was not at the forefront of the ambition of the explorers during the reign of Henry VII, and the chief aim was trade: establishing a direct trade route with Asia and in establishing new markets in North America. Ultimately neither was – nor could be – achieved.

The dismay, and lack of fulfilment of these explorers' goals, could lead us to view the discovery of the North American continent as a major disappointment. The explorers could not be satiated in their designs at finding a way through or around it, and there was no money to be made from what already existed. This remained a problem a century later under the Stuart monarchy, with the first successful and permanent colony Jamestown (established in 1607) verging on the point of ruin on several occasions before stabilising. Colonisation and empire building, then, was a fraught process requiring funds and tenacity; it would not be for many years in which these North American colonies would begin to generate profit. Such an assessment would mean that it would be unfair to blame Henry VII or his son for not doing more to push forward an Anglo empire. Hindsight is a wonderful thing, and these early Tudors did not have the advantage of a crystal ball in which to see the improbable rise of the world power that became the British Empire.

With that in mind, let's establish the actual extent of success of the exploration attempts during the reign of Henry VII. Despite the failures, the efforts of Cabot, Weston and others were heroic, and as such, they deserve recognition for their efforts in the twenty-first century. More practically, Cabot was able to demonstrate that 'a substantial land mass did exist within reasonable sailing from Europe'.[75] More importantly, the claims of Cabot provided a historic basis on which the English Crown could support later colonial claims; the planting of Henry VII's flag in 1497 harked back to the ancient tradition of 'Finders, Keepers'. It was a modest beginning, but from this sapling the great oak of the British Empire would grow.

Chapter 7

Warrior King

Henry VIII's arrival on the European stage

In 1507, two years before his death, King Henry VII addressed the City of London:

> This our realm is now environed, and, in manner, closed in every side with such mighty princes our good sons, friends, confederates and allies, that by the help of our Lord the same is and shall be perpetually established in rest and peace and wealthy condition.

The address was in reference to the state of England in the closing years of the first Tudor reign. Enemies had been vanquished and stability had been achieved, with the use of new friends and allies that the Tudors could draw upon. The past had been conquered, and the future with the kingdom's 'wealthy condition' looked bright.

Within two years, Henry VII was dead, and responsibility for maintaining – and expanding – the Tudor empire passed to his son.

The Final Years of Henry VII

The first fifteen years of the Tudor dynasty were characterised by rebellions and threats, with Henry constantly on the edge of his seat in ensuring that his wider possessions remained intact. Although a degree of stability across the Tudor imperial possessions had been achieved, particularly in the North and Ireland, the final decade of Henry VII's reign continued to pose three significant problems. First, Henry suffered personal tragedies at the turn of the sixteenth century: in 1502, his eldest son, Arthur, died a handful of months after his marriage to Catherine of

81

Aragon; then in 1503, his wife died after giving birth to a son, Geoffrey (the son also died shortly after). These deaths unsettled the Tudor hold on their domains, with Henry now only having one fit male heir – the future Henry VIII – and they provided fuel for those who wanted to make a play for the throne.

This led to the second significant problem: the continuation of menaces to Tudor rule. Henry had dealt with a range of threats in the form of Lambert Simnel and Perkin Warbeck, and also had killed off other males who had royal blood in their veins, such as John de la Pole and the Earl of Warwick. In the early 1500s, John de la Pole's younger brother, Edmund, abandoned England in the hope of finding military support in Europe; although he had made his peace with the Tudors, he saw the deaths of family members as an opportunity to propel his own claim. Ultimately, Edmund de la Pole was unsuccessful in raising an invasion force, but the fear of being toppled from power never left Henry's mind. Some in the kingdom discussed what would happen when the king died, with a suggestion put forward that the throne should not pass to Prince Henry, but rather to a strong man who could lead England forward, such as Edward Stafford, the Duke of Buckingham.

The third problem was the breakdown of Henry VII's carefully crafted diplomacy with European monarchs, shown very clearly in his Spanish gamble that developed after the death of Queen Isabella of Castile in 1504. Isabella's husband, Ferdinand, was in a precarious position, with many switching support to his daughter, Joanna, as the true monarch to rule the united kingdoms of Spain. Joanna's candidature was further boosted by her marriage to Philip of Burgundy; as the son of Emperor Maximilian, Philip had the resources of the Habsburgs to strike at Ferdinand and remove him from power. While on his way to Spain to stake their claim, Philip and Joanna's ships were pushed onto the coasts of Dorset, where they required repair. Henry seized the opportunity to meet with Philip and to impress upon him a new deal: the English would recognise Philip as the King of Spain, but in return, Edmund de la Pole – who was sheltering in Burgundy at the time – would be arrested and sent back to England. When Philip and Joanna set off on the sea, it seemed as if Henry had concluded a good bit of business, particularly with ingratiating himself with the new power-couple in Europe; it would have been expected to see the pair rule in Spain for years to come, with the formidable Habsburgs allies of the English. But shortly after arriving in Spain, Philip died and Joanna's support fell away, which allowed Ferdinand to dominate Spain once again. This Spanish gamble did not pay off and the result was to see England becoming diplomatically isolated by the time of Henry VII's death in 1509; this is illustrated clearly in the creation of the League of Cambrai of France, the Holy Roman Empire, Spain, the Papacy, to which Henry was not invited.

But despite these issues, the reign of Henry VII cannot be described as anything less than a success: he had established the Tudor dynasty, obtained recognition from European monarchs, and had stabilised the wider domains. Henry's lasting legacy has been the subject of debate by historians for decades, with the traditional interpretation – from the likes of Polydore Vergil in the early 1500s and Sir Francis Bacon in the early 1600s – stating that he was a successful monarch, particularly in terms of his shrewd diplomacy and financial acumen. This continued into the twentieth century, with S.B. Chrimes believing Henry's 'steady purposefulness saved England from mediocrity',[1] and with R.L. Storey arguing that his reign 'must still be regarded as one of the great landmarks in England's political development', particularly in being the difference between the old medieval world and the new modern world.[2] More recent interpretations have not been as kind to Henry VII, with fewer historians today agreeing with the view that it was a reign that decisively broke with tradition, with many highlighting that there was more of a continuation than change. In a similar manner, the belief that Henry VII was a man of peace was dominant for centuries; it was Polydore Vergil who wrote that 'Henry was a lover and ... a son of peace',[3] and this portrayal was celebrated in the royal court during Henry's reign with the poet laureate of the period – Bernard Andre – hailing the Tudor king as *'Rex Pacificus'*. However, others have pointed to Henry's actions in diplomacy, particularly the Breton Crisis and the French War of 1492, suggesting that the peace-loving portrayal is not consistent with his actions.[4] What is clear is that Henry VII was constrained from being proactive with his foreign policy due to a weaker military and economic capability; but his son, Henry VIII, had greater freedom on the European stage. In 1509, *Rex Pacificus* gave way to *Rex Imperator* ... the Warrior King.

Rex Imperator

Many had high hopes for the new reign, with Thomas More penning a poem for the coronation in which he wrote: 'This day is the end of our slavery, the fount of our liberty; the end of sadness, the beginning of joy.'[5] The general view was that the final years of Henry VII's reign had been pessimistic and unsettled, particularly with his parsimonious penny-pinching ways; the historian Thomas Penn has written in terms of the father being 'the Winter King', with Henry VIII offering the promise of a fresh, reviving summer.[6]

Such expectations of a fresh start were reflected in the king himself: young, bold and strong. In 1515, a Venetian ambassador commented on Henry's appearance:

> His majesty is the handsomest potentate I ever set eyes on; above the usual heigh, with an extremely fine calf to his leg, his complexion very fair and bright, with auburn hair combed straight and short in the French fashion, and a round face so very beautiful, that it would become a pretty woman, his throat being rather long and thick.

And that was not all, with the ambassador continuing:

> He speaks French, English and Latin, and a little Italian, plays well on the lute and harpsichord, sings songs from book at sight, draws the bow with greater strength than any man in England, and jousts marvellously. Believe me, he is in every aspect a most accomplished Prince.[7]

Henry's education was second to none, as highlighted in the reputation and expense of his tutors. As such, Henry was able to style himself as a Renaissance king, particularly with the finesse of his artistic gifts. However, there was also a darker side to his character, as evidenced from his youth. The historian John Guy writes of Henry's 'egoism, self-righteousness, and capacity to brood', particularly in terms of wanting to impress others – particularly those in Europe – of his brilliance and might. And what better way to achieve this than on the battlefield? John Guy comments:

As his reign unfolded, Henry VIII added 'imperial' concepts of kingship to existing feudal ones; he sought to give the words *Rex Imperator* a meaning unseen since the days of the Roman Empire. He was eager, too, to conquer, to emulate the glorious victories of the Black Prince and Henry V, to quest after the golden fleece that was the French Crown.[8]

Henry's imperial aspirations were clear to see from the moment of his coronation in 1509, in which 'the nine children of honour' on horses 'apparelled on their goldsmith's work', on which the words of various imperial domains belonging to the king were highlighted: 'England, and France, Gascony, Guienne, Normandy, Anjou, Cornwall, Wales, Ireland.'[9] Of course, the English monarch did not actually control many of these areas, particularly the French ones; however, his intention was loud and clear: he had high ambitions of projecting his rule across a wider empire. As such, talk of war was brewing in England.

War

Within a handful of years, the old wait-and-see policy of Henry VII was discarded in favour of a proactive approach with Henry VIII launching an invasion of northern France in 1513. How did it come to this? A major factor was Henry being heavily influenced by an Anglo claim to the French throne; this claim stretched back more than a century to the beginnings of the Hundred Years' War, particularly due to the exploits of Henry V in uniting the crowns of both England and France in the Treaty of Troyes in 1420. Since that point, various English monarchs had pushed forward this claim or conveniently discarded it depending on their relationship with France; Henry VII was quick to drop it after securing a favourable settlement in the Treaty of Etaples in 1492. But Henry VIII seized on the aim of making the dream a reality: he would rebuild the old empire in France.

An instrumental part of the countdown to the French war was Henry's closer relationship with the Spanish monarchy, particularly after his marriage to Catherine of Aragon in 1509. A final significant factor was the changing of the old guard of advisors of Henry VII's reign – who had largely favoured a peaceful, reactive approach to foreign policy –

with fresh blood who were more willing to agree with Henry's military ambitions. And there was no one who climbed faster in the court than Thomas Wolsey; the churchman was both intelligent and cunning, and knew that advancement would happen if he could give the king what he wanted.

All of these factors coalesced into the first military action of Henry's reign, when in 1511 he sent 1,000 archers and 500 other men into the Low Countries to assist Emperor Maximilian in his war against the Duke of Gueldres, while a further 1,000 men were sent to Cadiz to help King Ferdinand's fight against the Moors. Henry himself wanted to join the Spanish expedition, but was convinced against it; although the entire venture 'swiftly descended,' states one historian, 'into farce', with the English soldiers drinking themselves stupid. Both expeditions were, on the whole, unimportant; however, they signalled Henry's intent to become a far more proactive monarch than his father in terms of international affairs. Furthermore, his friendships with Maximilian and Ferdinand suggested a larger plan was forming, particularly in the anti-French alliance developing in the shape of the Holy League led by the Pope. In 1512, a formal declaration of war was delivered to France, with Henry agreeing to plans to send 12,000 men to Spain with the view of an invasion of southern France that would lead to the recovery of the lost province of Aquitaine. It had belonged to the English monarchy for three centuries, before the French took control of it during the Hundred Years' War.

However, the entire venture failed: there were problems transporting the men, and more serious issues with supplying the army. The English wanted to strike into Aquitaine, but Ferdinand used the English troops as a diversion for his own schemes to obtain the territory of Navarre. One of the English commanders, Thomas Howard, Earl of Surrey, feared the spread of sickness among the men, noting how the men wished 'they would never have been sent to this ungracious country where the people love a ducat better than all their kin'.[10] The Spanish and English didn't mix, leading to incidents of English soldiers pillaging and looting, before the men returned home having achieved nothing other than suffering 1,800 deaths. Henry was incensed on reading the reports; great cost had been spent sending an army to Spain, only for English honour to be 'besmirched, its discipline despoiled'.[11] King Ferdinand excellently summed up England's military problems:

They are very excellent men and only want experience. England has had no wars – the English do not know how to behave in a campaign. Unaccustomed as they are to warfare, they show a marked dislike to perform such labours as are inevitably entailed on soldiers.[12]

Ferdinand's summary, then, was that the long years of international peace under Henry VII had led to England becoming meek and stale in warfare.

Henry, however, was not finished with his military exploits; 1512 turned into 1513, and a fresh campaigning year offered new alternatives to make his name. Rather than return to Spain, England decided on invading the north of France by using Calais as the suitable starting point. Wolsey was involved in the logistics of organising a vast military undertaking: ships, 12,000 infantry, 4,000 cavalry, artillery, and thousands of suits of armour.[13] This time Henry himself would direct his troops in the field; however, there were issues regarding the slow speed of the English army's progress through northern France. The king spent three weeks in Calais parading his imperial might, rather than actually getting stuck into fighting; by the time he left the Pale – in late July – valuable weeks of the summer campaigning season had been lost.

Five days into his march the English suffered a setback when supplies coming from Calais were attacked by the French; 150 wagons were taken with 300 killed. Then, soon after, Henry was threatened by being overrun by a French force, forcing him to find cover with his foreign mercenaries, 'whom Henry regarded as better fighters than his countrymen'.[14] In early August, Henry arrived at the ongoing siege of Thérouanne, which held out for three more weeks; when it finally fell it became the first French town taken by an English force since the final days of the Hundred Years' War. The town was dealt harshly by the English, as explained by C.S.L. Davies: 'The fortifications were destroyed and the houses burnt, leaving only the cathedral and the adjoining clerical residences standing.'[15] It was during the siege when the much acclaimed 'Battle of the Spurs' happened, when the French sent knights to relieve the town; the English charged:

sending one body of French horsemen back into the others and causing wholesale panic. Within minutes the whole

French host was galloping back madly across the fields whence they had come, shedding their standards and lances and even the bardings of their horses.[16]

Although the skirmish may have been heavily exaggerated, the outcome was a success for Henry's Tudor force: standards were taken, as well as 100 prisoners for ransom. But more was to come when Henry headed to the larger city of Tournai, taking it in late September. Henry enjoyed a victory procession as a conquering hero through the town, with historian John Matsuiak noting how 'the king, wearing a full suit of richly decorated armour, rode a magnificent courser, as his henchmen carried his weapons before him'.[17] Henry celebrated his success by gifting titles to his closest nobles, particularly with Charles Brandon being made Duke of Suffolk. In the autumn, the king returned to England intent on resuming military activities against France in 1514.

But this new campaign did not transpire. Both Maximilian and Ferdinand settled their scores with France, and in doing so renounced their former deals with England. Importantly, Henry had spent the financial reserves carefully built up by his father throughout his reign. As such, there was no other option than to come to the negotiating table. The peace treaty was a generous one: Henry kept both towns, his claim to the French throne was recognised, and he received a pension (just as his father had at Etaples in 1492). Furthermore, Henry's younger sister – Mary – was married off to 'the toothless and lecherous' French King Louis XII.[18] Henry had experienced the taste of war in his northern French campaign, and England was able to enjoy a further historical military victory against Scotland in the very same year.

The Thistle and the Rose

The Anglo-Scottish relationship was a difficult one, based on centuries of mistrust and war principally stemming from the English Crown's attempts to subdue and oppress their northern neighbours. This antagonism can be traced to events in the late thirteenth century when, in 1286, King Alexander III died without a clear successor. The throne was to pass to a toddler, his granddaughter Margaret, the Maid of Norway; however, on the journey to Scotland in 1490 she died. Without a clear successor the field was open to thirteen different candidates, all of whom put forward their bid for the crown. Because of the fear of civil strife erupting, King Edward I of England was asked to arbitrate and help to find the most suitable candidate. However, as in keeping with Edward's aims of expanding his rule over Britain, he was able to manipulate the situation by only providing his support for a claimant if they in turn agreed to his position as overlord of Scotland. Edward eventually chose John Balliol, who became an English 'puppet', with Scotland being reduced in significance to 'vassal kingdom'.[19]

John Balliol eventually opposed Edward's schemes; however, an English invasion led to him being forced from the throne. Opposition to English domination continued to grow, resulting in the Wars for Scottish Independence, with help forthcoming from France, in establishing what became known as the Auld Alliance. New heroes were created, such as William Wallace and Robert the Bruce (a grandson of one of the original thirteen claimants), which culminated in the defeat of the English at the Battle of Bannockburn in 1314. After this point the relationship between both countries remained tumultuous, as evidenced by Berwick-upon-Tweed changing hands on several occasions. Border skirmishes were a constant issue; however, both countries were too weak and unstable to seriously threaten each other; during the fifteenth century, England was dealing with the fallout of the Hundred Years' War and the Wars of the Roses, while Scotland suffered from a succession of child monarchs (such as James II and James III).

Henry VII experienced his own entanglement with the Scottish when, in 1496, James IV agreed to support Perkin Warbeck in the quest to take the English throne. Perhaps King James believed Warbeck's story of being a wronged prince, leading to the bestowing of financial gifts on the pretender – paying for his household, servants and fine clothes – to the tune of £1,200 per year. Or perhaps it was due to the consideration of what could be gained from providing Warbeck with support; after all, Henry would be willing to 'offer any conditions ... for peace'.[20] If Warbeck was successful with his bid for the English crown then great rewards would be forthcoming; perhaps a large pay-out and extensive territory. But even if was all a failure, James may still also end up as a winner with a beneficial compensation settlement from Henry; perhaps the return of Berwick, or perhaps a juicy pension. James IV and Scotland had everything to gain.

After a stunted invasion of northern England, Henry prepared for an all-out invasion of Scotland in retaliation. He ordered his men:

> to make warre and to doo from hensfurth by land and by see all thanoyauance possible to the Scottis that ye can or maye.[21]

However, Henry's plans were scuppered in 1497 when the Cornish revolted in response to the call for taxation to provide the money to pay for the war. Men were diverted from heading to Scotland to instead head back south to deal with the rebellion. The events of the Cornish rising clearly scared Henry, and he changed tack and returned to his preferred method: negotiation of a treaty. Henry's one key aim was that James renounce his support of Perkin Warbeck, and in return the Tudor king was 'prepared to accept peace at any price'.[22] Luckily for James, he had already jettisoned Warbeck, having come to the conclusion that the pretender was far more trouble than he was worth. Polydore Vergil writes:

> the king wittily mocked the puerile man's empty-headedness, whom henceforth he neglected more each day, since his deeds failed to match his words, and his successes did not correspond to his promises.[23]

Negotiations led to the Treaty of Ayton, which established the first permanent peace settlement between the countries since 1328. Then, in 1502, the Treaty of Perpetual Peace was agreed, thereby confirming an agreement of James to marry Henry's daughter, Margaret.[24] On 25 January 1503, Margaret Tudor exchanged wedding vows with a proxy, leading to the formal marriage later in August. Richard Cavendish describes their introduction to one another:

> At Dalkeith Castle on August 3rd, King James himself, in a crimson velvet jacket, rode in with a train of horsemen. Margaret curtsied deeply and he bowed low and they kissed in greeting. They talked together privately and sat together at supper and afterwards he played to her on the clavichord and the lute. Two nights later she played for him.[25]

The difference in age – James was 30 and Margaret was 13 – was notable, although it is likely that the marriage was not consummated until years later; Margaret did not give birth for the first time until she was 17. James may have been underwhelmed by his 'small, dumpy' child bride,[26] but he would have been far more pleased with the handsome dowry that was attached to her, amounting to £35,000.[27] The occasion was celebrated with the writing of William Dunbar's poem 'The Thrissil and the Rois'; the thistle representing the Scottish royal emblem, and the rose portraying the house of Tudor.

Flodden

Despite this connection, it is clear the Anglo-Scottish relationship began to deteriorate in the final years of the reign of Henry VII, particularly due to the closeness of Scotland to France. The fear of the resurrection of the Auld Alliance never left English minds, and when Henry was committed to the invasion of northern France in 1513 the Scottish King James IV took the opportunity to attack.

Henry was at the siege of Thérouanne when a message was brought to him from James; the Scottish king asked for the English to return home and to make peace with France or else there would be consequences. The Tudor monarch was furious, telling the messenger that if James 'be so hardy to invade my realm or cause to enter one foot of my ground I shall make him as weary of his part as ever was man that began any such business'. Furthermore, Henry brought up Scotland's lowly position in a reference to the earlier claims of suzerainty of Edward I, declaring: 'I am the very own of Scotland', and that James 'holdeth it of me by homage'.

But James was not willing to let the prospect of a weakened and distracted England pass him by. In early August a force of Scottish border reivers crossed into Northumberland and pillaged numerous English settlements, which was followed several weeks later by a vast force of more than 30,000 men commanded by King James himself. Fortunately for the English, James' advanced warning of his intent to invade – as part of his belief in the chivalric code – provided England time to form a response force under the Earl of Surrey. However, James was confident in defeating 'a crooked old Earl in a cart', making reference to Surrey's advanced age of 70 years.[28]

The Scottish found a good position on an old Iron Age hill fort at Flodden Edge, near the Scottish border. Surrey didn't fancy his chances and tried his luck by sending a message to James to meet him in battle on a nearby plain. The Scottish king commented that it was 'not fitting for an Earl to seek to command a King', and assumed that Surrey and the English would scuttle off for resupply and safety at Berwick. But despite the temptation, Surrey was adamant that he could not avoid battle, particularly for the potential disgrace at refusing battle and the condemnation and wrath of Henry himself. Therefore, Surrey put together a plan to flank the Scottish, in which it seemed as though he was heading to Berwick, before he was able to turn around at the Scottish rear. Fearing encirclement, the Scottish were forced from their secure position; however, they were unable to maintain discipline, and with James on the front-line, disarray ensued in the strategic overview of battle. In the wet and windy conditions James was killed – he was later found with an arrow wound in his jaw – and alongside him fell a high number of Scottish officers and nobles.

The loss of so many leaders dealt a massive blow to the Scottish kingdom. Their king was dead and in his place was a 17-month-old boy, James V. The Earl of Surrey was celebrated and rewarded for his exploits, leading Henry to allow Surrey to reclaim his father's dukedom of Norfolk. It was a vast turnaround for the fortunes of the House of Howard, having fought against Henry Tudor at Bosworth in 1485 to become firmly embraced to the regime.

Henry VIII ended 1513 in a position of contentment: he had realised his dreams of going to war and chalked up victories against the French on foreign soil, while also having the additional pleasure of seeing the Scottish kingdom significantly weakened. The warrior king had arrived on the international stage. The challenge now was to maintain this position of power for the remainder of his reign.

Chapter 8

Peacemaker

Thomas Wolsey's diplomatic direction

On New Year's Day 1515, the French King Louis XII heard the final sacraments, before dying later that evening. His marriage to Henry VIII's sister, Mary Tudor, had lasted a handful of weeks; although Louis had been optimistic about finally obtaining a male heir, he died without a successor. The French throne passed to his cousin and son-in-law, Francis I.

The arrival of Francis on the European scene was a game-changer: he was younger than Henry and he had big ambitions to increase the prestige and power of France. Henry no longer faced a weak and ailing monarch in his quest to recover the French kingdom, and as such, his goal became more difficult. Then, a year later, King Ferdinand died, leaving the Spanish throne to his teenage grandson, Charles. Within a handful of years, Charles became the strongest ruler in Europe with his mouth-watering inheritance: the Spanish throne and the growing New World colonies, alongside Burgundy and then in 1519, election as the head of the Holy Roman Empire. The relative weakness of the Tudor empire is highlighted in a comparison with revenue generated elsewhere: England could raise £110,000 per year, whereas France could obtain £350,000. Then there was the matter of population size: England's 2.5 million was dwarfed by France's 15 million, whereas the Habsburg domains included up to 23 million people.

From being the new kid on the block who seemingly had the impetus to impose himself on Europe, Henry was now up against younger and more powerful rivals. This changed the dynamic of European power-politics, leading the English to attempt a different approach in remaining a central part of Continental diplomacy. The warrior king made way for the peacemaker.

Peace in Our Time

Having tasted victory in northern France in 1513, as well as success against Scotland, Henry would rightfully have felt content about his first military adventure when returning to England. There may have been a part of him that regretted having missed out on participating at Flodden; after all, the taking of a couple of French towns could not eclipse the vanquishing of a kingly rival. But, on the whole, he would have been satisfied that he had made a clear statement.

However, the military campaigns of 1513 came at a huge financial cost. His father's carefully constructed inheritance was gone, with £922,000 spent in the period 1511–13. The cost of fortifying Tournai alone cost £230,000, demonstrating to Henry that war was an expensive business.[1] The lack of continuing funds was the principal reason Henry negotiated a peace settlement with France, leading to a truce in 1514. Henry kept his newly taken French possessions, while his sister, Mary, was married off to the ageing French king. Henry's military goals were now substituted for belt-tightening peace policies; the trick was to make himself relevant and to exert himself on the European stage without resorting to an army.

By far the greatest success of this peace policy was the signing of the Treaty of London in 1518. Key states of Europe, including France, the Holy Roman Empire, Spain, Burgundy and the Papal States, came together to outlaw war; everyone agreed to not attack one another, and to come to the assistance of anyone under attack. It was, in many ways, an earlier prototype to the twentieth-century organisations of the League of Nations and the United Nations, although many historians have cynically viewed the entire treaty 'as a mere exercise in egoism'.[2] The treaty was the brainchild of Wolsey, who was currying favour from the Pope, and Henry was able to bask in the glow of plaudits from his fellow European monarchs.

However, this posturing came at a price: the expensively garrisoned and refurbished Tournai was handed back to the French. For a handful of years the town was viewed as part of the wider Tudor empire, a segment of Henry's French kingdom domains alongside the Pale of Calais. Although Tournai and Thérouanne had been referred to as expensive 'ungracious dogholes', it is clear that Henry valued them highly; it appears that Tournai even sent representation to the English Parliament during this short period.[3] The return of Tournai helped to keep the peace, with the English only slightly compensated with the French paying £120,000 for their former possession. It wasn't destined to remain in French hands for long; in 1521, it was captured by Charles V's imperial troops.

For Wolsey, the peace approach was personally advantageous: by providing his king with a platform for plaudits he enhanced his own position at the royal court, leading to the further advancement of power in England. Furthermore, the brokering of peace in Europe advanced Wolsey's reputation in Rome, with the recently created cardinal having an ambition to one day become the pope. One Venetian ambassador said of Wolsey's willingness to become involved on the European stage: 'Nothing pleases him more than to be called the arbiter of the affairs of Christendom.'[4] Many historians are sceptical about Wolsey's true commitment to the wider goal of peace; however, as J.J. Scarisbrick notes that neither 'Wolsey's evident desire to parade himself, nor his use of dubious methods, prove that the whole project was fraudulent'.[5] Wolsey was juggling the demands of two masters – Henry and the Papacy – and it was a job that proved to be more and more difficult with every passing year.

Henry v Francis

The reality was that this spirit of cooperation and non-aggression was destined to fall apart; within a handful of years diplomats were plotting behind closed doors, including Wolsey himself when negotiating an anti-French alliance with the Holy Roman Empire. The coming together of the English and the French at the spectacular extravaganza of the Field of the Cloth of Gold in 1520 was an attempt to continue the good feelings of the Treaty of London.

Henry viewed Francis with great suspicion and jealous envy, which only served to increase the national enmity between the two nations. But there was also a personal reason for Henry's hatred when, just two months after the death of Louis XII in 1515, Mary Tudor married Charles Brandon, the Duke of Suffolk. The match was made possible by Francis, who attended the wedding in person; Henry was angered at the trampling of his own feudal rights, particularly after he had previously sworn Suffolk away from his sister.

However, Wolsey hoped that the summit meeting on the outskirts of Calais would help restore good faith, and although the two-week event in 1520 was nothing more than a glorified jousting, wrestling and archery tournament, it did demonstrate the imperial magnificence of the English monarch. Around 6,000 people attended on Henry, with the budget for hosting the Field of the Cloth of Gold costing the equivalent of a year's revenue. Relations between the two kings became tested when Henry offered his rival to a bout of wrestling, which ended with the English monarch being thrown to the ground. However, rather than sulk, Henry appears to have found common ground with Francis, with time spent drinking and eating with one another. But despite this, little of diplomatic value came out of the meeting; although, Wolsey made sure that he had other irons in the fire.

Charles V's position as the most powerful monarch in Europe brought about a rivalry with the French kingdom, and in April 1521, Francis declared war on Charles, thereby igniting a decades-long feud. This placed Henry in a fortuitous position in which he was courted by both monarchs, which helps explain the eagerness of the French to come to an understanding at the Field of the Cloth of Gold. In May 1520, a month before that summit meeting, Charles travelled to England to speak with Henry in the hope of becoming friends. Henry appears to have continued to juggle the two camps; in the summer of 1521 a conference was held between England and France at Calais, and then just two days later Wolsey headed to Bruges to meet Charles. Wolsey was impressed by Charles' commitment to England, in which England and Charles agreed to attack France if Francis refused to agree to peace. Furthermore, it was also agreed that Charles would marry Princess Mary when she came of age, which was an offer that Henry could not refuse. Having attempted the path of peace, Henry was now returning to his default position of going to war.

Henry's second French war started with his declaration in 1522, leading to the landing of English troops in Picardy. In the campaigning season of 1523, the Duke of Suffolk attempted to march on Paris itself, which could have led to the realisation of Henry's dreams of realising his claim on the French kingdom. However, the promised imperial troops were not to be found, which led to the collapse of the entire enterprise. It appeared that Charles was more focused on the gains to be made in northern Italy, and that the English presence in France was simply a mere diversion tactic.

Despite Henry's anger, Charles' own powerbase continued to expand, as shown in the defeat of the French at the Battle of Pavia in February 1525. Francis was captured and the English feared that the Habsburgs would dominate all of Europe. The Treaty of More, signed in the summer of 1525, ended Henry's war with France, but the English continued to watch on as spectators at the imperial rise of the period; in 1527, imperial troops marched into Rome and sacked the city, leading to their control of the Papacy. By this point, Wolsey was scrabbling for the semblance of a coherent diplomatic policy, with the English forced into the arms of France to help combat Charles' power. The cardinal's ambition of becoming pope appeared to be slipping from his grasp, particularly with England's opposition to Charles, and by the late 1520s, Wolsey was facing knives out from all directions.

The Fall of Wolsey

Henry VIII tasked Wolsey with a clear instruction: obtain an annulment from the Papacy to end the king's marriage to Catherine of Aragon. In times of old, when the Papacy was more inclined to the English king's whims, it may have proved a straightforward process; after all, it was Pope Julius II who granted papal dispensation to allow Henry to marry his brother's widow in 1509. However, in the context of the late 1520s the assumption that Henry could simply ask the Pope for a favour in providing the approval of an annulment soon proved to be naïve. The European geopolitical map had greatly changed, with Charles V now triumphant across the Continent and with the Pope firmly under the Habsburg thumb. As such, the Pope was reluctant to provide dispensation for an annulment because it did not suit the wider Habsburg plans: first, family honour was at stake, and Charles V was reluctant to see his aunt discarded in such a shameful manner; second, keeping Henry chained to his marriage would mean that he would be unable to marry others and have the chance of heirs, which would, by logic, keep England unstable and weak. There was no need for new heirs when there was a perfectly good one waiting in the wings; Princess Mary may have been female, but she was also half a Habsburg, which counted for much more.

So, the Pope used a variety of delaying tactics, dragging out the case for several years, until Henry and his advisors realised what game was being played, leading to the formulation of more drastic policies to provide him with the freedom to marry Anne. But for Wolsey, the failure to use his papal connections was the final straw for Henry's patience; in 1529 his governmental powers were taken from him, and after spending time in York he was ordered to London to face charges from his courtly enemies. On the journey south he fell ill and died, speaking the following words shortly before his death: 'If I had served God as diligently as I have done the King, he would not have given me over in my grey hairs.'

Wolsey's downfall was not a result of his foreign policy initiatives, but rather his inability to secure Henry's divorce to Catherine of Aragon. He was the director of English diplomacy for a fifteen-year period; however, the trouble in serving two masters – his king and his pope – ultimately proved impossible. The extent of the success of his diplomatic manoeuvres can be questioned: the peace initiatives were temporary, while the quest to find a suitable ally, in the form of both Charles and Francis, also failed. Ultimately, the set-piece events, such as the Treaty of London of 1518, were hollow due to Henry's over-riding hunger to prove himself on the battlefield. The king's core position, especially if he had resources to fund it, was to go to war. The claim of Henry being a man of peace proved inaccurate; the burning longing to become *Rex Imperator* could not be contained.

Chapter 9

Expanding the 'Imperiall Crowne'
The enlargement of Britain in the 1530s

'Mine own sweetheart', begins one of Henry's undated love letters to Anne Boleyn, in which he pleads his sorrow at being parted from her:

> these shall be to advertise you of the great loneliness that I find here since your departing, for I ensure you methinketh the time longer since your departing now last than I was wont to do a whole fortnight

Henry continues:

> Wishing myself (specially an evening) in my sweetheart's arms, whose pretty dukkys I trust shortly to kiss. Written with the hand of him that was, is, and shall be yours by his will.

Henry VIII's marriage to Catherine of Aragon was into its eighteenth year when the king's attention was captivated by the alluring eyes of Anne Boleyn. Anne's refusal to simply become another royal mistress forced Henry to decide to annul his marriage with Catherine. This switch of affections was, in many ways, the logical move: the marriage to Catherine had only led to one child – Princess Mary – but no sons, and by the late 1520s it seemed as if Catherine's childbearing days were now past. But Henry underestimated the difficulty of obtaining an annulment from the Pope, and his desire to legally wed Anne had profound consequences on religion, politics and society. This one romance would transform all of Britain.

The Henrician Supremacy

The frustration of the King's Great Matter led Henry to consider alternatives ways to free himself from his marriage and to allow him to marry Anne. Archbishop Cranmer provided him with the means: by using the arguments of the growing Protestant movement, he could simply renounce the authority of Rome and establish himself as the head of the Church of England. The justification came in promoting the idea that England was not a mere kingdom, but rather an empire with a history that stretched far back into the past beyond the formation of the Catholic Church. This was highlighted in legislation in the form of the Act of Appeals in 1533, in which Henry was stated as both the king of England as well as the head of the English Church due to 'the imperial crown of his realm'.

With these new powers, Henry obtained an annulment from Catherine, married Anne, and by the end of 1533 had a new child: Princess Elizabeth. More importantly, his position as the head of the English Church, as defined in the Act of Supremacy of 1534, created vast new powers that had previously been untapped by Henry's kingly predecessors. Church land was sold and religious doctrine was altered, all of which tampered with the way religion had stood in England for centuries.

Either by design or by accident, the 1530s became a transformative decade. This is also true of the Tudor empire, with Henry – emboldened by his new status – taking decisive steps in reasserting and redefining his relationship in three corners of his empire: Wales, Ireland and the North.

The 'Dominion of Wales'

The relationship between Wales and England remains as odd in the twenty-first century as it did in the Tudor era. Both are countries, but yet unequal in size; both are nations within the United Kingdom, yet Wales was annexed and absorbed within the English political and legal system. However, clear differences remain and although the devolution changes of recent decades have provided the Welsh with greater control of their laws, it has also muddied the water further. Ultimately, who holds the power: Westminster or the Welsh Parliament? One small, recent event may help to illustrate this confusing relationship; in 2020 the football club

Chester FC ran into difficulties when it became tangled in attempting to follow the COVID restrictions provided by the Westminster government and the Welsh Parliament. The Deva Stadium straddles the English-Welsh border, with the pitch being entirely on Welsh soil, while the team plays in the English football system; as such, the stadium is considered English. This led to the football club becoming entangled in disputes with both the Westminster and Welsh governments. The boundary can be traced back to the 'Acts of Union' of Henry VIII's reign, when he attempted to remove 'Discord, Variance, Debate, Division'; as with his religious control, Wales would be reformed and remoulded.

By the time of the reign of Henry VIII, the Welsh had largely embraced the Tudor state. Their vital role in Henry Tudor's victory at Bosworth in 1485, particularly with the impact of Sir Rhys ap Thomas, and the links of the Welsh ancestry of the Tudors was a source of pride for many; after all, one of 'their own' had claimed the throne. This general mood was echoed by a Venetian envoy of the period who wrote of how the 'Welsh may now be said to have recovered their formal independence, for the most wise and fortunate Henry VII is a Welshman'.[1] However, there does not appear to have been what historian P.R. Roberts called a 'distinctive Welsh policy', with Henry VII preferring to reaffirm the existing status quo.[2] There may have been concerns regarding Henry VIII's position on Wales, particularly with the new king not appearing to share the same affinity as his father.

The constitutional position of the Welsh within the Tudor empire remained peculiar, with the relationship being roughly the same as established by Edward I at the end of the thirteenth century. Wales was annexed to the English Crown, but there remained notable differences between those who lived in Wales and those who lived in England; these included the difference under the law, as well as the complete lack of parliamentary representation. Furthermore, the country was divided between the Principality of Wales and the increasingly anachronistic feudal marcher lordships. The Marcher Lords had previously played important roles for English monarchs, particularly in maintaining the peace, but their powerbase had been badly eroded during the Wars of the Roses, with many lordships finding their way back into royal hands.

For the first decade of his reign, Henry VIII was content to allow matters in Wales to continue as they had done under his father, as seen in the form of Sir Rhys ap Thomas, who retained his influence until his death in 1525. However, Rhys ap Thomas' grandson was not as successful in winning over royal favour, leading to his trial for treason and then execution at Tower Hill in 1531.[3] The status quo was further rocked with the impact of the Break with Rome; the natural Tudor suspicion of nobles escalated due to questions of the religious allegiances of the Marcher Lords. Would these lords remain loyal to their king, or would they retain their Catholic faith? Religious division could lead to rebellions and could also lead to the invitation of Catholic monarchs to land an army in Wales, thereby cutting straight into the heart of Henry's kingdom, just as his father had demonstrated in August 1485.

Such fears were played out in the form of James ap Gruffydd ap Hywel. Descended from gentry in south Wales, James ap Gruffydd became estranged from the court due to the Break with Rome, leading to an abandonment of Wales to go into foreign exile in the hope of obtaining support for a Catholic rebellion. A government informant wrote of his arrival in Scotland in 1533, calling the Welshman 'the gretest man in Wales'.[4] Although nothing came of these plots, it was worrying enough to acknowledge that all was not well in the Welsh region.

This may help explain the reason for Henry VIII taking 'an extended progress' to the Welsh borders in 1535 in an effort to win over the hearts of the people.[5] More importantly, the entrance of Bishop Rowland Lee into Welsh politics in 1534 as Lord President of the Council of Wales highlighted the Crown's intention to stabilise law and order. Lee had risen to prominence under the patronage of Thomas Wolsey, and after Wolsey's fall from power he continued under the protection of Thomas Cromwell. Lee had proven himself a team player during the religious changes of the early 1530s, having officiated the wedding of Henry to Anne. Lee's time in Wales was a particularly disruptive one, leading historians to deem him the 'Hanging Bishop' due to the ferocity of the executions he meted out to felons in the aim of restoring order to the region. Some historic claims have placed the number of executions at 5,000 – a thousand for every year Lee was in his post – although this number is likely to have been exaggerated. But Lee's sadistic behaviour can be sampled in his proud boast of having hanged 'four of the best blood in the county of Shropshire', while on another occasion he ordered the hanging of a corpse, after the offender died before conviction. Throughout it all, Lee reported back to Cromwell on a daily basis, writing how 'the outlaws submit themselves or be taken. If he be taken he playeth his pagent. If he submit himself I take him to God's mercy and the king's grace upon his fine.'[6]

However, the Hanging Bishop was not enthusiastic about the Crown's plans to reform the political relationship between England and Wales in the shape of two acts – the 'Acts of Union' – between 1535 and 1542. It was Henry VIII's attempt to eliminate the 'great Discord, Variance, Debate, Division, Murmur and Sedition' that had 'grown between his said Subjects'. The two acts provided clarity for the relationship between England and Wales, with the annexed smaller country becoming officially absorbed into the English state, thereby becoming fully subjected to the 'imperiall crowne of this realme'.[7] Key changes included the abolishing of the old Marcher Lordships; the division of Wales into shire counties, thereby mirroring the English county system; the provision of representation in the House of Commons for the very first time; and bringing Wales into the same legal framework as in England. As the 1535 Act noted, this would mean that Wales 'shal be, stoned and contyne for ever frome hensforthe' united to England.[8]

These changes were supported and embraced by the Welsh lords and gentry, particularly due to their easier access to patronage and political posts. However, there were negative consequences as a result of these acts, particularly in terms of Welsh identity. Although Wales' former distinct political character had been reduced, it was its cultural and social character that had been primarily threatened. The acts had specified that all political, professional and legal documents were 'to be given and done in the English Tongue', which prevented those who only spoke Welsh from holding any high office (and this was not officially repealed until the Welsh Languages Act of 1993). Although the primary aim was to eliminate 'great Discord, Variance, Debate, Division', many Welsh people were now effectively excluded from legal access and political power, which is illustrated in the make-up of the Court of Great Sessions established in 1542; 217 judges on the benches in 288 years of the court's existence, and from this number only thirty were Welshmen.[9] Although historians have stated that there was no systematic conscious attempt from government to eradicate the Welsh language, these changes did establish a clear distinction between the English language of the elites and Welsh language of the lower orders.[10] This, then, was Tudor imperialism in action: Tudor influence was spread throughout Wales, with Henry increasing his hold on the region.

Ireland and the Geraldine Insurrection

Across the Irish Sea was the 'disturbed land', which had been relatively calm since Henry VII's problems in the 1490s. The restoration of the Fitzgeralds had led to decades of stability under their leadership; after Gerald Fitzgerald died in 1513, his position was filled by his son, also Gerald Fitzgerald – 'the Younger Gerald' – who became the ninth Earl of Kildare. He was well regarded by the English Crown, as illustrated by his attendance at the Field of the Cloth of Gold in 1520. But the religious changes of the 1530s added pressure to an island infamous for its tendency to disrupt into open rebellion. However, the immediate cause of the problems in the 1530s was not religion but rather the re-emergence of the never-ending Geraldine-Butler feud. Fitzgerald was shot during an attack on one of the Butler allies, leading to a deterioration in his health, particularly his speech. Fearing that he was losing control, Fitzgerald was summoned to London where he was committed to the Tower.

Back in Ireland a rumour circulated that Fitzgerald had been executed. This led to outrage, with his son, Thomas Fitzgerald, raising a rebellion against the English Crown in protest – the first serious anti-English rebellion on the island since Henry VII's reign in the 1490s. The rumour was false, although Fitzgerald died soon after due to his earlier injuries; it was enough to bring about a rising of anti-English resentment that had been bubbling under the surface since Henry's Break with Rome. Ultimately, Thomas Fitzgerald attempted the very same tactic that his grandfather had used four decades earlier: showing the Tudors that governing Ireland was impossible without the support of a Kildare.

In June 1534, Thomas Fitzgerald used a council in Dublin to obtain support and outline a strategy on how to deal with the English. He was accompanied by more than a hundred armoured gallowglasses who sported silk fringes on their helmets; this gave rise to Thomas' nickname 'Silken Thomas'. Fitzgerald symbolically threw the sword of state to the floor and declared that all royal belongings were to be forfeited, with the long-term aim of exiling or executing all of those born in England. The Pale was besieged by the rebels, with only Dublin Castle holding out.

However, the Silken Thomas rebellion was unable to fulfil its ambitious aims. First, the Butlers refused to be tempted by the offer of dividing all of Ireland between the two feuding clans. Second, the rebellion was ill-equipped for a long campaign, as highlighted by its organisational difficulties. One tragic incident illustrates the confusion within the ranks of the rebellion; Archbishop John Alen was held hostage by the rebels and mistakenly murdered. Tradition notes how Alen's killers misunderstood Thomas Fitzgerald's order to 'take this fellow away' as the signal for murder, rather than to simply remove him from Fitzgerald's sight.

In the summer of 1534, the rebels attacked Dublin Castle, before Fitzgerald retreated to his stronghold of Maynooth Castle. A year later, an English force under Lord Deputy Sir William Skeffington marched towards it, with the castle falling due to the bribing of its constable. The garrison surrendered in the mistaken belief that they would be pardoned; however, they were either beheaded or hanged, including the bribed constable himself.[11] Fitzgerald saw that his days were numbered, and with his support slipping away he asked for a pardon. The newly installed Lord Deputy of the Pale – Lord Leonard Grey – agreed, guaranteeing Fitzgerald's personal safety. By the end of 1535 the Silken Thomas rebellion was over, with Thomas Fitzgerald now safely confined to the Tower of London. However, unlike his grandfather, he was not pardoned and absolved of his sins. His family were attainted, with their title of Kildare and lands stripped away from them. Then, in 1537, Thomas Fitzgerald and his five uncles were:

> draune from the Tower in to Tyborne, and there alle hongyd
> and hedded and quartered, save the Lord Thomas for he was
> but hongyd and hedded.[12]

Between 1536 and 1540, Lord Grey was energetic in his efforts to restore stability in Ireland. However, his methods were brutal and many within the administration clashed with him, particularly the former Lord Deputy, William Skeffington. Skeffington was reluctant to remain in charge of duties, especially due to his advanced age of 70, and the quarrels that he held with Grey are said to have dramatically shortened his life (he was dead by the end of 1535). Grey's actions while campaigning against the Irish clans were bloody, particularly in the killing of women and children. In the words of historian David Edwards, Grey 'saw all killing as virtuous, an achievement worthy of commemoration'.[13]

However, support for the Fitzgeralds was not fully extinguished and by the end of the decade the Geraldine League had been established with the aim of having lands restored in the form of Gerald Fitzgerald, the future eleventh Earl of Kildare. Two important Irish nobles – Conn O'Neill and Manus O'Donnell – united to invade the Pale in 1539, but Tudor control was eventually restored after Grey's absent army returned to Dublin. The Irish forces retreated to their lands, stocked up with treasures and spoils from their ransacking of the Pale; however, the English overtook them at the ford of Belahoe. The resultant battle saw the Irish completely overwhelmed, leading to hundreds of casualties, but the rebellion was not fully eradicated.

The situation was further confused due to Lord Grey's sister; Elizabeth Grey was the widow of the ninth Earl of Kildare who had passed away in the Tower in 1534, which made her stepmother to Silken Thomas and mother to the younger son, Gerald Fitzgerald. Gerald went on the run, escaping Ireland and spending the next decade on the Continent; Lord Grey was accused of allowing his nephew to escape, with the Crown recalling, attainting and executing Grey for treasonous actions. Grey's successor – Anthony St Leger – continued the fight against the Irish rebels, and his brief was similar to his predecessors: to restore order to Ireland and to obtain submission from the primary clans. St Leger had a more conciliatory approach, particularly in his promotion of the need to make bridges; the carrot, rather than the stick, would help the English regain control of Ireland. In 1541 the O'Neills and O'Donnells were finally defeated and both submitted to Tudor rule once more.

The 1530s reveals a chaotic approach from the Crown to the problems in Ireland. Just as Henry VII himself had attempted a range of approaches in the 1490s, Henry VIII's government used a mixture of 'threats and inducements'; pardons for those who would surrender, and execution for those who continued to oppose him.[14] But big problems remained, particularly in terms of the constitutional position of Ireland within the Tudor domains. After Henry's excommunication in 1533, many in Europe wanted the Papacy to proclaim Ireland's separation from the English throne; it was a pope who had granted Ireland to the English in the twelfth century, and as such, the papacy could simply take it back. A solution was found in the reorganisation of the island as the Kingdom of Ireland, in which Henry made himself king in 1542. English law would be imposed, providing the Irish with the same legal protections as those in England and Wales; although, unlike Wales, Ireland would retain its own parliament.

As Henry VII realised in the 1490s, the key to obtaining control of Ireland was the relationship with the Irish lords. This led to the development of the surrender and regrant policy, in which Irish lords surrendered their lands and had them regranted to them under a royal charter while swearing loyalty to Henry. The intention was to transform the ruling system in Ireland away from the old clan loyalties to become more akin to the English feudal system. The old Irish tradition of electing their kings had clashed with the English tradition of primogeniture, and furthermore, the lack of a clear successor led to feuding and bickering; this new policy would limit this instability. Furthermore, it also ensured that the Irish lords would become assimilated into English ways, such as with English manners and customs. In return, the Irish lords and gentry benefited in similar ways as with the Welsh elites; they became better treated and protected within the Tudor state.[15] Initially, the policy worked in terms of bringing Ireland to heel, as shown in the example of Conn O'Neill; he crossed the sea to personally submit to Henry VIII, converted to Protestantism, and was made the Earl of Tyrone in return. It had been a difficult decade, but Henry ended his reign with a tighter grip on Ireland.

The Pilgrimage of Grace

However, the biggest test of Henry's power grab in the 1530s came not from his Celtic subjects but rather from those in the north of England. Since those early hectic days of opposition against Henry VII, the North had been largely quiet and had accommodated itself within the Tudor empire. However, outrage at the Henrician religious reforms led to the largest rebellion the Tudors would ever face.

During 1536–7, a series of risings in the North, primarily concerned with opposition to the decision to dissolve the monasteries, became a serious threat. In October 1536, the Bishop of Lincoln was murdered by rebels under the leadership of 'Captain Cobbler', a shoemaker called Nicholas Melton. The numbers swelled to more than 10,000 and a list of grievances was hastily put together; however, when the Duke of Suffolk was sent into the region with an army the entire venture collapsed. But other risings in the North – from Yorkshire, Durham, Northumberland and Lancashire – coalesced into what has been labelled the Pilgrimage of Grace; by the middle of October 1536, this rebellion amounted to more than 30,000 men led by a Yorkshire lawyer, Robert Aske. On 21 October, the rebels took control of Pontefract Castle, signalling to the government that they were not to be underestimated.

Henry's initial reaction on hearing of the Lincolnshire Rising was fury, as evidenced in his reply to their demands:

> How presumptions then are ye, the rude commons of one shire, and that one of the most brute and beastly of the whole realm, and of least experience, to find fault with your prince, for the electing of his councillors and prelates.[16]

However, news of the Pilgrimage of Grace left him shaken; he could not hope to match the mighty number of the rebels, and so he used a different tactic: stall for time. The Duke of Norfolk was sent to listen to their demands, with articles referring to how the 'suppression of so many religious houses' being 'a great hurt to the common wealth', as well as another referring to an economic grievance in the form of sheep tax.[17] A temporary truce was agreed; however, Aske wisely retained his rebel forces rather than have them disperse.

By the time of December 1536, the rebels took the chance to finalise their demands in the form of the twenty-four Articles, which substantially beefed up the earlier points. The second article was clear: 'to have the supreme head of the church ... restored unto the see of Rome', with other articles asking for the legitimisation of Lady Mary, the abbeys restored to their former position, 'the liberties of the church to have their old customs', while also ensuring that Henry's chief minister, Cromwell, was punished.[18] Norfolk issued a general pardon with the promise that a future parliamentary session would discuss the articles raised, all of which led to the rebels returning home.

Henry requested that Aske travel to London, where he spent Christmas at Greenwich Palace. 'Be you welcome, my good Aske,' said the king to the rebel on meeting, 'it is my wish that here, before my council, you ask what you desire and I will grant it.' Aske pointed the finger of blame at Cromwell himself, the architect of the vast changes during the decade. In response, Henry appeared to empathise with Aske and the plight of the rebels, even going to the extent of providing valuable gifts to the Yorkshireman. As can be seen by later events, it was all a public relations exercise; keeping Aske sweet to ensure that the North did not boil over. When Aske returned to the North in January he did so as a firm supporter of the Tudor king, but what Henry wanted was the rebellion itself to become divided to give him a chance to capitalise.

He did not have to wait long, for in February 1537 Sir Francis Bigod, disgusted at the truce agreed in December, decided to kick-start the rebellion. He had ambitions to take Hull and Scarborough, but the entire project completely unravelled in a handful of days. The reaction of the Tudor state was vicious: using the argument that the rebels could not be trusted, the ringleaders were rounded up and arrested, with more than 200 executed. Despite all of his hard honest work, the sentence on Aske spared nothing:

> You are to be drawn upon a hurdle to the place of execution, and there you are to be hanged by the neck, and being alive cut down, and your privy-members to be cut off, and your bowels to be taken out of your belly and there burned, you being alive; and your head to be cut off, and your body to be divided into four quarters, and that your head and quarters to be disposed of where his majesty shall think fit.

The Pilgrimage of Grace, as with other opposition to authority in the 1530s, concluded with another victory for Henry VIII and the Tudor cause.

A Transformed Kingdom

The 1530s was an important decade in the development of Britain, with Henry VIII taking full advantage of the opportunity to exert his own imperial rule. In many ways, the Tudor state had enjoyed three successes, in Wales, Ireland and the North: Wales became fully absorbed within the Tudor empire, with Henry achieving his aim of creating 'amicable Concord and Unity'; the Kingdom of Ireland appeared to have settled Henry's concerns of continued instability from across the sea; and the North's religious opposition was pacified.

However, these developments came at a cost to each of the areas. Both Ireland and Wales suffered in terms of the impact on their own language and culture, with English customs imposed upon them. Furthermore, both nations, as well as the North, were affected in terms of the attack on their old religious traditions; at the top of society, Catholicism was replaced by Protestantism. It was a revolution installed from above, although the Tudor government would have been naïve to have assumed that there would be no retaliation in return.

Despite vast changes, the Irish Question remained an enduring concern for Henry and his successors. First, expenditure remained high. Second, the allegiance of the Irish lords remained fragile, as Henry's daughter, Elizabeth I, was to discover during her reign. Third, many European Catholic monarchs refused to acknowledge the establishment of this new kingdom, which continued the fear that foreign rulers may use Ireland as a base of operations for rebellions and potential invasions. Fourth, and perhaps most important, the changes unleashed by the Tudor government in the 1530s–1540s had severe long-term consequences, particularly in the division between a Protestant, pro-Anglo elite and the more impoverished Catholic lower-orders. As such, problems of stability in Ireland were not solved by the reforms under Henry VIII, only simply paused.

On the whole, the Tudor empire was expanded during these years. No new territory was added to the portfolio of the Crown, but the reorganisation and consolidation of Wales, Ireland and the North provided a firm base for the Tudor dynasty within the British Isles. It was not revolutionary, in that Henry VIII was continuing in the footsteps of his medieval predecessors – notably Edward I – in giving focus to the potential of a British imperial project; but it was largely effective. Further developments in the 1540s provided Henry VIII with the vision of adding Scotland to this collection.

Chapter 10

The Rough Wooing

Henry VIII's attempt to subjugate Scotland in the 1540s

In September 1541, Henry VIII spent a fortnight waiting for his nephew, the Scottish King James V, to arrive in York for a meeting. It was the first time that Henry had visited the northern reaches of his kingdom, and having spent a small fortune on refurbishing an old abbey he believed that it was all worth it just so he could finally talk to this nephew face-to-face. Henry was keen to prise Scotland away from their pro-French policy, thereby bringing James more closely within the Tudor orbit.

However, Henry waited and waited.

After two weeks had passed, he realised that James V had once again evaded him. In the words of historian David M. Head, Henry had to admit that 'his nephew had made a fool of him'.[1] On 29 September, Henry departed to return to the south. After years of vain attempts to bring the Scottish under his tutelage he had come to a decision: only violence would bring them to heel.

The Origins of War

Throughout Henry VIII's reign the Anglo-Scottish relationship proved to be a difficult one. The Battle of Flodden Field provided the opportunity for a reset in the relationship; the quarrelsome James IV was dead and Scotland was weakened, thereby providing Henry with opportunities to meddle and to dominate. The Scottish court was riven with divisions in the subsequent decades, with Henry's sister – Margaret – being a major figure in events. At times, Henry toyed with the idea of invading, particularly in the early 1520s when he threatened to attack Edinburgh from the sea, but such plans fizzled out due to Henry's overriding preoccupation with France.[2]

111

After James V assumed full control of his kingdom in the late 1520s, Henry sought to give him strong guidance in terms of moving toward a pro-Anglo perspective rather than continue with the Auld Alliance. There were clear reasons for this approach, particularly in terms of avoiding becoming encircled by a Scottish-France alliance, but also because of the value of James V himself; before the birth of Prince Edward in 1537, James was the next available male heir for the English throne. Henry pushed for a summit meeting to speak to his nephew directly, no doubt hopeful that the force of his personality would convince James to join his side. However, the various attempts, from the late 1530s onward, were continually dodged by James, who had a litany of excuses.

James could not resist the temptation of being captivated by the French kingdom, particularly in making a notable marriage with a daughter of Francis I. He was determined to take the hand of Madeleine of Valois; however, Francis was worried about allowing his sickly daughter to move to the unrelenting Scottish environment. James was determined, to such an extent that he travelled to France in person in 1536 to claim his bride. Eventually Francis agreed, and James renewed the Auld Alliance, then married at Notre Dame, before returning to Scotland armed with a new wife and a handsome dowry. But Francis' fears were realised; within a month of arriving in her new kingdom Madeleine was dead. James then asked Francis for the hand of his second daughter, and, understandably worried of bad omens, the French king offered the hand of one of the kingdom's noblewomen, Mary of Guise, instead. The marriage produced two sons who died prematurely, before Mary was pregnant once more in 1542.

More worryingly for Henry was the manner in which James was courted by the other monarchs of Europe. In 1537, James was made Defender of the Faith by the Pope; no doubt Henry was slightly riled, having once been gifted that same title in the early 1520s. Then a year later many of the major European leaders – such as Charles and Francis – issued a joint declaration of cooperation against the enemies of Christendom. And enemy number one? Perhaps Henry himself. By 1539 there were real fears about the various Catholic powers of Europe – with Scotland – joining up to lead an invasion against the heretical English king. In February, a survey of defences was made, more money was pumped into fortifications and the royal navy was prepared for war. In May, more than 16,000 soldiers marched through London in a parade before the king, as a show of force that England was not to be messed with. The fear soon subsided, particularly due to the notoriously erratic relationship between Charles and Francis, but Henry realised that he was short of friends.

By 1541, Henry believed that he had finally caught his fish; James agreed to a summit meeting in York. But after two weeks of waiting, Henry realised that his nephew had snubbed him. The English monarch retaliated by issuing a proclamation that expelled all Scottish residents from Northumbria, while also preparing his border defences. Then, in October 1541, Henry's sister Margaret died. With her passing went a key cog in the link between the two countries. Within a year England and Scotland would go to war.

Solway Moss

Throughout 1542, tensions on the English-Scottish border reached fever pitch. In August an English force under Sir Robert Bowes was ambushed at Haddon Rig, near Kelso, with 500 men captured. Although the English were clearly the aggressor – after all, they were on Scottish soil – Henry saw the incident as Scottish provocation and therefore the key reason for war.[3] Henry sent the aged Duke of Norfolk north – just as his father before him – with an army to force the Scottish to come to a favourable settlement. The demands included the freeing of all English prisoners, the Scottish giving up all claims to English-held lands, and to also provide prominent bishops and earls as hostages for good behaviour. Furthermore, Henry demanded that his nephew come to London by Christmas to seal the peace personally.[4] The Scottish were not won over with such demands, and understandably refused. James himself feared that if he set foot in London then he might not ever return home again.

Although Henry wanted Norfolk to sack Edinburgh, all Norfolk could do was burn Kelso and ravage nearby lands. It was late in the campaigning season and the poor preparations meant that the English army had to return south for the winter. The Scottish were encouraged by this lacklustre attack, which led to a counter-attack of around 15,000 troops heading into Cumbria. In November 1542, this army met a much smaller English force of just 3,000 at Solway Moss, and despite being confident of victory the result was a huge defeat for Scotland, leading to one early twentieth-century historian to deem it a 'discreditable episode in Scottish history'.[5] A key reason for the defeat was the division within the leadership of the Scottish army, with it rumoured that James himself was more interested in meeting one of his mistresses. One of his favourites, Oliver Sinclair, was declared as the commander, but this led to questions of credibility: 'Who was Sinclair? ... Every knight and gentleman, every common clan follower, felt himself and his kindred insulted.'[6] This was compounded when many Scottish soldiers became trapped in boggy terrain. Many in the army preferred to surrender or flee rather than fight, leading to several hundred drowning in nearby marshes. All of this warrants the assessment of one historian: 'The Scottish army had ceased to exist through a sequence of incompetent actions that were almost unparalleled in the annals of war.'[7]

Worse was to come when just days later news poured through that James V had died at the young age of 30. Many believed that his death was connected to the defeat at Solway Moss, and that he had died of a mixture of grief and shame; this interpretation continued into the twentieth century, with one historian noting how the king 'died partly of melancholy'.[8] But the likely cause of death is either cholera or dysentery, rather than despair. The heir to a throne was a baby girl who was just 7 days old: Mary, Queen of Scots. The events of November 1542 enticed Henry to delve further into his Scottish adventure to take full advantage of Scotland's weak and vulnerable condition.

Dynastic Union

Now in the driving seat, Henry hatched a new plan to subjugate Scotland and to bring it firmly under his control. This policy centred on the future marriage between his son Prince Edward and James' daughter Mary; this marriage would seal peace between the two countries and bring all of the British Isles under Tudor control. Support for this ambitious plan was echoed in Parliament, which supported Henry's claim to his 'right and title of the saide Crowne and Realme'.[9]

Henry treated the Scottish prisoners from Solway Moss in a benevolent manner, entertaining 'them royally on Christmas Day' and giving them 'gold chains, money and horses'.[10] These prisoners were to be the basis of a pro-English group, and having been won over by Henry's charms, they returned to Scotland in the spring of 1543 to promote Henry's marriage match. Furthermore, some – including Oliver Sinclair – agreed to a secret treaty in which Henry would become King of Scotland if the young Queen Mary was to die. Henry attempted to press some of these lords further by suggesting that they organise a coup d'état in Scotland, leading to the capture of the anti-English Cardinal Beaton, Mary herself, as well as principal castles.[11] The Scottish regent – Lord Arran – was himself sympathetic to Henry's demands, leading to Cardinal Beaton's arrest.

The spring and summer of 1543 focused on the formation of the Treaties of Greenwich; key terms included Scotland renouncing the Auld Alliance and confirmation of the future marriage between Edward and Mary (furthermore, Queen Mary was to be sent south to England on her tenth birthday). All of this would leave Henry holding all the aces in terms of his control of Scotland. However, many prominent Scottish lords took their time in discussing the treaties, providing those north of the border with opportunity to catch their breath and to build up a resistance to Tudor demands. The English ambassador Ralph Sadler was told by one Scottish lord that everyone in Scotland would resist this hostile takeover:

> For, there is not so little a boy but that he will hurl stones against it, and the wives will handle their distaffs, and the commons universally will rather die in it, yea, and many noblemen and all the clergy be fully against it.[12]

Then, in September 1543, Arran and Beaton reconciled, with Arran doing a complete flip-flop in converting to Catholicism and joining the pro-French faction. In December, the Scottish Parliament revoked the Greenwich treaties and once again reaffirmed the Auld Alliance. All of Henry's schemes collapsed, leading to a renewed phase of war.

Scorched Earth

The term 'Rough Wooing' was invented, as with most wars, many years after the actual event itself. It describes the English approach to beat Scotland into submission after the failure of the Greenwich treaties, with

Henry keen to punish the Scottish for their refusal to support his dynastic plans. The Privy Council issued a clear instruction for the invasion:

> Put all to fire and sword, burn Edinburgh, so razed and defaced when you have sacked and gotten what ye can of it, as there may remain forever a perpetual memory of the vengeance of God lightened upon [them] for their falsehood and disloyalty.[13]

The man tasked with punishing Scotland was the uncle of Prince Edward, Sir Edward Seymour, Earl of Hertford. Seymour had milked his position as the brother of Jane Seymour, using it to advance his own career; but he had also proved himself to be a valuable servant of the Crown. In May 1544, his English force landed in Scotland – estimated to have been between 5,000 and 10,000 strong – with the army sacking Leith and Edinburgh. The English were largely unchallenged until they became exposed to artillery fire from Edinburgh Castle, which remained defiant. The area was torched, with English soldiers noting how they could hear women crying out in pain and anguish. By the time the English left the area a week later, further damage was done to the harbour and piers of Leith, as well as surrounding infrastructure. No doubt the English were hoping that Scottish politics and society would become destabilised, and this is illustrated clearly in Arran's civil strife and fights against internal enemies during 1544, and the murder of Cardinal Beaton in 1546. However, despite their continual quarrels, the Scottish became united on one crucial issue: opposition to the English.

This renewed position was evidenced at the Battle of Ancrum Moor in February 1545. Sir Ralph Eure commanded a force of around 5,000, with the intention of controlling and harassing the Scottish border. The quarrelsome Scottish nobility had united with the intention of fighting back, and having learned from the mistakes of Solway Moss, the Scottish army performed a tactical masterclass. A small force approached Eure, making a feint attack, before retreating; the hungry English followed in pursuit. However, as the English advanced they realised that the full force of the Scottish army was hidden on the far side of the hill. The advantage of surprise confused the English soldiers, with men scattering and fleeing for their lives. The result was the death of around 800 Englishmen – including Eure himself – with a further 1,000 taken prisoner.

The defeat at Ancrum proved that Scotland would not be a pushover. What was more, Henry had other military factors to consider by 1545, with his attention diverted once more to the French kingdom.

'Oh, my gallant men'

While Seymour was busy preparing his raid on Scotland, Henry focused on his final French campaign. Two decades had passed since his last war against France; however, the key players of Europe remained the same; his rival, Francis I, retained the French crown, and the third part of this twisted and conniving triumvirate, Charles V, continued on as the most powerful monarch. Although the late 1530s had planted a fear in Henry that Francis and Charles might team up on a Catholic crusade to invade England, the reality was that the pair had fallen out once again, going to war with one another in 1541. As in earlier decades, this presented Henry with an opportunity to interfere in wider European affairs.

In February 1543, an Anglo-Imperial anti-French alliance was signed. The plan was for the two armies to march together in northern France and strike at Paris; however, the Scottish problem delayed Henry's preparations by a year. By the summer of 1544 he had amassed a colossal 48,000-strong army, with Henry conscious that this was his final chance to demonstrate to Europe and to posterity that he was a warrior king of the highest calibre. Such was his personal involvement that he decided to lead the invasion himself. However, the Henry of the 1540s was not the man of his younger years, and he was continually plagued with poor health due to substantial leg injuries. As historian J.J. Scarisbrick notes, by this time 'he was becoming a man of huge girth, eating and drinking prodigiously … just as he was about to set out on his last campaign … the ulcer flared up once more and the fever returned'.[14] Such was Henry's condition that he was reduced to being carried around in a chair and was moved upstairs with the use of machinery. However, as Alison Weir states, the invasion of France gave him a renewed 'zest for life',[15] even if he had to be winched onto his horse, with armour cut away to relieve pressure on his leg. And yet he could still operate in the heavy armour, 'and those who saw them marvelled that any man could lift a lance of such huge dimensions'.[16]

In June, Henry set off for Calais; he did not join with the imperial army to march on Paris, however, for he had other ideas. The English army remained within the confines of northern France, laying siege to nearby towns such as Montreuil before capturing Boulogne in September. Charles was understandably miffed at being slighted by Henry, leading him to sign a separate peace with Francis by the end of the year. In many ways, Henry's lack of coordination with the imperial army suggests that he was focused on short-term aims and easier targets, but some historians have suggested that Henry had learned from being backstabbed by Charles in previous campaigns, and so on his last military throw of the dice he decided on completing the invasion on his terms only. Having secured French territory for his empire, he garrisoned Boulogne and headed home to celebrate.

However, by the end of the year Henry now faced an unshackled France while also becoming bogged down in an endless slog with Scotland. In 1545, Seymour returning to raze and pillage Scotland once again, and then in the summer it was the turn of France to put pressure on England. The French intended to sail a large fleet toward Portsmouth, principally to destroy English ships, and then to potentially land an army. However, as would happen later in the century with the Spanish Armada, poor winds meant that the French were unable to engage the English in battle; the most they could do was to land a small raiding party on the Isle of Wight, which was, so states a local plaque, 'repulsed by local militia'.

By far the biggest tragedy of the year was the sinking of Henry's flagship the *Mary Rose*. Henry was present at Southsea Castle in July 1545 where he watched the disaster with his own eyes; the ship was sunk not due to French cannon but rather in confusion when manoeuvring in Portsmouth harbour. Six hundred men were drowned, leading Henry to lament: 'Oh, my gentlemen! Oh, my gallant men!'[17]

Both sides reached stalemate, which led to the signing of the Treaty of Ardres, signed in 1546 near the location of the Field of the Cloth of Gold. It was agreed that Henry would hold on to Boulogne and that France would settle all outstanding pension payments. Furthermore, the treaty also saw an end to the Scottish war. Everything, then, had returned to just as it had been before back in 1541 when James V had snubbed Henry's meeting, albeit now the English held Boulogne. Henry had achieved a slice of military glory, but the question must be asked: was it all worth it?

The founding father of the Tudor dynasty: Henry VII (1505, Unknown Artist, National Portrait Gallery). *Wikimedia Commons*

Lord Stanley crowns his stepson Henry Tudor at Bosworth in 1485 (c.1858, Unknown Artist). *Wikimedia Commons*

Henry VII's mother, Margaret Beaufort (1650–1700, Unknown Artist, National Portrait Gallery). *Wikimedia Commons*

Lambert Simnel: the first pretender to challenge Henry VII's throne in 1487 (Unknown Date, Unknown Artist). *Wikimedia Commons*

Above left: Henry VII's second pretender, Perkin Warbeck, who troubled him throughout the 1490s (Fifteenth Century, Unknown Artist). *Wikimedia Commons*

Above right: Anne of Brittany: Henry VII's ally during the Breton Crisis of 1489–91 (1503–08, Jean Bourcdichon). *Wikimedia Commons*

The Cornish rebels of 1497 – Michael Joseph and Michael Flamank – are immortalised in a statue in St Keverne, Cornwall (2009, Trevor Harris, photograph). *Wikimedia Commons*

Above: John Cabot's statue in Bristol (2015, Adrian Pingstone, photograph). *Wikimedia Commons*

Left: The young Henry VIII before taking the reins of power in 1509 (c.1509, Meynnart Wewyck). *Wikimedia Commons*

King Henry VIII at the peak of his power (1540, Hans Holbein). *Wikimedia Commons*

ANNO · ÆTATIS ·

· SVÆ · XLIX ·

The Battle of the Spurs. Despite its exaggeration, the Battle of the Spurs in 1513 provided Henry VIII with a taste of military glory (c.1513, Unknown Artist). *Wikimedia Commons*

THE BATTLE OF FLODDEN (*see page* 125).

Above: The Battle of Flodden Field. Despite not being present, the victory at Flodden gave Henry VIII a great victory (1873, from British Battles on Sea & Land, Vol. 10). *Wikimedia Commons*

Left: The French King Francis I was one of Henry VIII's most long-enduring rivals (1539, Titian). *Wikimedia Commons*

Emperor Charles V: the most powerful monarch in Europe during Henry VIII's reign (1514–1516, Unknown Artist). *Wikimedia Commons*

Thomas Wolsey served as Henry VIII's right-hand man from the 1510s–1520. *Wikimedia Commons*

The Field of the Cloth of Gold in 1520 was Henry VIII's attempt to exert himself on the European stage without resorting to warfare (1545, Unknown Artist). *Wikimedia Commons*

Thomas Fitzgerland – aka Silken Thomas – led a rebellion against the Tudor Crown in Ireland during the 1530s (1530, Anthony van Dyck). *Wikimedia Commons*

The Pilgrimage of Grace in 1536 threatened to loosen the Tudor hold on the North of England (1913, Fred Kirk Shaw). *Wikimedia Commons*

James V snubbed Henry VIII and then soon after died after the Scottish defeat at Solway Moss in 1542 (c.1536, Corneille de Lyon). *Wikimedia Commons*

Left: Edward Seymour took control during the early years of the reign of Edward VI, but became engulfed with war, rebellion and division (Sixteenth Century, Artist Unknown). *Wikimedia Commons*

Below: Siege of Calais, 1558. Having been held by the English for two centuries, Calais fell to the French in 1558 (1838, Francois-Edouard Picot). *Wikimedia Commons*

Death of Sir Hugh Willoughby. Sir Hugh Willoughby set out to find the Northeast Passage, but ended up meeting his death on the north Russian coast (c.1554, Unknown Artist). *Wikimedia Commons*

Ivan the Terrible wanted a closer alliance with Elizabeth I, despite her reluctance (1897, Viktor Mikhailovich Vasnetsov). *Wikimedia Commons*

Left: Sir John Hawkins initiated England's first involvement with the African slave trade in the 1560s (1581, Artist Unknown). *Wikimedia Commons*

Below: John White's striking watercolours revealed a foreign and exotic world of North American natives to a Tudor audience (1585, John White). *Wikimedia Commons*

Sir Francis Drake plays his legendary game of bowls before taking the fight to the Spanish Armada in 1588 (1880, John Seymour Lucas). *Wikimedia Commons*

Portrait of Elizabeth I ('The Armada Portrait'). The defeat of the Armada in 1588 provided Elizabeth I with her greatest victory (c.1588, Artist Unknown). *Wikimedia Commons*

Robert Dudley, Duke of Leicester, remained a favourite of Elizabeth's for three decades, despite his misstep in the Netherlands in the 1580s (c.1575, Artist Unknown). *Wikimedia Commons*

Sir Walter Raleigh played a large role in the growth of the Tudor empire; however, his attempts to find the City of Gold ended in failure (c.1588, Artist Unknown). *Wikimedia Commons*

James VI of Scotland inherited the Tudor throne on the death of Elizabeth I in 1603, thereby bringing an end to 118 years of Tudor rule (1621, Daniel Mijtens). *Wikimedia Commons*

Henry VIII's Legacy

Henry VIII's reign came to an end on 28 January 1547. During his reign of four decades he attempted to expand the Tudor empire in a variety of directions; there was no coherent, consistent policy, but always a clear hunger to prove himself on the battlefield and to expand his imperial domains. His British project – which had seen such success in Wales and Ireland – came to a halt in Scotland; however, his policy of the Rough Wooing was continued in the reign of Edward VI. Edward Seymour, now the number one noble in the kingdom (and having rewarded himself as the Duke of Somerset), headed back to Scotland in an effort to finish what he had started. He experienced a brilliant victory at the Battle of Pinkie Cleugh, but soon realised that he was unable to control Scotland; his military ventures proved costly, which economically unsettled the kingdom, and by the end of 1549 he had been removed from his position of power. His successor, John Dudley, Duke of Northumberland, sought a conclusive end to the Scottish war, thereby leading to the abandonment of Henry's earlier dream.

Dudley also had a hand in cleaning up another area of Henry's messes: the captured town of Boulogne. As Eric W. Eves points out: 'Henry became the only king to win territory in France for more than a century';[18] however, it had been achieved at great cost. More than £2 million was spent in the 1540s on his military exploits, equivalent to a decade's worth of a normal government expenditure;[19] this was covered by Henry's windfall of the sale of monastic land, but the Crown also resorted to increasing taxation and raising loans, leading to one historian to state how 'the future was mortgaged and confidence in the country's financial system was undermined'.[20] The economy became problematic, leading to serious issues during the reigns of Henry's children; Dudley dealt with the costly issue of garrisoning Boulogne by simply passing it back to the French.

Within a handful of years after his death, Henry VIII's attempts to control Scotland and to make an impression in France had been reversed. Uncharitable observers would estimate his true legacy not in battles won or territory conquered, but rather in the money wasted on such vain gambles. It may not have been worth it, but it is clear that nothing would have deterred Henry VIII from trying.

Chapter 11

An Anglo-Cornish War

A different perspective of the
1549 Prayer Book Rebellion

Under the heading 'The Death Squads', one Cornish historian recently compared the actions of the Tudors to those of the SS in Nazi Germany, arguing that the aftermath of the 1549 Prayer Book Rebellion led to the murder of thousands:

> They faced an awful future. Their rights had been torn up before their eyes; a death blow had been dealt to their language and identity; and thousands of families, deprived of a breadwinner, could only look forward to misery and starvation.[1]

The events of 1549 were not simply a rebellion, argued the late historian Craig Weatherhill, but rather a war in which the Cornish fought the English to preserve their freedoms and heritage. The resulting slaughter, which led to the death of 10 per cent of Cornwall's population, 'labels this episode to be one of the worst acts of genocide in the history of the world'.[2] As such, the rebellion of 1549 deserves to be recognised as a wider conflict, after centuries of being 'minimised':

> It was nothing less than all-out war, instigated by injustice and fuelled by outrage, but most books say little about it and, sadly, our schoolchildren are told even less.[3]

This, then, is the story of the 'Anglo-Cornish War' of the summer of 1549.

The Murder of William Body

The year 1497 saw the West was in flames; two rebellions were raised against Henry VII, and although he was triumphant on both occasions – with the second one leading to the final capture of Perkin Warbeck – the fragility of Tudor rule in the West Country was exposed. However, after shaky beginnings, the region accommodated itself with the Tudor dynasty, as shown with the Charter of Pardon of 1508, which restored ancient freedoms in the form of the Stannary Parliament to Cornwall. Highlighting Cornwall's position within the wider imperial domains, Cornwall was portrayed as one of the nine children of honour in Henry VIII's coronation service, taking place alongside other nations, such as Ireland and Wales.[4] While other regions, notably the North, gave Henry VIII problems after the religious changes of the 1530s, the West remained largely tranquil. So peaceful, in fact, that when the wider centralisation reforms of the period took place in the North, Wales and Ireland, the creation of the Council of the West was quietly forgotten about.

However, the religious reforms during the early years of the reign of Edward VI roused the region into anger and outright rebellion. On his death, Henry VIII left an English Church that remained largely Catholic in outlook, but this conservative approach was abandoned with his death, with Archbishop Cranmer and the new rising Protestant elite, led by Edward Seymour, recently created Duke of Somerset, unleashing new religious reforms. Having seen the monasteries dissolved in the 1530s, the country faced the impact of the removal of chantries, as well as instructions to draw up inventories of various church items, 'such as bells, vestments, ornaments and plates'.[5] Many in the Celtic periphery of the kingdom viewed these changes suspiciously, but nowhere more so than in the far-west of Cornwall.

In 1548, royal commissioners were appointed to remove items – such as Catholic images – from churches; the man appointed to the task in Cornwall – William Body – provoked the Cornish with his actions. It did not help matters that Body was a thoroughly unlikable individual, as highlighted in his conduct while serving in Ireland under Lord Grey in the 1530s; Grey complained 'about Body's drunken behaviour, abominable language and lies'.[6] In April 1548, Body found himself 'confronted by an angry mob', where he was 'dragged outside' of a house before being stabbed to death.[7] This 'angry mob' soon swelled to 3,000 people, with much discussion held about rebelling so 'they would have all such laws as was made by the late King Henry VIII and none other until the King's majesty accomplished the age of twenty-four years'.[8] The local gentry in the region acted fast, and soon a messenger from the government offered pardon to those who gave up talk of revolt and went home. However, there were exceptions to the pardon, with the ring-leaders arrested and executed:

> They were drawn through the town on a hurdle behind a horse; at the gallows they were hanged by the neck, but cut down while still just alive, and thrown to the ground. Then they were disembowelled and their entrails were burnt in front of their still-seeing eyes. Finally, they were beheaded. The mutilated corpses were cut into four quarters, to be displayed wherever the king wished to make a point about the unwisdom of adventuring against the Crown.[9]

Twenty-eight were executed at Launceston; a pro-Catholic priest was taken to London, and his head impaled on London Bridge; another execution was conducted on Plymouth Hoe, with the quarters sent across the West. As the historian John Sturt notes, 'the rising had been quelled virtually by a trick', leading to widespread anger in Cornwall.[10] The 'Cornish Commotion' may have ended, but more was to come the following year.[11]

'And so we the Cornish men ... utterly refuse this new English'

In January 1549, the Act of Uniformity passed in Parliament. It led to further religious changes, moving the Church of England toward a Protestant one. A key part of this reform was the publication of the Book of Common Prayer, which all churches in the kingdom were ordered to use. This was the logical continuation of the Henrician reforms of the 1530s – both in terms of politics and religion – with more power centralised in the hands of the Tudor state. The reforms were not received well in Cornwall; the region was still brooding and the changes were the spark required to bring about a new wave of dissent. Religious grievances were the key elements within the early list of articles sent to the government, with points relating to the availability of baptism services, the holding of mass, the continuing use of holy water and bread, and a statement that religion should remain as it was in Henry's day until the young king came of age himself. However, there were further issues behind the protests, including the need for land reform, a reduction in tax and concern about wheat price quadrupling.[12] Also important was how the new English prayer book was to be 'imposed upon a population that was only partly English-speaking', with the Cornish language being dominant.[13] Archbishop Cranmer appeared to be confused when learning of this particular disagreement, noting how the Cornish were hardly fluent in Latin, the language of the Catholic Church. However, Cranmer missed the point; as historian Philip Payton states, 'Latin was familiar (if not always understood) all across Cornwall, whereas English was not.'[14] The change in language, along with the alterations to religion, were attacks on key longstanding elements of Cornish culture and identity. Within their petition the rebels stated that the new service was:

> like a Christmas game... we will have our old service of Mattins, Mass, Evensong, and Procession in Latin as it was before. And so we the Cornish men (whereof certain of us understand no English) utterly refuse this new English.[15]

The protests appear to have centred in Bodmin, with some local gentry members and Catholic priests becoming leaders. Sir Humphrey Arundell was a 36-year-old with soldiering experience whose grandfather had played a part in the 1497 rebellion; this pedigree led to one historian to declare that Arundell 'had rebel blood in his veins'.[16] He had a somewhat complex reputation in Cornwall, having been 'charged with forcible entry upon other people's lands' and had withheld 'money under his mother's will to his younger brothers'.[17] Arundell later claimed to have only joined the rebellion to prevent it from becoming too unruly; however, his actions and involvement show, in the words of one historian, that 'his whole-hearted allegiance to their cause could not be questioned'.[18] Operating as the ying to Arundell's yang was John Winslade, another member of the gentry who has been described as being 'generous, impulsive, well-liked'.[19] Alongside his son, William, Winslade bet the entire fortune of his family on the success of the rebellion.[20]

Arundell sent the list of articles to London and initially planned to remain in Cornwall to await a reply. However, the response was not well received; the government offered a pardon for those who laid down their arms and went back home; but many remembered what had happened after the 'pardon' of 1548. The men 'were growing restive', and so the Cornish took the decision to march into Devon;[21] just as, notes A.L. Rowse, 'their grandfathers had in 1497'.[22] The army grew in number and enjoyed early successes, including the capture of key castles in Cornwall (such as St Mawes and Pendennis) as well as the settlement of Plymouth. The next stop was Exeter, the central hub of the West Country.

The Siege of Exeter

While the Cornish were rising, trouble was brewing in Devon in the village of Sampford Courtenay. Word spread of what was happening in Cornwall, which increased the anxiety in the village regarding the introduction of the new service with the church 'packed, and buzzing with speculation'.[23] Sensing anger in the room, the vicar resorted to conducting the service under the old rules; however, fearing an outbreak of violence, justices of the peace arrived in the village in an attempt to maintain order. William Hellyons, a local yeoman, told the protestors that he disagreed with their law-breaking antics, and this protest escalated to an incident in which Hellyons was 'hacked to death' with a pitchfork outside the church.[24] The rebels of Sampford Courtenay met with the arriving Cornishmen, and the momentum carried away a number of men, with the intention of marching on Exeter to remonstrate and to have their voice heard. By the end of June 1549, the rebels controlled the surrounding countryside around Exeter; the capital of the West was now under siege.

Edward VI's government struggled to understand the severity of the situation. This was no doubt due to other pressing issues, such as the continuing war with Scotland, the fear of the military entrance of France, as well as a lack of funds; furthermore, other disturbances were breaking out in England. Local lords were sent to the region to speak to the rebels, carrying a pardon from the king to disperse. The Carews – Sir Gawen and Sir Peter (who was on honeymoon in Lincolnshire when called into action) – rode 200 miles on eleven changes of horses to reach Exeter by 21 June.[25] They went to Crediton to talk with the rebels; however, they were unceremoniously dismissed, leaving the pair 'shaking with rage'.[26] Their encounter led to the burning of barns in the town; however, this incident had a large impact on improving the position of the rebels, with many other locals now fearing that their own barns and livelihoods would also be torched by infuriated lords. The Duke of Somerset was particularly miffed on hearing of the incident, noting: 'peaceful and conciliatory measures ... were to have been used towards these poor deluded people'.[27] At the end of the month, Lord Russell was sent to the West with the brief of stabilising the situation and ensuring that Exeter did not fall; unfortunately, Russell was sent without the required men to take on the rebels directly in battle.

On 2 July, the mayor of Exeter ordered all the gates to the city to be shut, with the 3,000-strong population up against a rebel army of up to 10,000. The rebels hoped that the city would declare for them and their religious cause; and if it did not, then the town would be starved into submission. John Hooker was an eye-witness who chronicled the experiences of these times, noting how the citizens were reduced to a lean diet of 'horse bread' made up of 'the poorest kind of dough, made from whatever could be procured: corn, beans, peas, bran, anything'.[28] The rebel army lacked siege weapons to break down the walls, and attempts at mining were prevented through counter-measures. As the weeks wore on, the defenders of the city acted heroically, despite suffering casualties, with one man 'shot through both cheeks with an arrow'.[29] One rebel sniper, a Breton with the surname Hammond, was particularly deadly, leading to a suggestion that he could shoot fireballs onto the roofs of Exeter's thatched buildings to smoke the citizens out. To demonstrate his accurate aim, Hammond positioned himself on St David's Hill, 'singled out a man standing in North Street, a good 400 yards away, and promptly blew him away with one shot'.[30] However, a local vicar – Father Welsh, a 'short, thickset' Cornishman by birth – persuaded the rebels to avoid such carnage, which saved the city from becoming an inferno.[31]

While the siege continued, Russell made nearby Honiton his headquarters, frantically writing to London requesting reinforcements. He was aware of the repercussions if Exeter fell – that a regional rebellion potentially would become a wider national revolt – however, he was cautious to act before he felt able to do so. In late July, boosted by German mercenaries, Russell finally moved toward the relief of Exeter; his route was blocked by Arundell, leading to battle at Fenny Bridges. The rebels attempted to take the initiative but were pushed back by the royal force; however, the mercenaries – who were 'underpaid, brutalised, and without any higher motivation' – turned their focus to looting and 'set to work stripping corpses, slitting throats here, wrenching off rings there, and generally collecting up the day's profits'.[32] This allowed the Cornish to make a counter-offensive, catching the mercenaries off guard, before Russell was able to regain control of the situation by sending in fresh reserves. John Hooker recorded his comments on the battle:

> The fight for the time was very sharp and cruel, for the Cornishmen were very lusty and fresh and fully bent to fight out the matter.[33]

However, the rebels realised that they were outnumbered, and so retreated back to Exeter. Around 300 men from each side were reputed to have lost their lives. Russell, fearing becoming encircled in rebel territory, returned to Honiton. However, he was not long waiting for the solid reinforcements that had been promised: Lord Grey arrived with more than 1,000 men, fresh from putting down risings in Oxfordshire and Buckinghamshire, and there were additional Italian and Spanish mercenaries, along with the promise of a further thousand Welshmen under the leadership of Sir William Herbert. Power had now shifted from Arundell to Russell and his bolstered army.

In early August, the royal force advanced once more on Exeter, deciding to camp on Aylesbury Common.[34] The rebels attempted a surprise attack but suffered heavy losses, both in terms of men killed and others taken prisoner. On 5 August, Arundell reordered his men at Clyst St Mary, but then faced an assault from the royalists, leading to a bloody outcome in which a further thousand were killed and many hundreds taken prisoner. At this point, with hundreds of prisoners under their control, Lord Grey ordered their murder; in the space of ten minutes, 900 throats were slit. The Cornish were outraged at this massacre, and on 6 August a new battle took place at Clyst Heath, in which the rebels threw everything at the royalist army:

> Outmanoeuvred, outgunned, outflanked and outnumbered,
> the Cornish fought like men possessed, burning with fury
> born of the previous evening's massacre.[35]

Such was the ferocity, Hooker commented that Lord Grey – a veteran of
the Scottish campaigns – 'reported himself that he never in all the wars
he had been in did know the like'.[36] But despite their bravery, the rebels
were no match for the royal army; 2,000 were killed in what became
a 'hopeless battle'.[37] Diminished and demoralised, Arundell ordered
a retreat from the area, leaving Russell victorious; after weeks under
siege, Exeter was saved.

The 'Killing Squads'

Lord Russell and his royalist army marched into the city of Exeter,
ending the summer's siege. Russell spent ten days in the city, in which
any lingering rebels were punished and the king's justice was restored.
It was an unfortunate end for Father Welsh, the vicar who had prevented
the town from being set on fire; he was hanged, with Hooker noting how
his corpse was surrounded by 'a holy-water bucket, a sprinkle, a sacring
bell, a pair of beads and such other like popish trash'; the body reputedly
swinging on the gibbet for years after.[38] However, celebrations were
somewhat premature, for the rebels used this time to lick their wounds,
regroup, and to pose a threat once again; reports came to Russell that
Arundell and his men were ready to make a final stand back at the village
of Sampford Courtenay.

On 16 August, Russell headed to the village, armed with 8,000 men
and boosted by the addition of Herbert's troops. They pushed against the
rebels, leading to an initial retreat, before Arundell launched a surprise
attack on the flank. Initially the royal army was confused until Grey took
control, but the rebels continued to battle against the odds; according to
historian Craig Weatherhill, the Cornish were 'seemingly fighting to the
death'.[39] The contemporary John Hooker noted how 'the Cornish would
not give in until most of their number had been slain or captured'.[40]
The rebels experienced big losses, leading Arundell, Winslade and other
leaders to escape to seek safety in Okehampton. Unlike with previous
encounters, this time Russell ordered a pursuit of the rebels; in total, a

further 700 rebels were killed and another 700 were taken prisoner. The rebel fight was now fully extinguished and the ten-week war was over.

Arundell eventually found his way back across the Cornish border and into Launceston. But the local authorities in the town were not keen to shelter the rebels, instead taking the decision to arrest and detain them. Arundell's heartbreak was compounded when he discovered that his right-hand man had actually been an informant for Russell throughout the rebellion, passing on secrets of his movements and the rebel plans. The rebel leaders were transferred to Rougemont Castle in Exeter, with Arundell, no doubt, looking at the countryside beside him wondering what might have been. 'How bitter,' writes John Sturt, 'was the jeering of the people by the roadside, who until a few days before would surely have cheered him.'[41] By September, they had been transferred to the Tower of London, and they eventually faced traitors' deaths in being hanged, drawn and quartered in January 1550 at Tyburn, just like the Cornish rebel An Gof in 1497.

The punishment of rebellious Cornwall was not yet over, with many in the clergy deprived of their status, and a notable number of priests and mayors were hanged. The task of 'pacification' of the West was given to Sir Anthony Kingston, who 'set about his task with enthusiasm and diligence'.[42] Kingston had experience in suppression of rebellions after his involvement during the Pilgrimage of Grace, for which he was knighted by Henry VIII. Historians do not have a kind word to say about Kingston; John Sturt labels him 'one of the most gratuitously cruel men of a cruel age',[43] and Craig Weatherhill described him as being head of the 'killing squads':

> Cruel, inhumane, a man divested of common humanity – these are just a few historical descriptions of a man who would have been equally at home carrying out the worst excesses of Nazi Germany.[44]

Various stories of Kingston's actions were passed down to future generations, with his visit to the mayor of Bodmin's home illustrative of his conduct. The legend describes how Kingston:

> wrote to the mayor to say that he and some important guests were coming to Bodmin and would appreciate lunch. The

mayor arranged a lavish meal. Just before they ate, Kingston took the mayor aside and told him that there had to be an execution and would he please arrange for the construction of a gallows, to be ready at the end of the feast. The mayor gave the necessary orders and all sat down to the food and wine.

And this is when the story takes a dark turn:

> At the end of the meal Kingston asked to be shown the gallows. 'Are they strong enough, do you think?' he enquired. When the mayor assured him that they were, he was told: 'Then climb up to them, for they are for hanging you.'[45]

'I trust you mean no such thing to me', the mayor reputedly pleaded. Kingston responded: 'Sir, there is no remedy. You have been a busy rebel, and therefore this is appointed for your reward.'[46] It just one of several stories of Kingston's sadistic measures.

An Anglo-Cornish War?

Is it accurate to revise this rebellion as a war? For hundreds of years it has gone under various labels – such as Prayer Book Rebellion, Western Rebellion, Western Rising – but all of these titles are united in their treatment of the event as a revolt. Weatherhill's reassessment does have merit, particularly in reframing this summer beyond being primarily about religion; other factors are incorporated, including the fight for a distinct Cornish identity. In this light, the events of the summer of 1549 were actions in opposing a dominant, centralising Tudor force, with the Cornish adamant about retaining their own language and cultural beliefs.

Weatherhill's argument develops this further beyond a war, stating the actions of the English are more accurately described as 'one of the worst acts of genocide in the history of the world', when considering the percentage of Cornwall's population that was killed.[47] The historian makes explicit comparisons to Nazi Germany, particularly in stating that Kingston was the head of the 'death squads'. It is estimated that around

5,500 died during the rebellion, with Kingston's actions possibly adding a further 1,000 to the total; this places the figure killed at around 10 per cent of the Cornish population. The murder of 900 prisoners at Clyst Heath – which Weatherhill deemed 'one of the worst atrocities in British history' – provides evidence for the claim of genocide; that the English were not simply engaged in the act of putting down a rebellion, but rather were focused on putting down an entire people. The frenzied killings of 900 men in ten minutes is suggestive of the murderous intent of the English soldiers. Why was this kill order given? In many ways, it made little sense, especially for the mercenaries who presumably preferred prisoners to live to extract a ransom.

There is further support by the orders provided by the government to Russell: to 'shall not suffer those rebels to breathe'.[48] However, there are other lines in correspondence from the Duke of Somerset, particularly in the early phases of the rebellion, for peace. 'Bring the people,' wrote the duke, 'with gentleness to such conformity as appertaineth by travail and gentle persuasions.'[49] It was only when the rebellion escalated that the government resorted to tougher measures. Of course, the actions at Clyst Heath cannot be easily explained away, although other reasons are provided: fear that the prisoners may escape, as well as anxiety and anger over not being able to easily topple the rebels. But it is clear that the royal army treated the Cornish in the same manner that they would treat the other peoples within the Tudor imperial orbit, particularly the Irish: harsh punishment to beat them into submission.

There are many problems with suitably labelling the summer of 1549 as an Anglo-Cornish War, particularly in considering the actions of those from Devon who fought for the rebels. But simply viewing the rebellion in a religious frame does not suffice either. Ultimately the Cornish – and those in Devon – were fighting for more than religion; they were fighting for a way of life. Unfortunately, this life was abruptly ended during the middle years of the Tudor century; as with other areas of the empire – the North, Ireland, Wales – the Tudors ended the conflict as the victors. The years 1497 and 1549 were hair-raising for Tudor monarchs, but Cornwall was neutered to such an extent that it no longer posed a threat to the Tudor state.

Chapter 12

Tudor Brexit

The imperial implications of losing Calais in 1558

The summer of 1346 was a busy one for Edward III's army during the early actions of what would later become known as the Hundred Years' War. They had landed in northern France and enjoyed success at the Battle of Crécy before then heading toward the French town of Calais. The settlement held out against the English and their allies for more than a year, before surrendering the following summer in August 1347. It capped off Edward's *annus mirabilis*, becoming one of the highwater periods of English military might in the fourteenth century.

Now in English hands, Calais was heavily fortified and became an integral cog in England's conduct in the future decades of the war. Furthermore, it also played a key role in the promotion of trade, and also highlighted England's imperial commitments outside of Britain. The town was to remain in English hands for a further two centuries until the reign of Mary I.

Mary

Mary was born in 1518, the daughter of Henry VIII and his first wife, Catherine of Aragon. She was the apple of her father's eye; however, her father's developing romance with Anne Boleyn had severe repercussions for the princess and her status at the royal court. Her mother was ruined by the years of plotting and rumours, dying in 1536, while Mary became a bystander to the unfolding religious and political transformation in Tudor England. The change in religion during Henry VIII's later years, and particularly during the reign of her younger half-brother Edward VI, meant that Mary's devout hold onto the Catholic faith made her alienated within her own country. If Edward was to have reigned for many decades – not entirely improbable, considering he was only 9 years of age when becoming monarch in 1547 – then Mary would have undoubtedly faded into the footnotes of history books. However, Edward's death at the age of 15 in 1553 saw the throne passing – after an attempted subversion of the succession – to Mary.

Mary was deemed by many within the political establishment to be too simple minded, too devoted to religion, and ultimately too naïve to survive the scheming of the Tudor court. Her reign lasted just five years and during this short period she has become known to history as a notorious monarch, particularly with her nickname 'Bloody Mary'. This was due to her obsession to revive Catholicism in England, notably the formulation of the Heresy Act, which saw 300 Protestants burned to death for their beliefs. However, it is Mary's choice of marriage partner that ultimately led to a foreign policy blunder in the loss of Calais in 1558.

Mary married Philip of Spain, the son of her cousin, Charles V. In many ways the match was a considerable one: the Tudors were now strongly allied with the mighty Habsburgs. If the marriage was successful in yielding a child, then England might have become one of the many territories within a wider imperial network, which would have included the Austrian and Germanic lands, Spain, the Netherlands, Italian states, as well as the vast and growing New World domains. However, a child was highly unlikely; Mary was advanced in years, being 38 years old at the time of her marriage, and Philip was not entirely keen on fulfilling his husbandly duties. But Mary was now firmly ensconced within the Habsburg orbit, and when war reared its head against the French it meant that England was ultimately brought into the fight. The 200 years of Calais nestled within the English empire was soon to be at an end.

The Pale

Calais occupied a peculiar part within the English monarch's list of territories. It was never wholly absorbed within the English kingdom, even though there were attempts to tie it more closely with England during the Tudor period; this is particularly seen with the return of two MPs to Parliament from 1536 onward. There were more statements on Calais' position within the Tudor empire in the sixteenth century, particularly during the reign of Henry VIII; in 1512 the children of Calesians were declared to be 'good English', while in the 1530s Parliament hailed Calais as 'one of the most principal treasures belonging to this his Realm of England'.[1] This clearly links with Henry's obsession in wanting to take the French throne, and as such, Calais was treated highly alongside other captured territories, including Tournai in the 1510s and Boulogne in the 1540s.

However, historian David Potter states that Calais was 'never totally anglicised'; although the garrison was thoroughly English, the town itself and the wider Pale remained French in character.[2] This can be clearly seen in the ease with which the French removed English traces when they reoccupied the settlement; despite two centuries of being under English control, the English merchants were booted out and the territory was quickly reorganised.

Henry's death in 1547 coincided with the growth of French enthusiasm to have their captured towns returned. In 1550, Boulogne was restored to France in a peace treaty with England, thereby ending the War of the Rough Wooing. France paid 400,000 crowns for the honour, which was a boon for the struggling English economy at that time. French eyes then turned to Calais, further up the coast, to a suitable opportunity for its recovery.

The Fall of Calais

Having tired of his role as Mary's neutered consort, Philip's priorities changed when in 1556 his father, Charles, abdicated the Spanish throne; Philip became one of the strongest monarchs in Europe, controlling Spain, the Americas, as well as the Netherlands. It also meant that he was now front and centre of the never-ending Habsburg-Valois feud, which renewed once again later that summer. Despite neglecting Mary and England, Philip was keen for the English to help him with his war; in January 1557, England sent troops to the Netherlands to help defend it from French eyes, then in March, Philip made a rare visit to his wife in England primarily to drum up further support. Mary and her advisors were reluctant to join an all-out war against France, particularly because of the papacy's alliance with the French king. Mary had fought hard to reconnect England with the Catholic faith and this war would likely jeopardise this. In many ways, Mary was caught between a rock and a hard place, between choosing her husband or her pope. However, events escalated after the incident of Thomas Stafford.

Thomas Stafford was a dissatisfied noble who had earlier joined the Wyatt Rebellion in 1554, which had attempted to remove Mary from the throne. He was initially imprisoned for his involvement, before he then took the opportunity to abscond for France. While there, he met with other English exiles and sought the support of the French to help him make a triumphant return to England so that he could claim the throne for himself. In April 1557, Stafford landed in Scarborough with a small group of men, took control of the castle and declared himself the Protector of England. However, his reign of power did not last long and within a handful of days the Earl of Westmorland took control of the castle and arrested Stafford; he was later beheaded at Tower Hill. The whole incident was a pathetic failed repeat of what Henry Tudor had achieved back in 1485, and although the French were not as generous with men and ships in 1557 as they were for the first Tudor king, it was clear that England could not simply sit by and allow this French aggression to go unpunished. As such, war was declared.

The navy was placed on alert in the Channel, while the Scottish activated the Auld Alliance and took advantage by raiding the north of England. The Habsburg side experienced the greatest joy in the summer of 1557, when the French were decisively beaten at Saint Quentin in Picardy. Northern France was weakened as a result, with Paris looking particularly vulnerable. As a result of defeat, the French reorganised their northern defences, with Francis, Duke of Guise, redirected from heading south to the Italian theatre. A decade previously the duke had been seriously injured while laying siege to English-held Boulogne, when a lance went through his helmet; despite the surgeon's initial concerns, the duke made a recovery, with the scar leading to his nickname 'Le Balafré'. On the duke's appraisal of the condition in the north, the French started to seriously consider a direct attack on Calais itself.

During the months of war in 1557 Calais had been largely neglected. The settlement was exposed due to a lack of natural defences, and although 2,000 troops were stationed there, no winter reinforcements were provided. The Deputy of Calais, Thomas Wentworth, had previously complained about the poor state of affairs, but did not expect a direct attack during the winter months. The historian David Potter writes that

Wentworth was complacent in taking 'the view that, should the French attempt anything against him, the weather would sweep them away'.[3] However, it was clear that the French were exerting pressure on the Pale, having already captured a couple of strongholds that autumn.

By the final day of the year the French amassed more than 20,000 men under the leadership of the Duke of Guise. Despite the unorthodox timing – in mid-winter – the attack was unstoppable. The speed was enough to surprise Wentworth, who surrendered Calais a handful of days later, before the French then continued onward, mopping up the Pale by taking the fortress of Guines. By the end of January, the French king Henry II arrived in Calais for the celebration of the reclaiming of this lost French territory.

The speed at which the Pale was captured caused suspicions to be raised about Wentworth's loyalty, leading to charges of treason while he remained a prisoner of war. However, by the time he returned to England there had been a change of queen and he was acquitted of earlier charges. It was a better fate than the one that awaited the conqueror of Calais; in 1563, the Duke of Guise was assassinated. For Mary, the loss of Calais was a humiliating blow. On her deathbed, later in the year of 1558, the queen reputedly told her ladies-in-waiting: 'When I am dead and cut open, they will find Philip and Calais inscribed on my heart.'

The wide embracing peace settlement of Cateau-Cambrésis ended the war in April 1559, and Calais was recognised as an English territory that was in French hands, with 500,000 gold crowns to be paid by the French for compensation. This suggests, then, that the English had not yet completely wiped their hands with Calais, although the new monarch – Queen Elizabeth I – was not keen to push the matter further.

Elizabeth took a proactive approach to assisting Protestants in the early years of her reign, as shown in her involvement in Scottish politics and then later in France. The Huguenots sought her protection, leading to the sending of ships and men in 1562 and the occupation of the port of Le Havre. Elizabeth used this as the basis of reviving her claim to Calais, intending to keep hold of Le Havre until the Pale was restored. This French gamble proved costly, however, and in 1563 the English were ejected from the port. The subsequent Treaty of Troyes in 1564 established a final settlement on Calais: the French would retain it and a payment of 120,000 crowns was made to England. After this point, Elizabeth made no further claim to Calais, thereby ending two centuries of history of its association with England.

A Tudor Brexit?

Historians have debated the overall impact of England losing Calais; the loss of its market has been highlighted as an economic blow, but the reality was that trade centring on the town had been in decline throughout the century. In financial terms, the costs involved in defending and garrisoning Calais were not fully offset by the income derived from trade. As such, it is more accurate to view the loss of the Pale in terms of its military value; the town provided English monarchs with the opportunity to become involved in the northern European theatre of war. This is highlighted most clearly with Henry VIII's French wars, particularly his invasions of northern France in 1513 and in the 1540s; opportunities were available to link up with imperial troops and for the English to take an active role in the continual Habsburg-Valois wars. However, the alternative view is that Calais was a temptation that Henry was unable to ignore, which led him to commit troops and expense on what were vanity projects for little real gain.

The loss of Calais removed any future temptation for an accessible invasion of northern France. But this loss turned out to be England's advantage; Elizabeth was not hampered with the legacy of her father or half-sister, and as shown in the 1564 treaty with the French, she was on the whole content to see Calais become a part of history. Freed from having to maintain and defend it, Elizabeth had a freer hand in terms of European diplomacy. In the long view, this helped England in its shift from the French obsession to start considering what lay in the oceans away from Europe. The decade after the loss of Calais saw communication opening with Russia, West Africa being plundered, and of ambitious dreams of colonising the New World. Of course, such developments did not automatically derive from the loss of Calais, but being weaned off its unhealthy fixation with the Pale allowed the English to direct their energy to other pursuits.

As with Brexit in 2016, the loss of its connection with the European continent provided England with an opportunity for a reset in terms of its international position. Elizabeth I made the most of this freedom, although it remains to be seen if the United Kingdom in the twenty-first century is able to do the same.

Chapter 13

'The Discovery of Russia'

England's Russian connections and the Northeast Passage

Every spring the fishermen from northern Russia headed northward with the aim of exploiting the fresh opportunities of the thawing landscape. In the spring of 1554, however, these fishermen were to encounter something rather different, when they spotted two strange, foreign ships in a bay. They ventured further and saw no signs of life, and on entering the ships they found sixty-two frozen bodies.

A year later the Venetian ambassador in London wrote of the rumours that had circulated of these mysterious deaths, describing he had:

> heard how the men who found them to return them to England narrate strange things about the mode in which they were frozen, having found some of them seated in the act of writing, pen still in hand, and the paper before them; others at table, platters in hand and spoon in mouth; others opening a locker, and others in various postures, like statues, as if they had been adjusted and placed in these attitudes. They say that some dogs on board the ships displayed the same phenaomena.[1]

The leader of this ill-fated expedition was Sir Hugh Willoughby. He was one of many Englishmen who lost their lives in the attempt to advance English interests in the northern Russian seas.

The Mystery of Sir Hugh Willoughby's Death

Decades after John Cabot's failed attempts to find the much-fabled Northwest Passage, England remained a distinctly second-rate power that could not compare to the strength of the Spanish and Portuguese empires. Spain had advanced in the New World, securing a virtual monopoly of imperialism, with England relegated to merely using the fishing grounds off Newfoundland. However, although the Northwest Passage appeared to be off limits, suggestions were put forward of looking in the opposite direction to establish a Northeast Passage to unlock the riches of Asia.

Suggestions of attempting a Northeast Passage were mooted as early as 1527, when Robert Thorne – the son of a Bristolian sailor involved in the earlier voyages to Newfoundland – promoted the idea of sailing north as the key to unlocking a direct route to Asia.[2] In 1531, Thorne wrote directly to Henry VIII:

> there is left one way to discover, which is into the North: for that of the foure parts of the worlde it seemeth three partes are discvoered by other Princes. For out of Spaine they have discvoered all the Indies and Seas Occidentall, and out of Portugale all the Indies and Seas Oriental: So that by this part of the Orient and Occident, they have compassed the worlde.[3]

Thorne stressed how England was well placed for this discovery, due to being 'the nearest and aptest of all other' kingdoms. His belief in the power of English sailors – that was 'there is no lande inhabitable [i.e. uninhabitable], nor Sea innavigable' – appeared to be ill-suited for the reality of the period, particularly when considering the personal interests of Henry VIII.[4] Thorne's plans fell on deaf ears, with Henry far too consumed with his other pet projects – religious supremacy, the invasions of France and the domination of the British Isles – to consider such a costly and time-consuming project.

However, after Henry's death in 1547, support grew for looking further afield beyond the immediate confines of Europe. There was a growing demand to find more markets for English cloth, particularly due to the volatile position of the key locations in the Low Countries. Furthermore, others advocated a more daring approach, notably in the early letters and correspondence of imperial advocate Dr John Dee, as well as in Eden's 1555 publication *Decades of the New Worlde*. Although North America was the primary focus of Eden's attention, he also mentioned the potential of the Northeast:

> by which vyage not only golde, sylver, precious stones, and spices, may be browght hether by a safer and shorter way.[5]

Perhaps the most significant event to highlight this wind of change was the return of Sebastian Cabot to English shores in 1548. Cabot had left England in the early years of the reign of Henry VIII, having become frustrated at the lack of opportunity; this led to three decades in the service of the Spanish in which he sailed to Brazil and was involved in an early Spanish settlement in South America. Cabot's return promised great things, particularly the knowledge of Spanish navigation techniques from the revered House of Trade in Seville. All of this is underlined by the 'warm welcome' that he received on returning to England, along with a handsome pension and the promise of playing a leading role in England's maritime future.[6]

This hope was evidenced in the publication of Cabot's new world map in 1549, in which 'a new chapter in English geographical thought and practice opened'.[7] Discussion began regarding opening up the Northeast Passage, with the Duke of Northumberland – England's most eminent and powerful noble – promoting the notion of connecting England to Cathay.[8] And so a plan came together to attempt the Passage, which in 1553 was cemented in the form of the 'Company of the Merchant Adventurers of England for Discovery of Lands, Territories, Iles, Dominions and Seigneuries Unknown, and Not Before that Late Adventure or Enterprise by Sea or Navigation Commonly Frequented.' Two hundred and forty people invested in the new company, with a minimum subscription fee of £25; £6,000 was eventually raised, which enabled the company to build three new ships.[9] They had big plans, with the charter giving:

> full power and authority to travel to these unexplored regions, there to seek such articles as we lack, and thither to bring from our shores such articles as these people may require.[10]

139

Sir Hugh Willoughby was an unlikely candidate to lead the first expedition into the northern seas. Quite worryingly, he had no maritime experience. But what he did have was the advantage of a connection to high places, particularly Edward Seymour, the Duke of Somerset, having served with distinction in the Scottish campaigns of the 1540s (for which he was knighted). The fall of Somerset meant that Willoughby was in need of a new backer and a new source of income, which led him to petition the newly formed Company of Merchant Adventurers to lead the expedition to strike out and establish the Northeast Passage.

The newly constructed ships – under the direction of Sebastian Cabot – were the *Bona Esperanza* (120 tons), the *Bona Confidentia* (90 tons) and the *Edward Bonaventure* (160 tons). Willoughby sailed on the flagship, the *Esperanza*, whereas the *Edward Bonaventure* was under the command of master Stephen Borough, with Richard Chancellor acting as second-in-command. The fleet left in May 1553 'amid great rejoicing on ship and shore' along the Thames.[11] However, progress was slow due to bad winds, with the ships not reaching the Norwegian coast until July 1553. A violent storm on 30 July separated the ships, although there was a plan to rendezvous at the settlement of Vardo. The only ship to reach the meeting point was Chancellor's; he waited a week for the others to arrive, before heading off alone.

The other ships were scattered but they did not surrender their mission, pushing onward into treacherous waters. Sir Hugh Willoughby's journal provides a clear overview of the expedition's whereabouts and actions in 1553, and on 18 September they anchored in a suitable harbour where a decision was taken to remain during the dangerous winter. Willoughby wrote of his impressions of the location:

> This haven runneth into the main, about two leagues, and is in breadth half a league, wherin were very many seal fishes, and other great fishes, and upon the main we saw bears, great deer, foxes, with divers strange beasts, as guloines, and such other which were to us unknown, and also wonderful.[12]

Willoughby continued:

> thus remaining in this haven the space of a week, seeing the year far spent, and also very evil weather, as frost, snow, and

hail, as though it had been the deep of winter, we thought best to winter there.[13]

Willoughby ordered groups of men to search the surrounding countryside, with the hope of establishing contact with locals; however, as Willoughby writes, they 'returned without finding people, or any similitude of habitation'.[14] It is at this point that Willoughby's journal ends. Fast forward to the spring of 1554 when Russian fishermen found the two ships anchored at the mouth of the river in Lapland; when they ventured onboard they found the bodies of Willoughby and sixty-one others.

There are many questions attached to the death of Sir Hugh Willoughby and his crew. First, when did they all die? Although the journal ends before the end of the year, a will found on the ship indicates that Willoughby was still alive in January 1554.[15] This suggests that the crew, and Willoughby himself, were not completely incompetent and had survived months of the harsh Russian weather.

The bigger question is: how did they die? For centuries it was accepted that the men had passed away in one of the following ways: of exposure to the cold, starvation, or of scurvy. The letter from the Venetian ambassador (written in November 1555) described how the men were found 'all frozen',[16] with the bodies immobile in positions such as the act of writing or in the middle of eating. This narrative became established in later accounts, particularly Richard Hakluyt's 1589 *Principle Navigations* in which he noted how they 'perished for cold',[17] and this interpretation became dominant in the following centuries, with minor amendments of starvation or scurvy. In the nineteenth century, historians described Willoughby dying 'in the act of writing his journal', and that everyone was 'frozen to death';[18] in the early part of the twentieth century, Inna Lubimenko noted how 'all the seamen died of hunger and cold';[19] and this belief continued into the second half of the century when other historians wrote of how 'all the men were frozen to death'.[20]

However, the work of Eleanora C. Gordon in the 1980s led to a reassessment of original documents to advance a more convincing verdict: it wasn't the cold, starvation or scurvy, but rather death by carbon monoxide poisoning. Gordon notes how the earlier accounts of bodies being frozen to death were likely embellishments, and that if Sir Hugh and his men were suddenly killed then it was not logical to assume that it was from the cold. After all, the men were found 'in normal postures', rather than huddled together in an attempt to keep warm.[21] Furthermore, there was additional clothing in the stores of the ships, which would, no doubt, have been used if the cold weather was becoming severe. Also, she dismisses the notion that starvation was the cause, due to the 'ample' food supply (there were provisions to last for eighteen months), along with the opportunity to find meat on the coast (as noted in Willoughby's journal).[22] All of this led Gordon to conclude that it was accidental death by carbon monoxide; in an attempt to remain warm they blocked all air and access points, such as the chimney:

> Willoughby and his men may not have been the hapless victims of environmental circumstances beyond their control, but rather may have unwittingly brought about their own deaths in a freak accident.[23]

The attempt to find the Northeast Passage had led to the deaths of the first English victims.[24] But they were not to be the last.

An Englishman in Moscow

Two of the Company's three ships had succumbed; however, the third – commanded by Borough and Chancellor – continued onward, becoming the first English ship to enter the Russian White Sea. On 24 August 1553, the *Edward Bonaventure* dropped anchor near the mouth of the Dvina River in the White Sea, near present-day Archangel.

Chancellor was born in 1521, and like many of the Tudor seamen, he grew up in Bristol. He developed experience of voyages to the Mediterranean, which put him in the same circles as Sebastian Cabot and John Dee. Chancellor rose to prominence within the Company under the patronage of the Duke of Northumberland, and he was able to obtain a place in the expedition to find the Northeast Passage in 1553. After becoming disconnected with Willoughby, Chancellor may have been forgiven for having second thoughts about continuing on alone; in the Norwegian port of Vardo he met Scottish fishermen who strongly warned him of the dangers that lay ahead. But Chancellor did not heed their advice, continuing eastward.

Unlike Willoughby's empty reception, Chancellor met Russians who lived in the nearby Nikolo-Korelsky monastery. They informed him that he was now in a land under the control of a ruler named Tsar Ivan; Chancellor responded by declaring 'himself bearer of a letter from his sovereignty to the Czar'.[25] It was agreed that Chancellor would travel inland to meet the Tsar, and having initially visited the regional capital he then set off on the 600-mile journey by horse-drawn sleigh through ice and snow to Moscow.

What type of land was Chancellor entering? Russia today comprises a significant portion of land in both Europe and Asia, but Russia in the middle of the Tudor period was smaller and less powerful. The earlier Kiev Rus state was destroyed after the impact of the Mongol invasions in the 1200s, although by the time Henry VII came to the throne in 1485 a renewed focus was placed on the growth of the Grand Duchy of Moscow. When Chancellor arrived in Moscow, this duchy had been transformed into the Tsardom of Russia under the control of Ivan the Terrible. Chancellor recorded his own impressions of entering Moscow, noting how it was primitively built – with houses made out of wood rather than stone – but that the city itself was far larger than London. Furthermore, he was impressed by the luxury on offer at the palace. The historians Nicholas Casimir and Baron de Bogoushevsky describe the scene:

> the English strangers were dazzled by the unexpected splendour of the Russian court. Surrounded by the Boyars and dignitaries of his realm, clad in rich vestments of gold and silver brocade, the younger sovereign wearing a magnificent diadem sparkling with precious gems, was seated on a costly throne.[26]

However, Chancellor was less enthused by the Russians themselves, calling them 'barbarous Russes'.[27]

The letter confirming Chancellor's mission was written in several languages, being addressed to unspecified 'Northern and Eastern Sovereigns'.[28] The letter expressed the following:

> Moved by the desire of establishing friendly relations with foreign peoples, certain of our subjects have proposed a journey to distant maritime regions in order to open a trade with the nations … inhabiting those districts.[29]

It continued:

> Accordingly we beseech you, kings, princes, and all in
> authority in these regions, to grant free passage through
> your dominions to these our subjects. They will touch none
> of your goods without your leave.[30]

Ivan responded positively to Chancellor's offer of friendship and to
establish a trading relationship, promising trade privileges and the
access of England's merchants to 'have a free market through my
whole dominions, to come and go as they please'. No doubt, Ivan
was mindful of the instability of his tsardom at that time, as well as
dealing with looming threats of Sweden and the Polish-Lithuanian
Commonwealth. Furthermore, being located on the eastern edge of
Europe – their Baltic access at St Petersburg would only develop in
the early 1700s – meant that they were politically and commercially
isolated, particularly so due to the control that the Hanseatic League
held over Baltic trade. As such, the prospect of a direct trade deal with
the English clearly interested Ivan, and Chancellor was tasked with
returning back to England to set plans in motion, leaving Moscow on
15 March 1554.

When Chancellor arrived in England he learnt that the old monarch,
King Edward VI, was dead, and that his half-sister, Mary I, now sat
on the throne. His return was hugely welcomed by the Company, the
royal court and the general public.[31] It was a hero's welcome due to
the great feat of reaching Russia, and as with any modern celebrity,
Chancellor cashed in on his newly found fame by penning: *Booke of
the Great and Mighty Emperor of Russia and Duke of Muscovia, and of
the Dominions, Orders, and Commodities thereunto belonging*. More
importantly, it led to the elevation of his business associates; in February
1555, the Muscovy Company was granted a monopoly to establish trade
with Russia, with the Company licensed to:

> make discoveries in all manner of unknown countries in a
> northern, north-eastern, and north-western direction; to use
> the royal arms on their flags, and to subdue, possess, and
> occupy all townes, castles, villages, isles, and main landes
> of infidelitie.[32]

The 1553 expedition was one of hope and speculation, rather than of firm expectation. But now the Company had a clear ambition, and in Chancellor they had the man who made it all possible. Chancellor was sent back to Russia to take the relationship to the next level, leaving later in the year of 1555.

On returning to Ivan's court, Chancellor presented him with a letter from Mary and Philip providing gratitude for the developing friendship. Chancellor and his men were 'enterayned and banqueted … with all humanitie and gentlenes',[33] and after the merriment the different nationalities got down to business to agree a deal. This agreement provided English merchants with wide access to Russian markets, with a biannual market to be established at the regional capital near the northern coast, with privileges including free passage, the ability to build and inhabit houses, and freedom from arrest.[34]

In July 1556, Chancellor set off for England. This time he was joined by Osip Nepeya, the first Russian ambassador to England, along with the two recovered ships related to the death of Sir Hugh Willoughby and his crew. However, the return voyage was disastrous due to devastating storms; the two recovered ships sank off the coast of Norway, and although Chancellor's *Edward Bonaventure* crossed the North Sea, it was driven ashore near Aberdeen. The majority of the crew, along with Chancellor himself, lost their lives.

Osip Nepeya, however, managed to survive. After the sinking of the ship, he was initially taken hostage by locals in the area, before being permitted to travel south to London. He was able to attend Queen Mary's royal court, where he was presented with a gift: '2 pieces cloth of gold; 1 broad-cloth, scarlet; 1 ditto, violet; 1 ditto, blue; 2 suits of armour (sent by Philip); and a helmet studded with gilt nails, also a lion and lioness.'[35] The Muscovy Company presented the Russian ambassador with their own gift of gratitude, a 'chain of pure gold worth 100 guineas, and five magnificent drinking cups'.[36] Despite the cost of lives, it was the beginning of what would become a tense and tumultuous friendship.

'The notable and strange journey of Master Jenkinson'

Just as Sir Hugh Willoughby had seemingly handed the baton to Richard Chancellor, momentum then passed from Chancellor to Anthony

145

Jenkinson. Jenkinson was part of the group that brought the first Russian ambassador back to England in 1557. Before this he had already obtained a wealth of experience, having travelled through North Africa and the Middle East, which culminated in a meeting with Suleyman the Magnificent of the Ottoman Empire. On behalf of the Muscovy Company, Jenkinson performed vital functions in a series of expeditions to Russia, and during this time he developed a strong bond with Tsar Ivan. In 1558 he set off to Russia for his first expedition to Moscow. As with Chancellor, Jenkinson was met with an enthusiastic reception:

> he entered Moscow, and met a most gracious reception. He found the Czar disposed to grant all his requests, and do everything in his power to increase the privileges and advance the trade of the English residents.[37]

After completing business arrangements in Moscow, he then ventured further southward down the Volga armed with 'two English clerks and a Tartar' into territory recently conquered by the Russian tsardom: Kazan and Astrakhan.[38] From here he was able to consider other routes towards the much-valued Asian markets; if the Company could not sail around the landmass to China, perhaps it could establish a link through the heart of the Continent. On reaching the Caspian Sea, Jenkinson chartered a ship and sailed across it while proudly unfurling the flag of the cross of St George; 'which I suppose', later wrote Jenkinson, 'was never seene in the Caspian sea before'.[39]

On the other side of the sea, he packed goods on camels and struck out across the deserts of Turkestan to Bokhara. He remained there for two months to strike up trade deals, before then returning to Moscow via the same route, loaded 'with 600 camel-loads of Oriental merchandise'.[40] The entire expedition was an incredible success, but yet Jenkinson had gambled with his life by travelling into dangerous regions where he could have been attacked or killed. Then, on completing fresh trade agreements, he returned to Moscow before heading back to England in 1560 to tell the English of his discoveries.

The finds of this expedition enthused the Company, and Jenkinson himself was able to stimulate further interest with the publication of a map of Russia. In 1561, he set off once more to Russia, and after reaching Moscow he continued south with the aim of travelling to Persian lands.

He eventually found the court of Shah Tahmasp and ended up obtaining trade deals on behalf of the Muscovy Company. By July 1564 he was back in London armed with more knowledge and fame. Jenkinson's third expedition to Russia was in 1566; such was his importance that he was sent specifically to negotiate with Ivan over a trade dispute. The same problems and disagreements necessitated his fourth and final expedition to Russia in 1571; once more, Jenkinson left Moscow having restored good favour for the Company and for the Crown.

Jenkinson's expeditions were hugely influential in stimulating trade with Russia and in generating further interest in wider exploration, as shown in the publication of his maps. Perhaps Jenkinson's greatest success was in becoming the first Englishman to reach out to strange unknown civilisations in Asia, and in establishing a trade connection with Persia. More visits to Persian lands happened during the 1560s and 1570s, of Company men in small groups of up to ten; but the journey was fraught with difficulties due to the distance and uncertain conditions, with many men dying of 'fever and privations'.[41] By 1581, the connection was abandoned due to the political uncertainty in Persia itself. However, an Anglo-Persian connection was not entirely ended; toward the end of the Tudor period Robert and Anthony Shirley became involved in the organisation and training of the Persian army, and in the early seventeenth century the British East India Company was founded, which would develop and have a large role in the shaping of the British Empire on the Asian continent.

Elizabeth and Ivan

Anthony Jenkinson did his best to smooth over what was an unsteady relationship between Queen Elizabeth and Tsar Ivan. Agreements were agreed, torn up and rewritten during this period due to a difference of opinion as to what the Anglo-Russian relationship should be. For Elizabeth, the connection was purely a business one, whereas Ivan wanted something far more personal in the form of a political and military union. The letters sent between the two monarchs highlight this continuing conflict, with Elizabeth forever flattering and being non-committal, and Ivan insisting on the relationship becoming something more. As historian Inna Lubimenko notes, this is found in the style and writing within the letters themselves, with Ivan's letters 'full of energy and vehemence, they show a force, a vigour, characteristic of the man – the intelligent and proud despot'. Whereas Elizabeth's replies were 'short and simple'.[42]

No doubt Ivan benefited from the presence of the English, particularly in the financial interactions and in the sharing of knowledge. In a letter to Elizabeth in 1567 he asked her to send him 'an architect able to build castles, towers and palaces, a doctor, an apothecary, and other artificers, such as can seek for gold and silver'.[43] In 1570, she also promised to host Ivan and his family if the situation in Russia became so severe that he had to abandon his throne; Elizabeth stated that Ivan could stay 'as longe as ye shall like to remaine with vs'.[44] But Ivan's ultimate goal – his 'pet project'[45] – was to establish a firm diplomatic union with England:

> the said Emperor of Muscouia earnestly requireth that there may be a perpetuall frendship and kyndred betwixt the Q.ma-tie and him which shal be the begining of further matter to be done.[46]

But Elizabeth was not as keen to agree to Ivan's request that 'England and Russland might be in all matters as one'.[47] She wanted a market for English goods, not to become embroiled in Ivan's problems and becoming a defender against his enemies.

The inability of England to commit to a closer diplomatic bond led to disputes, particularly with Ivan taking offence at grievances. This led to various breakdowns in which the rights and privileges of the Muscovy Company were rescinded, with the threat of Ivan shifting his assistance to the rival Hanseatic League. At times, it would become particularly poisonous, leading to the confiscation of goods and the unease of English merchants present in Russia; this was particularly so due to Ivan's habit of imprisoning envoys 'under the pretext of being spies in the interests of Poland'.[48] Ivan was desperate for military assistance, and he was paranoid about Elizabeth's 'unsympathetic conduct toward him'.[49] Elizabeth's general approach was to avoid antagonising Ivan – 'our deare brother emperour'[50] – and at times she would cede to his demands, as shown in the 1580s when thirteen boats loaded with munitions were sent to help Ivan in his wars with Sweden and Poland.

So much depended on personality, particularly those who could build a rapport with Ivan. Both Chancellor and Jenkinson clearly had the knack of settling Ivan's outrage, and this was equally true of Daniel Sylvester, who was sent to Moscow in the 1570s to smooth things over; however, Sylvester met an unfortunate end when lightning hit and killed him when in northern Russia. Other diplomats were not as delicate and understanding, as in the example of Sir Jerome Bowes in the 1580s. Bowes was sent to negotiate a marriage deal between Ivan (now on wife number seven) and the English lady Mary Hastings; however, his boastful and vain approach – such as telling others that he had the ear of the Tsar – did not endear him to Moscow's elite, particularly as his main ploy was seemingly to delay the marriage indefinitely. An anecdote of Bowes' time in Moscow was recounted throughout the years, with Samuel Pepys recording in his diary in the late seventeenth century the aftermath of when Ivan was reputed to have nailed the French ambassador's hat to his head. Bowes was threatened with similar punishment; however, Bowes proudly claimed that he was not merely a servant of the weak French king but rather a subject of the mighty English queen 'who does not vail her bonnet nor bare her head to any prince living'. The boldness of the English diplomat is said to have won over the Tsar, who respected Bowes' bravery and honour.

Ivan's death in 1584 led to an anti-Bowes backlash; he was confined to his house for two months during which period the Russian politicians discussed whether the Englishman should be executed. However, Bowes was spared a death sentence, and instead he was humiliatingly ejected from Russia:

> they took from him his sword, and, not even letting him throw on his upper garment, dragged him before the Czar, without allowing him to be accompanied by his interpreter. Paying no attention to his refusal, they forced upon him a letter for the Queen, then seizing him by the arms, they turned him out of the palace, ordering him to quit Moscow immediately.[51]

Bowes is noted to have 'foamed with ... powerless spite', and he demanded that all English merchants leave Russia.[52] However, nobody listened to him, and after Ivan's death the Anglo-Russian relationship settled down to an era of greater stability during the remainder of the Tudor period.

There was also a deeper reason for these disagreements, particularly in the political systems of the two nations: Elizabeth ruled with the guidance of her councillors and Parliament, whereas Ivan was a despot who had greater control over the policies and direction of Russia. Many English were 'amazed at the subservience of the Muscovite aristocracy toward the tsar',[53] and one diplomat described the reign of Ivan as 'cruel, barbarous, and tyrannical'.[54] Many of Elizabeth's subjects commented on the strengths of the English political system, noting how the English had a clearer understanding of justice. On occasion, English merchants would complain of the 'animosity of the Russian people', and how they felt uncertainty regarding the Tsar's whims.[55] However, the lure of gold was enough to tempt the English, and as Chancellor himself stated, the Russians had great potential: 'If they knewe their strength ... no man were able to make match with them.'[56]

The Triumph of the Muscovy Company

Despite the success in establishing direct trade links with Russia, and by extension, Persia, the Muscovy Company did not abandon their initial aim of finding the Northeast Passage. Jenkinson advised the Company to focus its energy on establishing trade with Persia, rather than with fanciful risky adventures; however, success in finding the Northeast Passage would allow the Company, and by extension England, access to the wealth of Asia.

Stephen Borough was master of the *Edward Bonaventure* when it became the first English ship to sail into the White Sea in 1553; when Chancellor travelled to Moscow, Borough remained on the ship throughout the winter. On his second expedition in 1556 he sailed beyond the White Sea in the *Serchthrift*, a small vessel with a crew of fifteen; he discovered the Kara Strait between Novaya Zemlya and Vaygach Island; however, he was unable to proceed further due to blockage of ice. The Muscovy Company appointed him chief navigator and he undertook more trips in the 1560s; however, he was unsuccessful in his attempt to find the Northeast Passage. Despite this failure, Borough proved to be of great value to the advancement of English navigation. His expeditions brought about the return of observations and data, and he was able to publish a handbook to help sailors navigate the treacherous conditions of Lapland and northern Russia.[57] His visit to the navigation school in Spain, Sebastian Cabot's old stomping ground, led to the printing of the 'first navigation manual ever printed in England',[58] and his collection of a list of native words and expressions were later published by Hakluyt in 1589.

In 1577, John Dee remained hopeful of England's attempts to enter the Asian seas. In his book, *The Great Volume of Famous and Riche Discoveries*, he wrote:

> I trust with one or two complete surveys, after this to be performed by my travail ... that all the northeast part of Asia, with the two principal cities thereof, Cambala and Quinsay, will become to the Brytish natural inhabitants of this Monarchy so well known, as are the coasts of Denmark and Norway and their periplus.[59]

However, Dee's dreams were not to be realised during the Tudor century. Later attempts – such as those led by John Wood, Arthur Pet and Charles Jackman – all failed; as with so many others, Jackson was lost with his ship on the return voyage and Wood's expedition has been described as being 'disastrous and ill-concieved'.[60] The Company ultimately concluded that the Northeast Passage was impossible, and England's attention in the remainder of the century gradually drifted back to the other direction: the Northwest Passage. By the 1590s, it was the Dutch who were able to hail the greater success in the northern Russian seas, particularly with Willem Barentsz's voyages.

Despite the inability to find the Northeast Passage it is clear that England's 'discovery of Russia' in the 1550s led to great advances for both countries. Russia benefited with the creation of Archangel as the northern Russian port, of the development of Vologda and of Moscow's enhancement as a centre for trade. For England, there were notable trading advantages, with some Russian historians previously claimed how their homeland was 'ruthlessly exploited' by the English during the period, and that the northern Russian region had turned into 'a virtual colony'.[61] However, Ivan and the Russians simply ceded to English interests with the intention of kickstarting their own economy and infrastructure; they always retained the power to eject, as shown in the incident of Sir Jerome Bowes.

Interestingly, in the decade after Elizabeth's death there appears to have been serious discussion about England taking control of territory in northern Russia. This was due to the volume of problems that Russia experienced during the 'Time of Troubles' when it appeared to be close to collapse; this was due to the constant churn of tsars and the resulting problems, such as anarchy, lawlessness and famine. It is estimated that more than one million Russians died during the period, and matters were hastened due to the advancing Polish-Lithuanian troops. The government of James I concluded that it would have been preferable if the English military took control of land in northern Russia, particularly the important port of Archangel. As the historian Chester Dunning notes: 'strange as it seems, for a brief period of time King James I actually dreamed of adding part of Muscovy to his "empire"'.[62] However, the emergence of the Romanovs led to improved fortunes in Russia, and this pipe-dream was ended.

The heyday of the Tudor-Russian relationship was undoubtedly the first two decades after Richard Chancellor's visit to Moscow. Despite the problems with Ivan's shifting approach, this period enabled the Muscovy Company to position itself as an influential organisation. By the end of the century the exclusive privileges afforded to England were no longer present, and the English now competed with rivals – particularly the Dutch – for Russia's attention, as well as the fishing grounds and harbours. The Northeast Passage may have proved impossible, but the efforts of these explorers and diplomats stimulated trade and more importantly advanced England's courage to search further and wider than ever before. Many were killed in attempting their missions, such as Sir Hugh Willoughby and Richard Chancellor; however, as the historian Lubimenko writes, 'danger, fatigue, illness, nothing stopped them, nor diminished their enterprise and their energy'.[63] These feats captured the imagination of others, particularly the writers Dr Dee and Richard Hakluyt, which in turn inspired the next generation of explorers. At the end of the sixteenth century, Hakluyt proudly declared that the Muscovy Company had 'performed more than any one, yea than all the nations of Europe' in terms of opening up the vast Russian lands.

Chapter 14

The Birth of the English Slave Trade
The 1560s' voyages of Sir John Hawkins

More than four centuries after the Elizabethan seadog John Hawkins raided West Africa in search of slaves, one of his descendants was invited to attend a 'reconciliation festival' in the Gambia. Andrew Hawkins, who knew little of his connection to John Hawkins, provided a public apology for the crimes of his family, saying: 'I don't feel guilty about the slave trade personally. But I want to take the story seriously and learn from it.'[1] In front of an audience of 25,000 people, Andrew Hawkins wore a T-shirt stating 'So Sorry' in various languages, while being chained alongside other Europeans. As he explains:

> Walking for an hour like that, in that heat ... The feeling of dehumanisation really horrified me. Some people were laughing at us. My neck was burning. The chains bite into you. You get a mark.[2]

Back in the UK some sections of the press were scathing about Andrew Hawkins' involvement in the event. The historian A.N. Wilson wrote an article in *The Daily Mail* with the headline: 'Get off your knees!' Wilson wrote:

> All propagandists know that pictures speak louder than words. What does this picture say? It says that white men of today, and Englishmen in particular, should grovel in apology because of something which was done by a few old seadogs in the 16th century.[3]

The debate about the legacy of John Hawkins' actions in West Africa continue to be waged in the twenty-first century. However, the general public seemingly knows little of the role that he played in creating the birth of the English slave trade.

'Partly by the sword and partly by other meanes'

By the middle of the sixteenth century, West Africa had been the preserve of the Portuguese for more than a hundred years. They first arrived on the coast in the region in the 1440s, with King John II taking up the title Lord of Guinea in 1481; the 1494 Treaty of Tordesillas cemented the position of the Portuguese within this side of the world, and they engaged in trade in terms of ivory, gold, and of slaves.

Henry VIII's general unwillingness to promote wider exploration or trade did not help stimulate English attempts in the region, and as such, there were only a handful of voyages before the reign of Elizabeth I. In 1528–30, the first English ship sailed from Plymouth to the West African region, captained by William Hawkins, John's father. It stopped at the River Sestos in present-day Liberia before then moving westward to Brazil. It is believed that William Hawkins 'brought back home a savage king' as a marvel for the royal court.[4] In 1554–5, John Lok brought Africans from the region back to London with the intention of having them learn English so they could act as interpreters to help promote trade on the Gold Coast. Later in the decade William Towerson sailed to Guinea, took hold of four or five Africans, and brought them back to Plymouth with a similar intention as Lok. As historian P.E.H. Hair notes, 'it is unclear from the accounts whether they went voluntarily or semi-voluntarily, or were kidnapped'.[5]

Such ventures clearly excited the young mind of John Hawkins, and the influence of his father and home-town of Plymouth provided him with opportunity to advance as a sailor. He was born in 1532 and during his adolescence he became involved in various trading expeditions; it was while visiting the Spanish-owned Canary Islands that he learned of the potential of making money through selling slaves. This coincided with the Crown relying more and more on the use of privateers; essentially pirates who were provided with a licence from the government. John Hawkins' father had taken part in this development in the 1540s, when he was commissioned to harass shipping in the Channel during Henry VIII's final French war.

As with earlier Tudor voyages (such as with John Cabot in the 1490s or with the Muscovy Company from the 1550s), a group of financial backers was needed to help fund the expedition to West Africa. Enough was gathered to enable the launching of three ships in 1562, with the intention of capturing slaves to take them to the New World to sell for profit. The remaining cargo room would be filled with valuables such as 'hides, ginger, sugar, and some pearls', with the aim of selling to European markets.[6]

The first voyage was a financial success, with 300 Africans taken across the Atlantic and sold at the Spanish colony of Santo Domingo. The Elizabethan writer Richard Hakluyt described the people of Guinea, one of the central regions on which Hawkins focused:

> all blacke, and are called Negroes, without any apparell, saving before their privities: of stature goodly men, and well liking, by reason of their foode … These men are also more civill then any other, because of their dailie traffike with the Frenchmen, and are of nature very gentle, and loving.[7]

How were these slaves obtained? Later in the century Hakluyt wrote of Hawkins' voyages, noting how the people were obtained 'partly by the sword, and partly by other meanes'.[8] The mention of 'the sword' clearly refers to the use of violence, and Hawkins himself writes of a later attempt to forcibly take Africans. Towerson's earlier voyage was not shy about using force, as shown in the setting on fire of two villages because they refused to trade with the English. However, these violent tactics led to retaliation from the West Africans, leading to the deaths of those in Hawkins' crew. The 'other meanes' refers to trading with other Europeans, using them as middle-men to obtain the slaves required.

The success of the 1562 voyage led to a second 'dramatically larger and more powerful' expedition in 1564, as shown with the involvement of leading governmental figures such as William Cecil and Robert Dudley, Earl of Leicester.[9] Hawkins and his fleet headed to West Africa and obtained slaves by resorting to violent tactics, which wasn't always incredibly effective; as explained by one of his crew, John Sparke:

> The Captain, who, with a dozen men, went through the town, returned; finding two hundred Negroes at the waters side, shooting at them in the boats and cutting them in pieces that were drowned in the water: at whose coming, they all ran away. So he entered his boats; and before he could put off from the shore, they returned again, and shot very fiercely and hurt divers of them.[10]

Sparke writes as to how the crew were 'somewhat discomforted':

> although the Captain, in a singular wise manner, carried himself, with countenance very cheerful outwardly, as though he did little weight the death of his men, nor yet the hurt of the rest (although his heart inwardly was broken in pieces for it).[11]

Once the slaves were secured, Hawkins headed to the Spanish domains of the New World. Because of the Spanish monopoly, many were not welcoming of Hawkins' business, stating that they 'were forbidden by the King to traffic with any foreign nation, upon penalty to forfeit their goods'.[12] However, on payment of an additional tax, Hawkins was able to sell his slaves and load up new cargo to return to England, stocking up – as John Sparkes wrote – on 'gold, silver, pearls, and other jewels in great store'.[13] Sparkes also writes of one other item:

> These potatoes be the most delicate roots that may be eaten; and do far exceed our parsnips or carrots. Their pines by of the bigness of two fists, the outside whereof is of the making of a pine apple, but it is soft like the rind of a cucumber; and the inside eateth like an apple, but is more delicious than any sweet apple sugared.[14]

After completing his transactions with the slaves, Hawkins then had a side adventure to the French colony of Fort Carolina in Florida, established by French Huguenots. The French were demoralised and at their wit's end; they were short of food and some had mutinied and left the colony. Hawkins writes of their condition:

> that they were faine to gather acorns, which being stamped small, and often washed, to take away the bitternesse of them, they did use for bread, eating withall sundry times, roots, whereof they found many good and holesome, and such as serve rather for medicines then for meates alone.[15]

Hawkins offered to return them to Europe, but many refused, perhaps fearing that the English would take control of the colony. Instead Hawkins and the English helped by tending to the wounds of those who had been engaged in hostilities with the natives. Rene Goulaine de Laudonniere wrote of the assistance received:

> I may saye that wee receaved as manye courtesies of the Generall, as it was possible to receive of any man living. Wherein doubtlesse hee hath wonne the reputation of a good and charitable man, deserving to be esteemed as much of us all as if hee had saved all our lives.[16]

Hawkins returned to England in 1565 and received a hero's welcome. Despite the loss of twenty men, the entire venture was a great financial success. The Crown recognised Hawkins' exploits, providing him with a coat of arms, which consisted:

> of a black shield, with a golden lion walking in the waves; above the lion, three golden coins; for the crest, a figure of half a Moor, bound and a captive, with golden amulets on his arms and ears.[17]

Hawkins was riding high; his standing within England and the royal court were massively enhanced due to his slave trading actions. However, his third voyage was one of disaster; its impact had wider serious ramifications in terms of England's relationship with Spain.

The Battle of San Juan de Ulúa

Having secured funding for a third expedition, Hawkins and his fleet (including his cousin, Francis Drake) left Plymouth in October 1567 but experienced issues with a quarrelsome crew and an inability to obtain slaves. As Hawkins himself explains, he landed in Cape Verde:

> hoping to obtain some Negroes, where we got but few, and those with great hurt and damage to our men, which chiefly proceeded of their envenomed arrows: and although in the beginning they seemed to be but small hurts, yet there hardly escaped any that had blood drawn of them, but died in strange sort, with their mouths shut some ten days before they died, and after their wounds were whole; where I myself had one of the greatest wounds, yet thanks be to God, escaped.[18]

He then moved on to the coast of Guinea and into Sierra Leone, disappointed that he had only obtained 150 slaves by January 1568. He was able to exploit a civil war taking place between two tribes, with Hawkins writing:

> But even in that present instant, there came to us a Negro, sent from a king, oppressed by other kings, his neighbours, desiring our aid, with [the] promise that as many Negroes as be these wars might be obtained, as well of his part as of ours, should be at our pleasure.[19]

Hawkins ordered an attack on the rival town; however, there were further difficulties with the killing of six of his men and the wounding of forty others. Hawkins then led the second wave with more men, in which he:

> assaulted the town, both by land and sea, and very hardly with fire (their houses being covered with dry palm leaves) obtained the town, put the inhabitants to flight, where we took 250 persons, men, women, & children, and by our friend the king of our side, there were taken 600 prisoners, whereof we hoped to have our choice: but the Negro (in

whose nation is seldom or never found truth) meant nothing less: for that night he removed his camp and prisoners, so that we were fain to content us with those few which we had gotten ourselves.[20]

By February 1568 his fleet had obtained between 400 and 500 people, and they reached Santo Domingo in March 1568. Facing the same suspicions as in previous visits, Hawkins used his old connections and testimonials, handing out bribes to local officials when needed. He was able to sell the slaves and filled his ships with gold, silver and jewels, before departing in July 1568.

However, the Spanish government was keen to clamp down on any further Anglo incursions into their monopoly of the New World, particularly the Caribbean region. The French colony of Fort Caroline – the same one that Hawkins had previously helped – had already felt the wrath of Spain when in 1565 it was attacked, with several hundred Huguenots massacred. They were concerned about Hawkins' return to the West Indies, and soon they would have the opportunity to demonstrate their displeasure.

Stormy weather prevented Hawkins' fleet from attempting an Atlantic crossing, and a decision was made to head to a nearby small port – San Juan de Ulúa – to stock up on supplies for his fleet of six ships before trying again. Hawkins writes of waking one morning to find 'thirteen great ships' of 'the Fleet of Spain', including a galleon carrying the newly appointed Viceroy of New Spain, arriving in the bay.[21] Tension and fear was building, but Hawkins obtained an agreement to remain there alongside the Spanish ships in peaceful harmony. However, having finally saddled-up alongside Hawkins, the Spanish used the opportunity to hatch a plan.

A force of men gathered on the mainland, with the intention of taking the shore batteries that would provide them with the initiative to hit the English ships. A further 150 men were hidden on a hulk – the *San Salvador* – which was to be brought up between the anchored English and Spanish ships. Once everything was in position, a trumpet was to be sounded to start the attack, all while Hawkins and his men were eating their lunch. However, the English sailors became suspicious of the Spanish, leading to Hawkins sending the Spanish-speaking Robert Barret to talk to the Viceroy about these fears. The Viceroy could not keep his cool: Barret was seized, the trumpet was broadcast and the attack was launched.

Hawkins later explained the pandemonium:

> Our men, which warded ashore, being stricken with sudden fear ... fled, and sought to recover succour from the ships. The Spaniards, being provided before for the purpose, landed in all places in multitudes from their ships, which they might easily do without boats; and slew all our men ashore without mercy.[22]

English ships were boarded, with Hawkins' *Jesus of Lubeck* stormed. Hawkins wrote about how despite 'the loss of many our men', the *Jesus* was 'defended' and the Spanish 'kept out'.[23] Fire was exchanged between the two sides, with the Spanish ship *Santa Clara* catching fire and sinking, and their flagship *San Pedro* being badly hit in an exchange with the English *Minion*. But with the Spanish securing the coast, they used the cannons to fire on English ships, which succumbed to the onslaught. Robert Blondel, the French commander of the *Grace of God*, set the ship on fire before joining Hawkins on the *Lubeck*. The *Angel* sank, and the *Swallow* was seized. The *Jesus of Lubeck* was heavily damaged, to the point that it was positioned as a shield to allow the *Minion* to escape out of range. Hawkins gave the order to abandon the ships, with members of the *Lubeck* crew taken onboard a pinnacle to find safety on the *Minion*.

The only English ships to escape from the battle were the *Minion* and Francis Drake's *Judith*. Many were left behind, including the stranded *Lubeck* – which was seized on the second day – which had a significant number of her crew onboard. Due to the lack of supplies and the concerns about sailing across the Atlantic, Hawkins wrote of the despair of the survivors on the *Minion*:

> Some desired to yield to the Spaniards. Some rather desired to obtain a place, where they might give themselves to the infidels. And some hath rather abide with a little pittance, the mercy of God at sea.[24]

Due to overcrowding and a lack of victuals, more than a hundred men were abandoned on the Mexican coast. These poor men, who had only just escaped a battle, were then attacked by natives before being imprisoned by the Spanish; they were later sent to Mexico City where they were able to live freely, with some starting families, before the arrival of the Inquisition in the 1570s. Many were rounded up and imprisoned once more, with brutal punishments being meted out due to their choice of religion: William Collins was sentenced to ten years in the galleys; John Burton received 200 lashes and six years in the galleys; while John Morton was burned at the stake.

Francis Drake reached Plymouth in December 1568, believing that his ship was the only survivor. Having heard a rumour of his brother's death, William Hawkins wrote a letter to the queen's right-hand man, William Cecil, lamenting his loss: 'But if it should be true, as GOD forbid! I shall have cause to curse them whiles I live, and my children after me.'[25] However, John Hawkins appeared a month after Drake, with the crew of the *Minion* reduced to fifteen men. No doubt, Hawkins had some stiff words for his cousin, and it is believed that Drake's quick escape cast a shadow over his reputation for years to come. San Juan de Ulúa was a watershed moment for the Elizabethan seadogs; more than 300 Englishmen lost their lives in the encounter, leading to Hawkins and his fellow seadogs to never forget the treachery of the Spanish.

The Troubled Legacy of Sir John Hawkins

The twenty-first century has seen a vast reappraisal of John Hawkins' legacy, with place names such as schools and squares being renamed to disassociate themselves with his troubled history. How are we to judge Hawkins and his legacy? One argument is regularly deployed with the actions of Hawkins and other slave traders: is it appropriate for a modern society to judge those who lived in the past under different values? One historian from the 1930s wrote:

> We should bear in mind that no opprobrium was attached to slave-trading. It does not seem to have occurred to Hawkins or to his contemporaries that the traffic was anything reprehensible; indeed, it was regarded almost as a crusade.[26]

The explanation here is that the God-fearing Hawkins was taking heathens and placing them in a Christian society. There are some examples of Africans settling in a form of domestic life in England after being taken, including one man who married an English woman with whom he had a son.[27] However, Hawkins engaged with the slave trade for profit, not with the aim of civilising people.

The extent to which he was the originator of the English slave trade can be questioned. He engaged with three different voyages in the 1560s, with the first two generating a handsome profit for himself and his backers; however, the impact of the disaster of 1568 ended any future slave expeditions. During the remainder of the Elizabethan period, voyages to Guinea were unusual, and English involvement in the transatlantic slave trade resumed much later in the middle of the 1600s. Although the principle remained the same – to turn a profit at every port despite the human cost – there was a clear interruption of several decades. As P.E.H. Hair explains, out of twenty-five direct voyages in the years before 1600, only three or four were focused on the slave trade: 'This has certainly persuaded some modern scholars that slaving was the normal and regular English practice in Guinea long before this was actually the case.'[28]

As such, Hawkins' involvement in the 1560s was a prologue of the future. As with other aspects of empire, the English lagged behind their rivals – the Spanish and Portuguese – in terms of expanding the slave trade as a sustained profitable business. But despite the successes or failures of these voyages, there is no denying that John Hawkins was a slaver; his actions in the 1560s led to the transportation of 1,500 Africans across the Atlantic. Despite his other deeds in service of the Tudors, it is the crimes of the slave trade with which his legacy will forever be associated.

Chapter 15

The King of California

Sir Francis Drake's Claim to Nova Albion

In 1772, the Spanish missionary Juan Crespí explored the area of San Francisco, where he made a startling discovery. Living among the natives were those who were 'bearded and fair-skinned', which seemed inconsistent with the other inhabitants of the area.[1] An old native story was later told of how ancestors of the fair-skinned individuals were once left behind from a travelling ship that made landfall in California centuries before.

If true, these descendants were possibly connected to the worldwide voyage of Francis Drake when he landed off the west coast of North America in 1579. Back in a time when California was largely undiscovered and when Drake claimed the land for his queen and country as *Nova Albion*.

'Our voyage is made, lads!'

Francis Drake's story begins with his birth in rural Tavistock, Devon, in the 1540s. His family moved to Kent due to the disturbances associated with the Prayer Book Rebellion in 1549, and it was here where he was apprenticed to a master of a barque. It has been speculated that Drake was illegitimate, which may help explain the reason for his being placed in the household of his relative William Hawkins of Plymouth. He developed seafaring experience as part of various voyages during the 1550s, travelling across the coasts of England, as well as France and the Low Countries. Then, in the 1560s, he held a variety of positions as a seaman on Hawkins' voyages to West Africa and the New World; he even sailed on an additional voyage in 1566–67 under Captain John Lovell; however, the enslaved Africans they had obtained proved unprofitable.

Then came the disastrous 1568 expedition, in which the English were mercilessly attacked in the port of San Juan de Ulúa in the Gulf of Mexico. Drake's speedy escape from the battle led to accusations from Hawkins: he was a deserter and was greedy in wanting to take all the treasure. The whole incident led, believe some historians, to a change in his character in which 'Spain and all things Spanish became his prey'.[2] He wanted to atone for his mistakes and also exact revenge on those who had wronged him.

In 1569, Drake married Mary Newman in a parish several miles north of Plymouth, Devon; but Drake was never content with a domestic life, with the sea forever calling out to him. In 1572–3 he was back out in the New World, this time focusing on a 'train-heist' in Panama, at the location where the gathered gold and silver from Peru was transported, ready to be sent across the Caribbean and then onto Spanish galleons back to Europe. He was able to capture the town of Nombre de Dios, and despite being injured, he remained in the area for a year, raiding the Spanish and keeping his eyes open for the jackpot of capturing a treasure ship. His men were a motley crew: of French privateers and of maroons, escapee African slaves. One of the maroons, Diego, was to become a notable assistant to Drake.

In March 1573 he was able to attack the Spanish Silver Train, a mule convoy, which resulted in the capture of 20 tons of gold and silver. This led to a frantic and frustrating march across eighteen miles of jungle, dragging as much booty as they could carry while the Spanish pursued them, with the aim of reaching boats to take them to safety. However, on reaching the coast they found that their means of escape had vanished. With nowhere left to go, it was decided to bury the treasure on the beach. Drake was able to reach his ship out at sea, having built a make-shift raft, on which he crossed ten miles of sea beside the coast. When he reached the deck of his ship it is said that his men were astonished at his poor, beaten appearance. When asked how the heist had gone, Drake is said to have 'teased them by looking downhearted. Then he laughed, pulled a necklace of Spanish gold from around his neck and said: "Our voyage is made, lads!"'

After this, he was once again away from his wife, serving in Ireland. One incident highlights his malicious attitude when, at the siege of Rathlin Castle, he was involved in the murder of hundreds of men, women and children who had surrendered. As eventful as this Irish chapter was, Drake continued to itch to return to the New World. It was where the gold and silver was located, and where his hated enemies the Spanish were.

Circumnavigating the Globe

It was while on his Silver Train heist in Panama that Drake climbed a tree in a mountainous region and looked out to the other ocean that lay beyond the coast. In doing so, Drake became the first Englishman to witness the Pacific Ocean. Perhaps it was at this moment that an ambition was stirred within him.

The possibility of a venture to the 'South Sea' – the Pacific – was discussed in the Tudor court earlier in the 1570s. Another one of the West Country seadogs, Richard Grenville, received a royal patent in 1574 to undertake a voyage; however, this was cancelled after Elizabeth became reluctant to stir things having established a new understanding of peace with the Spanish. However, within a couple of years, the Privy Council were more amenable to such an undertaking – but the beneficiary was not Grenville, it was Drake himself. This was the start of a lifelong feud between the two seadogs, with Grenville vowing never to serve with Drake in any capacity. Grenville would have had cause to feel particularly bitter after the voyage turned into an epic circumnavigation around the world, although historians have noted that the sailors leaving Plymouth at the end of 1577 were 'under the illusion that they were embarking on a voyage of relatively moderation duration and peril'.[3] Little did they know that the next time they would see England, for those lucky enough to survive and return, would be in 1580.

Drake's famous *Golden Hind* was described as:

> The ship is about eighty feet in length between stem and sternpost. It is propelled solely by sail. It is manned by more than sixty men. It is victulaed with salt meat, sea biscuit, and other foods that will keep for a reasonable period. Water is carried in casks and penuriously rationed.[4]

The fleet included four other ships, adding a sixth when the Portuguese *Mary* was captured off the coast of Africa. Drake started with more than

165

160 men; however, the voyage south through the Atlantic was costly, with the loss of two ships, while the *Mary* was later set on fire due to its rotting structure. By the time Drake entered the Pacific in the second half of 1578, only three ships of his fleet remained. However, the violent storms destroyed one of the ships (the *Marigold*) and caused another (the *Elizabeth*) to turn back to England. The only remaining ship, then, was Drake's *Golden Hind*.

Drake had notable issues with his crew, as highlighted in the incident with Thomas Doughty. Doughty was Drake's second-in-command, but the two had a large falling out when, in the summer of 1578, Drake accused him of witchcraft and charged him with treason. In a trial, over which Drake presided, he sentenced Doughty to be executed, leading to his beheading. The ship's chaplain, Francis Fletcher, later reminded Drake of Doughty's death, suggesting that the problems that plagued the voyage were connected to the unfair sentencing and manner in which Doughty was handled. Drake, never one to suffer fools lightly, had the chaplain chained to a hatch cover, and excommunicated him for good measure. There were various occasions, particularly when the ship became loaded with Spanish loot, when Drake banished some of his crew on land or a smaller vessel; the eight poor souls who were placed in a small boat in October 1578 'to waite upon the ship for all necessary uses' became separated during a storm and were never seen again.[5]

Along the way, Drake made landfall in several places, such as Argentina, and also laid claim to several locations for the Crown, including Elizabeth Island. With only one ship remaining, Drake pushed on and sailed northward along the Pacific coast of South America, using the opportunity to attack Spanish ports and pillage towns. Some of the spoils included the capture of more accurate navigational charts, as well as a cache of Chilean wine. More important was the capture of a Spanish ship carrying 25,000 pesos of Peruvian gold, as well as the seizure of the *Nuestra Senora de la Concepcion*. Although it wasn't all without injury, with Drake himself being attacked by the natives of Mocha Island.

The Claim to California

By June 1579, Drake sailed away from the Spanish sphere of influence and made landfall in South Cove, in modern-day Oregon. The decision was taken to move further south to find a suitable harbour in which to repair his ship, before then figuring out the most convenient and safe route in which to return to England. The *Golden Hind* moved further south before eventually settling on a location in northern California in what Drake described as 'a faire and good Baye, with a good winde to enter', which has now become known as Drake's Cove.[6]

Drake claimed the land as *Nova Albion* (or New Albion) in the name of Queen Elizabeth. It is believed that he attached an engraved plate of brass to a large post, thereby staking England's assertion to California. The name Albion was given 'in respect of the white bancks and cliffes' that shared 'some affinity' with English locations such as the white cliffs of Dover and the coast of Dorset.[7] The region was deemed to have been outside any Spanish claims, with N.M. Penzer noting:

> The Spandiards neuer had any dealing, or so much as set a
> foote in this country, the vtmost of their discoueries reaching
> onely to many degrees Southward of this place.[8]

There are many question marks remaining over Drake's time in California, in what some historians have called 'the Drake controversy':[9] where did he land, did he leave a brass plate, and was he ever actually in California? One of the chief reasons for the continuing questions is the manner in which Drake's circumnavigation was hushed-up by the Elizabethan government, for fear of the Spanish and other rivals finding out about Drake's escapades. Drake's logbook was passed to the government for safe-keeping (and eventually lost) and his crew were pledged not to discuss their journey. It was only a decade later when information was reported in Richard Hakluyt's book, but the story was, in the words of historian Harry Kelsey, 'riddled with errors, exaggerations, and more than a few deliberate deceptions'.[10] All of which has plagued research and scholarly activity into Drake's voyage in the subsequent centuries.[11]

Drake and his crew remained in California for several weeks, using the downtime to clean and repair the *Golden Hind*. During this stay relations were made with the local natives, the Miwoks, and after the usual anxiety-ridden first meetings the two groups formed a profitable partnership. It is believed that Drake assumed that the natives deemed him a God; however, it appears that he misunderstood the meaning of the Miwoks' wailing and self-laceration; the natives were not worshipping but rather mourning, believing that the English arrivals were former relatives who had returned from the dead. However, there is much in common with Drake's time with the Miwoks, as with the Spanish and the Aztecs or Incans, with the natives said to have 'greatly wondered at the things' the English showed them.[12] As Drake's nephew wrote in the early seventeenth century:

> as men ravished in their mindes, with the sight of such things
> as they never had seene, or heard of before that time: their
> errand being rather with submission and feare to worship
> us as Gods, then to have any warre with us as with mortall
> men.[13]

Drake himself believed that the natives saw the English as more than mere mortals: 'nothing could perswade them, nor remove that opinion, which they had conceived of us, that wee should be Gods'.[14] One of the Miwok leaders visited Drake, and:

> with great reverence, joyfully singing a song, set the crowne
> upon his head; inriched his necke with all their chaine; and
> offering unto him many other things, honoured him by the
> name of HYOH.[15]

Drake accepted in the name of his queen, with the writer Penzer later adding how:

> that the riches and treasures thereof (wherewith in the vpland
> countries it abounds) might with as great conuenciency
> be transported, to the enriching of her kingedome here at
> home.[16]

The Tudor empire, then, now stretched – in theory at least – to the Pacific ocean; and in taking the crown Drake himself became, in historian William M. Hamlin's words, 'the king of California – or perhaps, more accurately, the Viceroy'.[17]

No permanent colony was established before Drake and the *Hind* left several weeks later, but this also has been an area of continuing debate over the centuries. It is clear the *Hind* was not equipped with the resources required to establish a colony, and there are no lasting archaeological remains to provide evidence of a settlement in California from this period. However, there is the existence of an old native oral tradition that suggests that the men left behind integrated with the natives, which was later partially supported by Juan Crespí's observation of fair-skinned natives in the San Francisco bay area.[18] This suggests that these fair-skinned natives were descended from some of Drake's crew in the Elizabethan era. It is believed that a dozen or so men may have been left behind after Drake's visit to California, either voluntarily or forcibly, and there are many reasons: a lack of space, perhaps they were too ill to continue to travel onward, or they simply decided that they would remain rather than face the perils of a Pacific voyage and a return to the drudgery of England. As noted previously, Drake had form with leaving men stranded in various isolated locations, and so the off-loading of a dozen men is plausible. However, any action such as this cannot be interpreted to have been the serious makings of a permanent colony. There is only one actual person who is named who was left behind in *Nova Albion*, who was in ill health and so left to fend for himself. It is believed that he recovered his health before setting out on a four-year journey across modern-day Mexico, ending in finding a Spanish settlement.

King for a Day

Having remained in California for a handful of weeks, Drake and the *Hind* left North America at the end of July 1579 and headed into the Pacific for home. They wouldn't reach Plymouth until September 1580 and the remaining fourteen months were filled with further adventure and drama: the ship became caught in a reef and was almost lost; Drake befriended a sultan in the Spice Islands of the Moluccas; and sadly, Drake's trusted companion, Diego, died of wounds.

Drake and his men (only fifty-nine remained) were treated as heroes on their return to England. The *Hind* was filled with valuable cargo: spices and Spanish treasure. Elizabeth was understandably thrilled at Drake's return, no doubt because her claim to half the share of the cargo surpassed the Crown's income for that year. Despite the attempts at secrecy – for fear that the Spanish would find out – Drake was handsomely rewarded: Elizabeth gifted him a jewel and he was knighted in 1581. Furthermore, Drake had enough money to buy a manor for himself, choosing his rival Grenville's home at Buckland Abbey in Devon; because of the animosity between the pair, Drake employed agents to make the purchase, while keeping his own name hidden. It was more fuel to the fire for Grenville, having missed out on the opportunity to etch his own name in international history.

But what had Drake actually achieved in terms of advancing the Tudor empire? No, there was not a permanent colony, and California itself would never become part of the English or British Empires (eventually becoming annexed by the Spanish). However, there were undoubted gains from the voyage, particularly with Fletcher's observations of a multitude of objects and animals, including the language of the natives, the climate, and unknown animals such as 'very large and fat Deere', which are likely to have been what we now call Roosevelt elk. But more importantly, Drake's voyage to the Pacific was a motivating factor for others, and his claim to California, no matter how loose and fragile, provided justification for later English claims to North American territory. Importantly, it gave an additional spark to the desires of other imperialists at the time, including Dr Dee and Richard Hakluyt. Although Drake's legacy has come under scrutiny in modern-times – such as with the renaming of place-names and schools, as well as the removal of a statue in California – there is no denying that his circumnavigation of 1577–80 was highly influential in the development of the English and British Empires. Although he may have been a king for a day (or more accurately, several weeks), his visit to California provided the next step in England's move toward America.

Chapter 16

American Dream

Elizabethan England heads out to North America

In August 1590, after three years of desperately searching for a means to return to the New World, John White arrived at Roanoke colony. But on making landfall he realised that something was wrong. The colony was deserted and all the people were gone.

Weeks were spent searching but the colonists – which included White's daughter and granddaughter – were nowhere to be found. The only clue was the word 'Croatoan' carved in a post. With the weather worsening, John White was forced to abandon the search, get back on the ship, and return to England. His dream of building a new life filled with opportunity in America had turned into a nightmare.

Learning to Redream the Dream

Since John Cabot's voyage to North America in the 1490s, the English connection had declined to such a point that other rivals, such as the French, were in a stronger position to take advantage. By 1580 the Newfoundland area was visited by more than 400 vessels and 12,000 men, searching for fish, whales and seals.[1] Despite Cabot's earlier claim, no single country dominated, with the area being regularly visited by the French, Portuguese and Spanish sailors. The earlier dream of wider colonial interests in the reign of Henry VII were never realised; however, the dream re-emerged in the 1570s, supported by the growth of English confidence.

The exploits of the Elizabethan seadogs in the 1560s helped to push forward the belief that England had a right to venture further afield. This was, in turn, picked up by writers who hailed their achievements and called for more action, thereby establishing a perpetuating cycle.

Dr Dee, court astronomer and royal advisor, had long been an advocate for empire, and his 1577 work *General and Rare Memorials Pertaining to the Perfect Arte of Navigation* promoted the idea of a strong navy and how Elizabeth's sphere of control could extend across North America. The cover of Dee's book portrays Elizabeth sitting 'at the Helm of the Imperiall Ship, of the most parte of Christendome; if so, it be her Graces Pleasure'. The writer Richard Hakluyt also urged the English forward to establish colonies in the New World, arguing the world – 'all the commodities of Europe, Africa, and Asia' – would help revive stuttering trade.[2] More importantly, it was England's duty to promote Protestantism, to 'enlarge and advance ... the faith of Christ'.[3]

However, despite the plaudits and the plans, Elizabeth herself remained cautious in sponsoring initiatives to the New World. Licensing the seadogs to conduct piracy was one thing; providing financial and political support for a permanent colony was something very much different. Richard Grenville was disgusted when his plans to set up a New World colony were revoked in the mid-1570s, with the principal reason being Elizabeth's desire to keep the peace with Spain; Grenville was outraged when his idea was later snatched by Drake in 1577. But the Crown became emboldened with the success of Drake's circumnavigation, leading to more and more calls for England to make a strong claim to the North American continent. The 1570s–80s would see the Tudor empire attempting to expand to the New World, having learned to reimagine their American dream.

Frobisher's Folly on the Unknown Shore

Unlike many other seadogs who were rooted in the West Country, Martin Frobisher was born in Yorkshire; he made three voyages to the New World in an attempt to find the Northwest Passage. Before this, Frobisher had been incredibly busy in obtaining seafaring experience; he was part of Thomas Wyndham's voyage to West Africa, and despite a series of misfortunes – Wyndham died of disease in Benin, and only forty out of 140 sailors returned to England – it was still considered a financial success. Enough so for Frobisher's patron, Sir John York, to fund another expedition to Guinea in 1554; although precious cargo of gold, pepper and ivory was returned, Frobisher himself was captured by natives before being passed to the Portuguese, before eventually making his way back to England by 1558.

In the 1560s, he turned his hand to privateering ventures, with a licence to seize ships from French Catholics. He was successful in capturing five ships, but on bringing them into Plymouth he was arrested because of his involvement in raiding a Spanish ship. He was caught red-handed, with the Spanish ship's inventory – including wine – enough to condemn him. After being released he purchased two ships with the intention of heading back to West Africa, having learned of the success of John Hawkins' slaving exploits. However, English officials were concerned about Frobisher's motives, and after a storm put him in Scarborough he was once again arrested. In the late 1560s he was imprisoned for a third time after he attacked French Protestant ships that carried English goods.

His freedom appears to have come at a price; during the early 1570s he was sent on assignments by the Privy Council, such as searching for smugglers on the English coast, and then in service in Ireland against rebellious clans. By the mid-1570s, his reputation had been repaired to the point that he was considered a capable commander of a fleet of ships to strike out to North America with the aim of finally discovering the Northwest Passage. In June 1576, Frobisher's three ships sailed down the Thames, with cannons firing salutes and people cheering, while Elizabeth waved from the relaxed confines of Greenwich Palace.

The fleet reached the Shetland Islands by the end of June, before touching the south-eastern tip of Greenland in July; Frobisher mistakenly believed that this land was the phantom island of Frisland. One of the ships, the *Michael*, sailed back to England after a violent storm, while Frobisher sailed onward, reaching the North American continent. On arriving at Baffin Island, Frobisher claimed it for England, and then landed in what is now labelled Frobisher Bay. Although Frobisher himself believed that the Northwest Passage lay further beyond, the violent elements of ice and wind prevented him from proceeding onward. After making landfall the men met local natives; despite the initial meeting appearing to be cordial, a scuffle ensued in which some of the Englishmen were captured. Frobisher attempted to recover them but failed. Oral tradition of the Inuit claim that these Englishmen lived among the natives for several years, but then died when attempting to leave Baffin Island on a poorly constructed boat.

Having obtained all the information that he could, Frobisher decided to head home, where he had an audience with Elizabeth that October. He had claimed this new land for England and his proof was a black stone taken from Baffin Island. The stone was initially believed to be worthless, but the Italian alchemist Giovanni Battista Agnello confidently announced that it contained gold. As such, encouragement grew for a future voyage.

The following May, Frobisher headed back to North America, and the queen herself invested money in the expedition and provided her 200-ton royal ship HMS *Ayde*. This time the fleet was stronger and equipped with a variety of men: mariners, gunners, carpenters, merchants, as well as thirty Cornish miners to dig for more precious metals. By July 1577, the *Ayde* was back in the mouth of Frobisher Bay, and weeks were spent collecting black ore, with the company bankrolling the expedition now more interested in immediate profits rather than pursuing the dangers of the Northwest Passage. Having collected enough samples – as well as having had a couple of skirmishes with the natives – Frobisher ordered the ships to depart for England in August. This time he brought with him three captured natives; however, all died soon after arriving in England. Frobisher was once more thanked by the queen, and the focus then shifted to the 200 tons of ore brought home.

In 1578, a third and – as it turned out – final voyage was undertaken by Frobisher. By now the new territory of Baffin Island had been granted a new name: *Meta Incognita*, the Unknown Shore. This was the biggest voyage yet, with a fleet of fifteen ships equipped with the means to establish a permanent colony; the roster included miners, blacksmiths and assayers. The fleet left Plymouth in June 1578 and this time Frobisher headed up the western coastline of Baffin Island in what was later named the Hudson Strait; however, he didn't believe it to be as promising as his previous discoveries, and so they turned back to return to their more well-acquainted area. Attempts were made to find a good location for a settlement, but there were disagreements regarding the spot, with the biggest effort exerted on mining black ore. The fleet returned to England without having established a colony, but the 1,350 tons of black ore offered hope of glittering fortunes for Frobisher and the company. The ore was taken to a smelting plant at Dartford where gold was to be extracted; however, five years passed before the sobering realisation dawned: the ore was worthless rock (it was eventually used for mundane tasks such as wall construction).

The result was the bankruptcy of the company, with the director Michael Lok spending time in a debtor's prison. Frobisher's reputation was damaged, as was his marriage – he seems to have abandoned his wife at some point in the mid-1570s to take to the seas – and although more was yet to come from him – such as his feats when fighting against the Spanish Armada in 1588 – he was never again to venture to North America. His 1570s voyages had helped to spur on England's hunger for America; however, beyond the naming of a handful of phantom islands the entire venture had failed. The baton for the attempt to discover the Northwest Passage would soon fall to another.

The Pomposity of Sir Humphrey Gilbert

Humphrey Gilbert was another of the West Country men from the Elizabethan era; born at Greenway – later to be the home of Agatha Christie – in Devon in 1539, he was half-brother to Sir Walter Raleigh. Gilbert was a well-connected gentleman, with family members involved in a variety of imperial schemes, such as those in Ireland and in the New World. He was at the siege of Le Havre, where he was wounded in 1563, and he later served in Ireland under his mentor Sir Henry Sidney. The legacy he left behind in Ireland was brutal: he was involved in a number of military campaigns that led to the deaths of women and children. It was claimed that he 'decorated the path to his tent with human heads',[4] and he boasted how this brought:

> greate terrour to the people when they saw the heads of their dead fathers, brothers, children, kinsfolke, and friends, lye on the grounde before their faces, as they came to speak with the colonel.[5]

After returning to England in 1570, Gilbert married, became an MP and saw military action in the Spanish Netherlands. He retained academic pursuits, such as writing and helping to set up an arts society, and during this time he never forgot his earlier dream of leading an expedition to the New World in pursuit of the Northwest Passage. He spent the remainder of his life – and a large portion of his family fortune – in attempting to achieve this ambition.

During Drake's circumnavigation of the world in the late 1570s, Gilbert obtained letters patent to sail to North America with a fleet of seven ships. However, storms scattered the fleet, and the only ship that traversed the Atlantic was Raleigh's *Falcon*. Gilbert's seafaring ability was further questioned when he got lost in fog off Land's End in Cornwall, having been commissioned to sail to Ireland to attack the Fitzgerald clan. Yet still Gilbert continued to push for his Northwest Passage voyage, and by 1583 – with a growth in England's confidence – he left with a fleet of five ships to set out for North America.

The fleet reached Newfoundland, just as John Cabot had done a century earlier. Gilbert wasted no time in making a formal claim to the land for the English Crown, before then asserting his authority over various fishing stations; this included the placing of taxes on the fishermen who operated in the area, whether they were English or foreign. Yet despite all of this bluster and swagger, no actual attempt was made to form a permanent settlement. Due to a lack of supplies, the fleet departed within weeks, and Gilbert was never to see the New World again.

The fleet suffered a catalogue of problems on the return voyage: miscommunication, poor directions and the acclaimed sighting of a sea-monster. Gilbert sailed in HMS *Squirrel*, rather than the flagship the *Golden Hind*, and although the smaller ship was nearly overwhelmed in the Atlantic, Gilbert refused to leave it (although having had the misfortune to step on a nail, Gilbert did visit the *Hind* to have his foot properly bandaged). The weather did not improve and Gilbert simply remained in the stern of the *Squirrel* reading a book, said to have been Thomas More's *Utopia*. The crew of the *Hind* called out for Gilbert, but Gilbert replied: 'We are as near to Heaven by sea as by land!' Ultimately, the storm claimed the *Squirrel*, with all men onboard being lost to the sea.

Roanoke: The Lost Colony

Although Gilbert's voyage was ultimately not successful, he played an important role in helping to start a shift in thinking in English imperial adventures: from the pursuit of a quick profit – in the form of plundering Spanish treasure or in finding the jackpot in a gold reserve – to the realisation that colonies would be needed to bring long-term prosperity. Hawkins' West African expeditions in the 1560s, Drake's initial impetus for setting off in 1577, and Frobisher's visits to Baffin Island in the late 1570s were all focused on immediate gains. Territory in the New World may have been claimed – such as Drake in California – but there was no actual way to control such distant lands. This shift in thinking led to the desire to form a permanent colony on the North American coast; Elizabeth granted Sir Walter Raleigh a charter for colonisation of North America (1584), which was called Virginia in her honour of the Virgin Queen.

The charter was a handsome reward for the newly arrived court favourite, with Raleigh described as being 'strikingly attractive, six foot tall with a trimmed beard and piercing blue eyes and a love of extravagant clothes, jewels and pearls'.[6] Before arriving at court in 1581, Raleigh saw action in a variety of locations, including France as well as Ireland. Similar to his half-brother, Gilbert, he became renowned in Ireland as a result of his brutal actions, including the beheading of 600 Spanish and Italian soldiers at the siege of Smerwick. Raleigh later became well acquainted with the queen, even receiving his own pet name of 'Water', which historian Anna Whitelock describes as being due to 'his ties to the sea and his West Country pronunciation of his name'.[7]

The region of Virginia was chosen because it was located further north outside the Spanish sphere of influence, with the region viewed by both the Spanish and French as 'of little value for colonies' due to being 'too cool for tropical crops but too warm for the best furs'.[8] However, the absence of rivals could provide the English with an opportunity to establish a permanent colony. Raleigh was authorised to explore and colonise any 'remote, heathen and barbarous lands, countries and territories, not actually possessed of any Christian Prince or inhabited by Christian People'. This new colony would make the dreams of Dee and Hakluyt a reality: trade would be stimulated, with a new market for goods, and the Protestant faith would be promoted. Furthermore, a permanent settlement in North America provided opportunity for wider claims across the continent. Curiosity was further stoked in 1584 when a small exploration expedition led by Philip Amadas and Arthur Barlowe visited Virginia and brought back two natives to England, Manteo and Wanchese.

Despite Raleigh's pedigree, he would never visit Virginia himself, with the task of establishing a permanent colony left to others; the fleet comprised seven ships with Richard Grenville placed in command. Although the one hundred colonists contained only men, Raleigh ensured that the mission would be supported as best as possible: the two natives from the 1584 voyage returned as interpreters, and accompanying the men was a mathematician and astronomer (the Oxford educated Thomas Harriot) and an artist (John White), thereby enabling the expedition to describe and draw the landscape.

The fleet left in April 1585 before arriving off the North American coast in July. The island of Roanoke – in modern-day North Carolina – was selected, in the words of historian Alan Taylor, because the location 'promised obscurity from Spanish discovery and attack' due to being 'buffed by dangerous shoals and long sandbanks'. However, this obscurity came at a cost: it was difficult to land supplies, as highlighted when the *Tiger* hit the sandbank, ruining its food supply, and the soil was not fertile enough to grow crops. The English had a simple solution: get the local natives to feed them.

As with Drake in California, the Algonquians were starstruck at English 'thinges', with Harriot later writing how the natives 'thought they were rather the works of gods then of men'.[9] However, relations were immediately put to the test by Grenville's violent reaction on realising that a silver cup had gone missing; he retaliated by burning a native settlement. Grenville left for the Caribbean in August to continue with his mission of harassing the Spanish, meaning that leadership of the colony fell on the shoulders of Captain Ralph Lane; Lane continued the same approach as Grenville, having been hardened in the various Irish campaigns of the period. He set to work on constructing a fort and settlement, with it now understood that the current location could not help with their success in the long-term. John White – far more amenable than Lane and Grenville – proved to be successful in meeting and greeting the different natives, spending the winter with them in the Chesapeake region. It was during this time in which he painted a series of striking watercolours, detailing the day-to-day lives of the natives.

However, tension between the colonists and the natives grew, particularly over the issue of food; there simply was not enough to go around. In the spring of 1586 the local chieftain Wingina refused to cede to English demands for food, leading Lane to launch a surprise attack in which Wingina and other native leaders were killed. Lane was employing similar tactics used to attempt to quell the Irish, but rather than obtain compliance, the natives were terrified and fled the area, which only served to deepen the problem of the food supply. The colony faced starvation when, fortunately, Sir Francis Drake arrived in June 1586; Lane and his men made a decision to head home. Then only a few weeks later Grenville returned to a barren Roanoke with fresh supplies, leaving behind fifteen men to hold the fort until more colonists arrived in the future.

The whole venture was not a complete failure. The return of Drake and Lane led to the introduction of new items to England, such as corn and potatoes. Raleigh, with the aid of John White, worked on plans for a second attempt, this time shifting the focus to a family-friendly colony. The ninety-four colonists would include women and children, thereby becoming the first English families to settle in America, while the position of leader was given to John White with the hope of removing the brutal military choices from the likes of Grenville or Lane. And what was more, the colony would be established further north on fertile land, with the city to be named after Raleigh himself.

However, this second attempt ran into similar problems, as shown from the very beginning. On arrival in the New World the colonists were left at the old site of Roanoke; historian Alan Taylor believes this was due to the gold-lust of 'impatient mariners' who didn't want to waste any more time in reaching the Caribbean.[10] It may be possible that White himself agreed to the location as an initial starting point, due to having Manteo assisting him (he had hoped to enlist the support of the natives in the area). However, there was no welcome from the hapless fifteen men left behind by Grenville, who had been 'presumably driven off by a now enraged native population'.[11] So the colonists faced an immediate uphill struggle: there were no crops and the settlement had not been maintained; the colony faced similar difficulties to the earlier colonists. However, the shift to focus on families led to the birth of the first English child born in America. The girl was a granddaughter of John White, and she was given the name Virginia, after the region itself.

White decided to return to England to drum up further interest and finance, with the aim of returning with a bountiful supply within the year. However, one year became two, and two years then became three; the Spanish war proved problematic and delayed White's return to the colony. By the time he reappeared at Roanoke in August 1590 he found the colony deserted. The only sign was the word 'Croatoan' carved in a post,

Croatoan being a neighbouring island on which Manteo's people lived. However, no trace was found of them there, or indeed anywhere. There are a range of theories relating to the disappearance of the colonists: that they migrated further inland or that they intermarried with the natives. It is believed that when the English established Jamestown in 1607 they were told of white people who had lived as refugees in the Chesapeake area, before being killed by the powerful chief Powhatan.[12] The historian Richard Middleton is more certain:

> either they died of starvation; or they were killed by hostile American Indians; or they drowned at sea while trying to make their escape. The last fate now seems the most likely, given the lack of any archaeological remains.[13]

For John White, the loss of the colonists was a personal tragedy: his family, including his granddaughter, were among those vanished. Despite frantically searching the area he eventually returned to England later in 1590, writing how the fate of his family was now passed 'to the merciful help of the Almighty, whom I most humbly beseech to helpe and comfort them'. He never gave up hope that they would be found, although he ended his days regretting the 'evils and unfortunate events' that had plagued his American dreams.

A Delayed Dream

By the end of Queen Elizabeth's reign – and the end of the Tudor dynasty – in 1603, North America remained empty of a permanent colony. This was despite the attempts and dreams of the likes of Dr Dee, Frobisher, Sir Humphrey Gilbert, Sir Walter Raleigh and poor John White.

Frobisher failed on two counts: to strike it rich in the New World – being duped by the vast quantities of worthless hornblende – and not finding the Northwest Passage. But within the limitations of the 1570s, he was compelled to search for a financial fix to provide stimulation for further voyages. Also, nobody would find the Northwest Passage, for it simply did not exist. As such, he deserves recognition for what he was able to achieve in being the person at the helm of important voyages to re-establish what John Cabot had started eight decades previously.

Despite Gilbert's pomposity, he was one of the first to understand that the direction of empire should not be focused on the searching for metal in caves, but rather in establishing permanent colonies. He failed in his only attempt to do so in Newfoundland, but his claim to this land is sometimes referred to as Britain's oldest New World colony. The failed attempt, however, was one part of a wider paradigm shift taking place, of moving away from get-quick-rich schemes to truly comprehending the enormity of the task required to establish a settlement thousands of miles from home.

Two attempts to establish a colony at Roanoke failed. Key reasons for this include the location and the approach taken with the natives. Furthermore, to what extent did luck play a part? With more fortunate timing – particularly without the hinderance of the Spanish war – Roanoke could have proved to have been successful. Plenty of 'what ifs' abound: what if John White had arrived in 1588 rather than in 1590; what if the colony had been founded on more prosperous terrain; what if Ralph Lane had employed more conciliatory tactics rather than resorting to violence? Setting up a colony in the New World was an incredibly difficult business: finance, the right crew, the ability to supply, and how to deal with the natives. The historian Richard Middleton suggests that a modern comparison is like sending people to the moon in the twentieth century; an undertaking fraught with difficulties.[14]

Dr Dee fancied the development of a British Empire, and although he was never to see it within his lifetime he was correct in the assumption that the English would not stop in their attempts to widen their sphere of influence in North America. The Tudor experiments were developed by their successors, the Stuarts, leading to the successful founding of Jamestown in 1607 and of Plymouth in 1620, which further developed into a powerful array of colonies by the dawn of the eighteenth century. The dream was not abandoned but was rather delayed.

Chapter 17

Day of the Dog

How the Spanish Armada almost ended the Tudors

Queen Elizabeth stood in front of her soldiers, clad in a steel corset and a helmet from which white plumes proudly sprung. By her side stood her ever-favourite, the Earl of Leicester. The Spanish had amassed the greatest naval armada the world had ever known, all with the aim of invading England and removing Elizabeth from the throne. All that stood between them and Elizabeth was the water of the English Channel.

Elizabeth addressed the assembled men, the capability of whom Leicester gravely doubted , and spoke to them. 'My loving people', she began, before telling them:

> I am come among you as you see, at this time, not for my recreation and disport; but being resolved in the midst, and heat of the battaile to live, or die among you all, to lay down for my God, and for my kingdom, and for my people, my Honour, and my blood even in the dust.[1]

And she declared the most famous sentence from the speech:

> I know I have the bodie, but of a weak and feeble woman, but I have the heart and Stomach of a King, and a King of England too.

As such, the English would fight to maintain what they had, with Elizabeth stating that she thought:

> foul scorn that … Spain, or any Prince of Europe should dare to invade the borders of my Realm, to which rather than any dishonour should grow by me, I myself will take up arms.

Which would ultimately lead to 'a famous victorie over those enemies of my God, of my Kingdomes, and of my People'. The year was 1588 and the Spanish Armada had arrived on the shores of England for a dramatic and crucial showdown. Three generations over a hundred years of extending the power of their Crown was in jeopardy; the Tudor imperium was in jeopardy. But how had it all come to this?

The Anglo-Spanish Cold War

If the clock reversed by thirty years – from 1588 to 1558 – the Anglo-Spanish relationship would be perceived in a much different light. At the start of 1558 the two countries were locked together by the 'Spanish Match' of Queen Mary I and Philip of Spain, and although this alliance had brought England into war with France and led to the loss of Calais, the English future appeared to be a Catholic one in which they lived in harmony with the greatest superpower in Europe. But Mary's death and her half-sister's accession in November 1558 brought about a clear change in policy.

Initially, the two countries maintained a cordial relationship. Queen Elizabeth was a relative unknown on the European stage and Philip watched with interest at the religious developments taking place, particularly with the confusion regarding Elizabeth's own religious convictions: was she a Catholic or a Protestant? The Elizabethan Settlement appeared to accommodate both positions, but as the 1560s continued it became clear that Elizabeth would not tolerate the return of Catholicism to England. This religious difference became all the more crucial after Mary, Queen of Scots' arrival in England in 1568, which became the catalyst for the Northern Rebellion in 1569 and the Pope's excommunication of Elizabeth in 1570. A line in the sand had been drawn, and attempts were made to convince Philip to join a crusade against the heathen English.

Further pressure was exerted due to the actions of the Elizabethan seadogs, who were to engage in what historian Christopher Lee calls 'that Elizabethan patriotic pastime: robbing the Spaniards'.[2] John Hawkins' incursion into the New World markets in the 1560s had been punished at the Battle of San Juan de Ulúa, but rather than be discouraged the seadogs wanted revenge on the Spanish. Elizabeth appeared to be caught in the middle of this tension; the seadogs brought in much-needed revenue to the Crown, but she did not want to antagonise Philip. As such, the relationship from 1568 into the 1570s remained fraught with difficulty, as shown in England's immediate reaction to hearing news of the defeat in 1568. William Hawkins, having heard a rumour that his brother had been 'put to the sword by the Spaniards', urged the government to seize Spanish ships pushed into English waters during a storm in November 1568.[3] The ships contained a whopping 400,000 florins from Genoese bankers, intended to pay for the Spanish army currently fighting against rebels in the Netherlands. Elizabeth impounded the money, thereby converting the loan from the Spanish to the English. The Spanish were outraged at this decision, leading to Philip's number one commander in the Netherlands – the Duke of Alba – seizing English ships in that region. Philip responded by encouraging English Catholics to topple the queen, particularly in the form of the 1571 Ridolfi Plot. However, before a permanent fracture was made, a peace settlement was reached that temporarily led to the closure of various schemes of the seadogs. This was much to Richard Grenville's chagrin when his plan to voyage to the New World was axed. However, within a handful of years, the English Crown was once more ready to give its blessing to the expeditions of Drake and Frobisher, thereby testing Spanish nerves again.

A third vital tension developed: the position of the Netherlands. This region had been incorporated into the wider Habsburg domains in the late fifteenth century; however, resistance began to grow against Spanish rule. A key sticking point was that of religion, with the mostly Protestant Dutch aiming for greater autonomy and ultimately a united, independent state. This tension led to the creation of the Dutch Revolt. England was regularly dragged into the Dutch debate due to Elizabeth's position as preeminent Protestant monarch, leading to the Dutch rebels regularly sending invitations to the English court. Many of Elizabeth's advisors, such as Cecil and Leicester, advocated stronger involvement, but the queen had her fingers burnt previously over help provided to the French Huguenots in the early 1560s. Importantly, helping out a rebel state within the Spanish sphere of influence would no doubt lead to the wrath of Philip, as well as potentially unleashing attempts for the Spanish to meddle in Tudor spheres of influence, such as Ireland. But the English were also aware that if the Dutch threat was extinguished it would act as a falling domino, thereby leading to greater pressure on England.

By the 1580s, the Spanish situation in the Netherlands advanced under the leadership of the Duke of Parma. The rebel position was bleak: only a couple of provinces held out and then in 1584 their leader, William of Orange, was assassinated. The Spanish appeared unstoppable: they had annexed Portugal; the Turks in the Mediterranean had been silenced; the coffers were brimming with Incan gold; and then in 1584 Philip signed an agreement with the Catholic League of France in what became known as the Treaty of Joinville. The Catholic forces of Europe had assembled, as urged by the Pope, and after the fall of the Netherlands, England would be next on the hit-list.

Faced with Catholic encirclement, Elizabeth and her advisors debated what was to be done. Having always kept herself at arm's length from the rebels in the Netherlands, it was time to militarily intervene. As historian Hiram Morgan writes, 'if England stood idly by, could she afterwards survive on her own under continuous threat from an even stronger foe?'[4] The English held out a hand to the Dutch rebels, leading to the formation of the Treaty of Nonsuch in 1585; troops would be sent to the Netherlands to defend it against the Spanish. This action led to the outbreak of the Anglo-Spanish War, a conflict that would last nineteen years and would outlive both Elizabeth and Philip.

Leicester's Dutch Foray

The Treaty of Nonsuch committed the English to helping the Dutch rebels; this came in the form of loans, as well as an expeditionary force under the leadership of the Earl of Leicester. At the end of 1585, Leicester headed to the Low Countries where he was immediately wooed with the offer of the position of Governor-General of the Netherlands; never one to look a gift horse in the mouth, Leicester accepted without first consulting with Elizabeth. When the queen heard of what happened she was sent into a rage, drafting a letter to Leicester that he was to resign his post immediately.

Leicester's elevation placed Elizabeth in a difficult position. With Leicester being subordinate to her, it effectively made her sovereign of the Netherlands. This was a situation she had been keen to avoid, having batted away previous offers from the Dutch. Elizabeth sent a messenger to the Netherlands to upbraid Leicester, before he eventually resigned from the position; he later wrote how his 'credit hath been cracked' with the Dutch.

The English involvement in the Netherlands was beset with other difficulties, particularly the tactical differences between Elizabeth and her advisors and those of Leicester and the Dutch. The queen advised against becoming involved in any large confrontation with the Spanish commander, the Duke of Parma, no doubt because of the superior quality of the Spanish army. However, Leicester thirsted for decisive action on the battlefield, rather than the series of skirmishes he was faced with. Furthermore, the English men regularly quarrelled with their allies, leading to the annoyance of the Dutch hosts. Worse was to come when two of the officers – William Stanley and Rowland Yorke – deserted to join the Spanish.

Ultimately, Leicester returned to England without the acclaim of having covered himself in glory. The entire expedition was an expensive business, both for the Crown and for Leicester personally; it was nothing more than a pricey sideshow to what was gearing up to become a decisive naval engagement between England and Spain.

The Singeing of Philip's Beard

By 1586, reports were coming into England that the Spanish were preparing a great fleet to launch an invasion on England. Tension grew when in February 1587, Mary, Queen of Scots was beheaded after her involvement in plotting the downfall of Elizabeth in the Babington Plot. Cardinal Allen, an enemy of the Tudor regime, put forward Philip's very own claim to the English throne. Momentum was now with the Spanish.

However, the English planned a pre-emptive strike on Spain, hitting the port of Cadiz with the hope of wrecking as much as havoc as possible. The man tasked with leading the expedition was Sir Francis Drake, who had already been busy in the early years of the war attacking Spanish colonies. In September 1585, he sailed at the head of a fleet of more than twenty ships, attacking Vigo in Spain and holding it for two weeks, before then plundering Santiago in the Cape Verde islands. Then they headed across the Atlantic, sacking the port of Santo Domingo and capturing the city of Caragena de Indias in modern-day Colombia. On the return voyage Drake stopped by the region of Spanish Florida, ensuring that another fort was raided, before then making his way to Roanoke where he took the anguished colonists back to England. These exploits enhanced his fame, but more was to come.

The Cadiz plan was far more important than the raids in the New World colonies; the plan was to end – or at the very least stall – the Spanish Armada preparations. Drake commanded a fleet with the possibility that he could be confronted with the Armada if it had already set sail. He arrived at Cadiz in April 1587, finding the harbour crammed with supplies and ships for the Armada, which was waiting for a kind wind to launch out for sea. In the early hours of the morning, Drake and his ships moved into the inner harbour and caused a torrent of damage. Historian Robert Hutchinson writes of the destruction of thirty-seven ships, 'setting them ablaze or blowing them up in an enjoyable twelve-hour orgy of demolition'.[5] The attack has gone down in history as the 'singeing of the King's beard', but Drake was not yet done, spending the following weeks harassing Spanish shipping; this included the capture of the *San Felipe* and its £114,000 cargo of spices and silks. By the time Drake and his men returned to England they were the darlings of the nation; the mission had been a great success and the Armada could not sail in 1587. However, Philip became more determined than ever to push forward with his plan to invade England.

1588

July 1588. The Armada set sail.

Destination: to meet with the Spanish army under the command of the Duke of Parma in the Spanish Netherlands.

Next stop?

England.

It had been a long time coming. The disaster of Cadiz in 1587 set the Armada back for more than a year, with the financial cost becoming extortionate in costing Philip 30,000 ducats a day.[6] The man in charge of the operation, the Duke of Medina Sidonia, prepared the fleet to sail: 130 ships and 19,000 men assembled at Lisbon, and a 27,000-strong army was waiting in the Spanish Netherlands to be ferried across the Channel. The size and the cost were phenomenal, with historian Hiram Morgan claiming that 'there was nothing to equal it in Western history'.[7] But even at that stage Medina Sidonia got itchy feet, believing that the weather conditions were not right to set sail. However, Philip had waited long enough; the Armada would be launched without further delay.

The Spanish Armada was first sighted off the coast of Cornwall on 29 July. The next two weeks would see a fierce encounter between the two fleets in the English Channel, with Elizabeth's instructions clear: prevent the Armada combining with Parma's army. The English troops awaiting the potential arrival of the Spanish were, in Leicester's estimation, not fit for the fight. 'If you saw how weakly I am assisted,' he wrote from Tilbury, 'you would be sorry to think that we here should be the front against the enemy, that is so mighty, if he should land here'.[8] Queen Elizabeth may have shouted out heroic words, but the reality was that the Spanish would likely overwhelm them if they reached English soil.[9] The biggest defensive shield that Elizabeth possessed was the fleet and the expertise and ingenuity of the seadogs.

The importance of the seadogs cannot be underestimated; only thirty of the 200 English ships were royal. The list of names was a long and notable one, including Hawkins, Drake, Raleigh, Frobisher, Grenville and others. John Hawkins had been busy since his slave trading voyages of the 1560s; he was promoted to a commanding position within the navy, bringing about crucial reforms that included better pay for the sailors, as well as a change of design of galleons. Such was the importance of his involvement, historians have stressed how Hawkins must take the credit for helping to put together the fleet that was used to defeat the Armada. Drake served as Vice-Admiral, under Lord Howard of Effingham, with the apocryphal story of him playing a game of bowls on Plymouth Hoe when he first heard news that the Spanish were coming. 'I have time enough to play the game and thrash the Spaniards afterwards,' he is reputed to have boasted. He was heavily involved in the fight against the Spanish, capturing a galleon (which carried substantial funds for men in Parma's army) and helped organise the fireship tactics at the decisive Battle of Gravelines. Martin Frobisher took command of the *Triumph*, the royal navy's largest ship, and was involved in action in July along with Grenville in the *Revenge*, and later engaged the Duke of Medina Sidonia's flagship *San Martin*. Lord Howard was suitably impressed, knighting Frobisher the very next day onboard the *Ark Royal*.

Westerly winds pushed the Spanish fleet up the Channel, with both sides engaging one another in a succession of skirmishes. A key objective for the English was to remain between the coast and the Armada, thereby preventing the Spanish from anchoring or landing. Throughout the first few days in August, the Spanish advanced further up the Channel, maintaining their formation and ships. On 6 August, the Spanish fleet anchored off Calais, closer to their goal of rendezvousing with Parma's waiting army. The English used the opportunity to put a scheme into practice: sailing old hulks carrying explosives to drift within the Spanish fleet. These fireships caused panic, with the Spanish desperate to cut their anchors to flee to safety.

On 8 August, the two fleets met one another off Gravelines. In a nine-hour engagement the English took their chance to close in on the Spanish ships, sinking twelve of them and wounding more than a thousand men. By this point the Armada had taken a serious battering, and with the wind continually against it, Medina Sidonia took the decision to retreat into the North Sea. This led the remaining Spanish ships on a large detour, moving around Scotland and Ireland to return to Spain; this retreat was particularly bruising, with 6,000 men – drowned, killed or captured – lost on the coasts of Ireland alone. When the defeated remains of the Armada limped back to Spain, only sixty ships out of the 130 that set out were returned, and an estimated 20,000 Spanish men were killed or lost in action. Medina Sidonia wrote to his king: 'The troubles and miseries we have suffered cannot be described to your majesty. They have been greater than have any been seen in any voyage before.'[10]

1588 will forever be etched in English history with other milestone dates, such as 1066, 1815 and 1945. The victory was celebrated in Elizabeth's Armada portrait, on which the queen rests her hand on a globe signifying the promotion of England's ambitions in the New World and beyond. However, 1588 also represents a climax of the Elizabethan period; Elizabeth ruled for fifteen further years, during which time the Spanish war continued to rumble on. The excellent generation of politicians and sailors died off, one by one, leaving Elizabeth largely alone to face the challenges of the new seventeenth century. 1588 was the highpoint of victory, but in the 1590s everyone became very much aware that the party was over.

Death of the Seadogs

The Spanish war continued into the new century, with England mostly conservative and defensive with their actions, and Philip attempting new armadas, but each one failing to make the impact needed. Many of the seadogs advocated an assertive naval policy, although Elizabeth continually shied away from this. Sir Walter Raleigh later commented on this issue:

> if the late Queen would have believed her men of war as she did her scribes, we had in her time beaten that great empire in pieces and made their kings kings of figs and oranges as in old times.[11]

Elizabeth's continual fear was of Philip sending out a successful armada and landing it in a difficult position, namely Ireland. The fear of invasion was never far from everyone's mind, with the Spanish making raids on the English coast, such as in Cornwall in 1595. Philip's death in 1598 did not bring an end to the war, with his successor underestimating Elizabeth as a dying and heirless woman. However, the death of Elizabeth in 1603 brought about the opportunity for peace, which was confirmed in the Treaty of London.

How successful was Elizabeth's war with Spain? Many historians are critical of Elizabeth's decisions, particularly her 'indecisive and stingy habits';[12] however, her achievements must be admired, particularly considering the reduced power of England when compared to the mighty Spain. On the whole, Elizabeth achieved her major objectives: to keep England safe from invasion, to challenge Spain's monopoly in the New World, and to keep the Netherlands from falling completely under the thumb of the Spanish. The Dutch question is one notable area of success; despite the continual problems and squabbling, the Spanish were expelled from the region in the 1590s. A new dynamic was established in the Netherlands: an independent Protestant state in the north, and the Catholic south remaining under Spanish control but with a degree of autonomy.

On the whole, the 1590s was a decade of decline and degeneration. This is seen throughout English society with the rise of poverty and vagrancy, of failed harvests and famine, and of a general unease about what would happen once Elizabeth passed away. This decline is characterised by a series of deaths, with Elizabeth's advisors fading away: Leicester, her firm favourite for more than thirty years, died in the same year as the Armada; Walsingham, her spymaster, followed in 1591; and then William Cecil – the ever-trusting hand – passed away in 1598.

And what became of the seadogs? Sir John Hawkins retained an active interest in the Spanish war; in 1589 (the same year of the death of his brother William) he sailed with Drake to attempt to intercept Spanish treasure ships, before realising that the Spanish employed a strong Atlantic fleet to protect them from greedy English eyes. In 1595, he raised a fleet to attack the Spanish in the West Indies in an attempt to recover his captured son, but the mission failed and Hawkins perished at sea near Puerto Rico. His son, Richard Hawkins, was eventually released and later enjoyed a notable career as a writer, in becoming an MP, as well as being one of the first to promote the idea that oranges and lemons could be a preventive for scurvy.

Sir Francis Drake died not long after his cousin, having found that his earlier luck had largely deserted him after 1588. In 1589, he laid siege to Coruna and fought in Galicia but at a heavy cost in terms of men and ships lost, leading to a relegation of duties when he returned to England. Then in 1595 he failed to conquer the port of Las Palmas and suffered a series of defeats in the Caribbean, although he managed to survive a cannonball being shot through his cabin. In January 1596, in his mid-fifties, Sir Francis Drake succumbed to dysentery while his ship was anchored off the coast of Portobelo. He was buried at sea in a lead-sealed coffin, with divers in the modern age regularly checking to see if they can uncover Drake's tomb.

Sir Martin Frobisher was involved in the 1590s in attempting to intercept Spanish treasure galleons, having seemingly disregarded his newly acquired status as the lord of a Yorkshire manor. He was involved in a series of actions in the Spanish war, and was notably annoyed at hearing that the *Madre de Deus* was captured by a rival. While serving in action in Brittany he suffered a gunshot to his thigh; the ball was extracted, but Frobisher could not fight the infection. Meanwhile Sir Richard Grenville met his end in 1591, fighting a superior Spanish fleet against the odds. Onboard the *Revenge*, Grenville faced fifty-three

Spanish ships, declaring that he 'utterly refused to turn from the enimie' and that 'he would rather chose to die than to dishonour himselfe'. Grenville and his crew fought bravely for twelve hours, before all of them were killed in battle.

And what became of Sir Walter Raleigh? That particular story will have to wait for the next chapter.

Chapter 18

The Search for the City of Gold

Sir Walter Raleigh's quest to find El Dorado

Sir Walter Raleigh's first words to the assembled crowd below the scaffold were: 'I give god thankes, I am come to dye in the light and not in the darknes'.[1]

It was 29 October 1618. The Tudors were now a memory, with the Stuart dynasty in the form of James I now on the throne in both England and Scotland. Raleigh had fallen out of favour with the new king and he accepted his fate; that morning he received communion, had breakfast, and was escorted to the scaffold. He used the opportunity for his final words, declaring that he was not an enemy of the king and that he was not in the pay of the Spanish. After praying, he requested to see the executioner's axe, running his finger along the blade, before saying that it was 'sharpe medicine … a physitian that will cure all diseases'.[2]

The historian Andrew Fleck writes of his last moments:

> Then he lay down on the block, stood up again to reposition
> himself to face east, gave the executioner a signal, and gave
> it again. The executioner decapitated him in two strokes.[3]

Sir Walter Raleigh, the last of the Elizabethan seadogs, was dead. He had attempted, on two occasions, to find the legendary city of gold in South America. However, as with many others before him, the whole enterprise ultimately alluded and frustrated him.

The Legend of El Dorado

The legend of El Dorado – meaning 'the golden one' – originated with the Spanish. It was rumoured that there was a prosperous monarch living in South America, in modern-day Venezuela, and that this leader had the peculiar habit of having himself covered in golden dust, such was its abundance. Over time, the legend morphed, moving from a single man to become a hidden golden city. This city of Manoa was regularly published in maps, located near the Orinoco river, until the entire legend was disproven at the turn of the nineteenth century. The riches that lay within it were said to have rivalled – even eclipsed – all the silver and gold found in the Spanish annexed Incan empire.

However, all attempts to find it were plagued with misfortune and failure. Diego de Ordaz explored the Orinoco river for more than a thousand miles without finding El Dorado, before dying at sea on the return to Spain; Alonso de Herrera was hit with a poisoned arrow fired by natives, later succumbing to death; the German Philipp von Hutten was wounded by natives before being executed by Spanish authorities on his return; Pedro de Orsua, a knight of Navarre, faced famine and ultimately suffered an overthrow by his own men; while Gonzalo Jiménez de Quesada was said to have spent a fortune searching with no result. Juan Martinez El Dorado enjoyed the greatest success, having been taken to the capital city where he lived for several months. He confirmed the extravagant parties that took place there, noting how the emperor and other lords has golden powder blown 'through canes upon their naked bodies, until they be shining from foot to the head'.[4] However, Martinez could not easily return; he had been blindfolded by the natives on his arrival to El Dorado and was forever destined to lament his inability to locate it.

The list of failures was long and notable. Sir Walter Raleigh had caught wind of the legend, and was willing to go further than any previous explorer. He would do it in the pursuit of rebuilding his reputation, but also for the glory of Queen Elizabeth and the Tudor empire.

1595: The First Voyage

Sir Walter Raleigh enjoyed his time as a favourite of Elizabeth's during his heyday in the 1580s: he was showered with gifts and rewards, being knighted in 1585, receiving the royal grant to establish the colony of Roanoke, as well as being made Warden of the Stannaries, which provided him with profit from the tin mines of Devon and Cornwall.

However, he suffered a fall from Elizabeth's favour when, in 1591, he secretly married one of her ladies-in-waiting, Bess Throckmorton, when their affair led to an unexpected pregnancy. When the marriage was uncovered, the queen punished the two of them by sending them to the Tower. Raleigh is said to have attempted to win back Elizabeth's affections through sending 'urgent messages and poems to the queen, assuring her of his love', but he was only permitted to leave the Tower for a brief time to greet his fleet at Dartmouth to welcome the captured ship *Madre de Dois*.[5] By the time Raleigh and Bess were released at Christmas, their son had died, and their invitation to the royal court was terminated. However, Raleigh had ambitions to be restored to Elizabeth's affections once more, and he would do so by executing a daring and dramatic plan: locating El Dorado. Raleigh later proclaimed that this land 'hath more quantity of gold ... than the best parts of the Indies, or Peru'.[6] The inclusion of this hidden land within the collection of Elizabeth's empire would boost the coffers of the Crown and make England a superpower to rival that of Spain. As Raleigh himself asserted, 'the shining glory of this conquest will eclipse all those so far-extended beams of the Spanish nation'.[7]

The plan was to head to South America and explore the Orinoco River, where the city of Manoa was said to be located. This would provide the key to unlocking what Raleigh called 'the large, rich, and beautiful empire of Guiana'.[8] Raleigh set out the details of his expedition in a book he had published on his return, titled *The discovery of the large, rich, and beautiful Empire of Guiana, with a relation of the great and golden city of Manoa*; otherwise, more succinctly known today as *The Discovery of Guiana*. It outlines his leaving England in February 1595, before heading out to the island of Trinidad. He had sent his servant, Jacob Whiddon, to the region a year earlier to obtain valuable information about the terrain and the natives that lived there, ensuring that he was aware of the political situation on the island in which the Spanish ruled with – claimed Raleigh – a firm fist.[9] He had a grievance with the governor of Trinidad, Don Antonio de Berreo, due to Berreo betraying Whiddon's men a year earlier. Raleigh learned of Berreo's cruelty, in which the 'ancient caciques' ('lords of the country') were 'their slaves; that he kept them in chains, and dropped their naked bodies with burning bacon, and such other torments'.[10] Raleigh hatched a plan to overthrow Berreo, in which he took control of the colony and set a Spanish city on fire.

Using a native interpreter brought from England, Raleigh addressed the natives of Trinidad:

> I made them understand that I was the servant of a queen who was the great cacique of the north, and a virgin, and had more caciqui [lords] under her than there were trees in that island; that she was an enemy to the Castellani in respect of their tyranny and oppression, and that she delivered all such nations about her, as were by them oppressed; and having freed all the coast of the northern world from their servitude, had sent me to free them also.[11]

Raleigh sweetened the deal by presenting them with a picture of Queen Elizabeth, which he noted 'they so admired and honoured'.[12] By hailing his queen as 'Elizabeth, the Great Princess' and 'Greatest Commander',[13] Raleigh created Elizabeth as a goddess; a tactic that he would regularly employ when meeting and greeting the various native tribes on his search for El Dorado. With Trinidad secured for the time being, the Tudor empire, on paper at least, now stretched to the waters of South America, but Raleigh intended to travel further onto the mainland to find his city of gold.

Despite initially being a foe of Raleigh's, Berreo became a valuable ally because the Spaniard himself had previously attempted the very same thing that Raleigh was searching for. Raleigh described Berreo as 'very valiant and liberal, and a gentleman of great assuredness, and of a great heart'.[14] Berreo provided information on El Dorado, although the Spanish governor did his best to convince Raleigh to turn back, 'that it would be labour lost, and that they should suffer many miseries if they proceeded'.[15] No doubt Berreo was thinking of all the other explorers who had come before Raleigh, and the great misfortunes they suffered. Berreo himself, after obtaining his freedom once the expedition was over, continued his own search, leading to his death in 1597.

The 'great river of Orenoque'[16] was the chief means by which Raleigh and his men were able to delve into the Continent. The river was said to be navigable for large ships for up to 1,000 miles, and 2,000 miles for small vessels, with many significant branches and with islands situated in between, 'many of them as big as the Isle of Wight'.[17] Raleigh wrote of what he saw on the river, of a 'great store of fowl, and of many sorts;

we saw in it divers sorts of strange fishes, and of marvellous bigness', such as 'lagartos' (meaning alligators).[18] Furthermore, they encountered other oddities, such as 'a nation of inhuman Cannibals',[19] and heard of 'a nation of people whose heads appear not above their shoulders', in which they were said 'to have their eyes in their shoulders, and their mouths in the middle of their breasts'.[20] However, the journey itself was tortuous and dangerous in parts, with food a continual problem; at one point, Raleigh writes of this issue:

> But so long we laboured that many days were spent, and we driven to draw ourselves to harder allowance, our bread even at the last, and no drink at all; and our men and ourselves so wearied and scorched, and doubtful withal whether we should ever perform it or no, the heat increasing as we drew towards the line.[21]

The pain was worse for Raleigh, he adds, because he had been more well acquainted with the food on offer at the royal court, being 'cared for in a sort far more differing' than most others.[22] And meal times were not the only problem, with the river itself being the home of predators; Raleigh wrote of one incident in which the alligators attacked 'a negro, a very proper young fellow', who foolishly leapt 'out of the galley to swim in the mouth of the river'. The outcome was not in doubt, with the man 'in all our sights taken and devoured'.[23]

Furthermore, Raleigh had the issue of attempting to keep his men under control to avoid them pillaging the settlements in the region. The lack of supplies clearly led to urges, including those of a sexual nature. However, in his book Raleigh is clear to affirm that English men did not assault or rape the natives, which was in contrast to the Spanish who 'took from them both their wives and daughters daily'. Raleigh wrote:

> But I protest before the Majesty of the living God, that I neither know nor believe, that any of our company, one or other, did offer insult to any of their women, and yet we saw many hundreds, and had many in our power, and of those very young and excellently favoured, which came among us without deceit, stark naked.[24]

However, Raleigh does admit that 'it was very impatient work to keep the meaner sort from spoil and stealing'.[25] It was important to Raleigh that the English were not shown to be the aggressors, to distinguish them from the actions of the Spanish, and to ensure that England would have strong allies when they returned in the future. Raleigh's book is an exercise in public relations, with a clear focus on highlighting the goodly ways of the English. Similarly, the natives of the region are often portrayed in positive terms, perhaps in an attempt to win interest from English readers and, more importantly, English financial backers for future voyages. One tribe of natives are described as 'a very goodly people and very valiant',[26] while a woman from another area is outlined in glowing terms:

> and in all my life I have seldom seen a better favoured woman. She was of good stature, with black eyes, fat of body, of an excellent countenance, her hair almost as long as herself, tied up again in pretty knots; and it seemed she stood not in that awe of her husband as the rest, for she spake and discoursed, and drank among the gentlemen and captains, and was very pleasant, knowing her own comeliness and taking great pride therein. I have seen a lady in England so like to her, as but for the difference of colour, I would have sworn might have been the same.[27]

Raleigh's aim, then, wasn't simply to locate the city of gold, but also to win over the hearts and minds of the natives. 'I have among them many more pieces of gold than I received,' he wrote, 'of the new money of twenty shillings with her Majesty's picture, to wear, with promise that they would become her servants thenceforth'.[28] He was reluctant to get involved in the internal politics of the region, particularly inter-tribal warfare, despite various offers. Raleigh played the diplomatic long-game, forever wanting to portray himself and the English as the saviours of the region, all in an effort to provide a firmer hold on the waiting gold and silver.

But despite all of this, the city of gold remained undiscovered, although Raleigh was at pains to point out that valuable resources were to be found in the region. He notes that they 'saw all the hills with stones of the colour of gold and silver',[29] and that he was 'assured' that the region 'hath more abundance of gold ... than all Peru and the West Indies'.[30] And so, the next step was to return once more to establish England's dominance in the region, with Raleigh pointing out how the tribes he had encountered had 'already become her Majesty's vassals',[31] and that an army of 3–4,000 soldiers would be able to take Manoa and hold it from the Spanish.[32] Surely, argued Raleigh, England must seize the opportunity; particularly, as he pointed out, due to the blunder Elizabeth's grandfather made when passing on Christopher Columbus' offer to explore the Atlantic. Despite there being a shift in the imperial efforts of the English – from pirates to colonisers – Raleigh points out that the rise in power of the Spanish was not due to 'the trades of sacks and Seville oranges', but rather the gold and silver found in the New World.

The whole of Raleigh's book is an attempt to win back Elizabeth's love and to lead to funds for future expeditions. But many contemporaries and historians have questioned the extent to which he exaggerated his claims; some of his enemies claimed that the gold specimens were taken from Africa. Ultimately, the boast of promising Elizabeth gold and silver, far beyond the scale of that obtained by Spain, proved to be completely empty. But does this mean that Raleigh was lying in his account? In many ways, Raleigh's book is similar to the writings of the ancient Greek historian Herodotus, with both interested in relaying tales of the fantastic. But Raleigh does provide a word of caution, noting on the veracity of his claims:

> it shall be found a weak policy in me, either to betray myself or my country with imaginations; neither am I so far in love with that lodging, watching, care, peril, diseases, ill savours, bad fare, and many other mischiefs that accompany these voyages, as to woo myself again into any of them, were I not assured that the sun covereth not so much riches in any part of the earth.[33]

Furthermore, Raleigh placed his reputation and position on the line when he boldly asserted that if gold was not found then he would 'lose her Highness' favour and good opinion for ever'.[34] But gold was never found, and in many ways the entire expedition could be considered a failure. However, as Winston Churchill once wrote, 'History will be kind to me, for I intend to write it'; similarly, Raleigh's chief success from the entire event was the publication of his account. Gold was not found, but Raleigh's writings placed him on the same level of the deeds of expanding the empire as the likes of Drake.

1617: The Second Voyage

Although El Dorado remained undiscovered, Raleigh was eventually restored to his position at the royal court. His glory days of being Elizabeth's favourite had long passed, but he was able to play a role in the remaining years of the Spanish war, being involved in the capture of Cadiz in 1596 – where he was wounded – and an expedition to the Azores. For the first couple of years after his return he harboured hopes of returning to find the city of gold, sending Captain Kemys – who had journeyed with him in 1595 – back to the region to keep in contact with the natives he had met. However, the government did not have the financial means to pursue Raleigh's designs, and with time the dream faded away. By 1600, Raleigh held the position of governor of the island of Jersey, and although the position was not as esteemed as other posts, the island was an important post in terms of the defence of England within the context of the wider Spanish war.

When James I came to the throne in 1603 as Elizabeth's successor, Raleigh suffered a drastic decline of fortunes. He became embroiled in the Main Plot of that year, in which some courtiers and politicians schemed to replace James with Lady Arbella Stuart; the venture was to be financially supported by Spanish cash, which would arrive in England via Jersey. Raleigh faced the full wrath of the enemies that he had accumulated over the years. The attorney general called him 'the spider of Hell'; however, there was a lack of evidence and the charges themselves appeared to be ridiculous, particularly the claim that he was in the pay of the Spanish.[35] He was condemned to death but was reprieved, leading to his return to the Tower where he remained for the next eleven years. Despite the lack of his liberty, life for an aristocrat such as Raleigh was not punishing and he continued living a leisurely life for the most part; he and Bess had another son, Carew, and he kept himself busy with the writing of several volumes of his *History of the World*.

Then, in 1617, Raleigh's dream of returning to Guiana was granted; he was pardoned and released from the Tower. It seems that by this point King James was ready to take Raleigh up on his offer of finding a city of gold, particularly because of the Crown's mounting financial problems. Raleigh gathered together a crew, including his son and his trusted deputy Lawrence Kemys, but this voyage was plagued with problems. Because of illness, Raleigh was unable to travel inland, choosing to remain at Trinidad; command was passed to Kemys, who took the rash decision to attack a Spanish settlement. Raleigh's son was killed, and although the settlement was burned, there was no clear way forward into Guiana. The attack was in violation of the mission, with the king ordering Raleigh to avoid confrontation with the Spanish. Kemys returned to Trinidad to beg forgiveness, and when Raleigh would not provide it he said: 'I know then, Sir, what course to take.' Later that night, Kemys drew his pistol and shot himself in the chest, before then taking a knife to stab himself in the heart.

When Raleigh returned to England he was arrested and taken to London. He wrote an apology, hoping to give it to James personally; however, the Spanish demanded punishment, and with James eager to keep the peace there was no chance this time for a reprieve from the scaffold. Raleigh accepted his fate, using his final speech as a last chance to confirm that he was not a traitor and that his words regarding Guiana were all genuine and in good faith. Having felt the executioner's blade with his finger, Raleigh said: 'What dost thou fear? Strike, man strike!' Two strikes later, Raleigh was dead.

Sir Walter Raleigh's boast that 'the shining glory of this conquest will eclipse all those so far-extended beams of the Spanish' was never fulfilled. He may have had a grand vision of the Tudor empire stretching and conquering the city of gold, but these remained a fantasy, much like his book. But his dreams of expanding England across the world would eventually be realised by later generations.

Chapter 19

Elizabethan Ireland

The training ground for the British Empire

In 1598 the Tudors suffered their biggest military defeat in Ireland at the Battle of the Yellow Ford. Of the 4,000 men who were in the English army at the beginning of that day in early August, only half returned home. The Irish, under the leadership of the rebellious Hugh O'Neill, now had momentum on their side, with Tudor power on the decline. There were calls for an independent Catholic Ireland, which would undo all the reforms of the past hundred years.

Queen Elizabeth saw the issue clearly. The Tudor hold of Ireland was on a knife-edge.

The Irish Question

The formation of the Kingdom of Ireland was to be the answer to the ongoing Irish Question: who was to rule in Ireland, either the English Crown or the Irish lords? Despite the initiation of the surrender and regrant policy, serious problems remained in Ireland that plagued Henry's successors in their attempts to maintain control. As realised by both Henry VII and Henry VIII, Ireland could not be treated in a similar way as with the other Celtic regions of Britain; Wales could be easily controlled because of its geographical connection to England, whereas the Irish Sea posed a considerable barrier. There were other serious problems, including the continuing high cost of maintaining an English presence in the Pale, as well as the fragile allegiance of the Irish lords. Most important was the growing religious split between a Protestant English elite and the majority of the Catholic Irish.

The accession of Queen Elizabeth in 1558 saw the fruition of these divisions in Ireland, with many historians critical of her policies; Hiram

Morgan states that Elizabeth's reign was 'calamitous for Ireland', whereas Wallace MacCaffrey wrote that 'her lack of vision condemned the second kingdom to penny-pinching, short-term policies'.[1] Perhaps if Elizabeth had used a similar approach to her grandfather, of providing stability by empowering the Irish lords, then she would have avoided a series of rebellions; however, Henry VII lived in different times, particularly before the problems caused by the Reformation. But the Elizabethan Tudor state pushed forward with their religious reforms and attempts to Anglicise vast swathes of Ireland during a volatile time; as such, they were met with firm resistance.

The English approach to Ireland was, understandably due to their limitations, a mixture of threats, violence and leniency. Garrisons were established by English troops that were given the power of martial law, allowing execution of Irish opponents without trial by jury. A particularly problematic policy was the introduction of plantations; confiscated Irish land was used by the Crown to introduce English settlers. The first plantations started during the reign of Mary I in the 1550s with the establishment of 'Queen's County' in Leinster; however, the historian Niall Ferguson notes that 'these were little more than military outposts'.[2] Later in the Elizabethan period, the idea of plantations was returned to; however, this led to firm resistance from the Irish against the attack on their traditions and culture. The Tudor state hoped that the allegiance of some of the Irish lords would be enough to overcome the bulk of the Irish population; however, it was a risky strategy.

The Desmond Rebellions

The Desmond rebellions were two revolts against Tudor rule, taking place in 1569–73 and then again in 1579–82. The origins came in the form of a clan dispute between the ever-warring Fitzgeralds and Butlers. Their battle in Affane in County Waterford led to Queen Elizabeth summoning the heads of the households to London; however, it is the difference in how Elizabeth dealt with each head that provided momentum for action. Gerald Fitzgerald, the fourteenth Earl of Desmond, was arrested and detained in the Tower, whereas Thomas Butler, the tenth Earl of Ormond, was simply pardoned. It didn't help matters that the Earl of Ormond was a keen favourite of Elizabeth's; nicknamed 'Black Tom',

Ormond contended with the Earl of Leicester for the queen's attention. His influence on Irish policy is undoubted, due to his continuing allegiance to the Crown during the difficult rebellions of the Elizabethan period.

With the Munster Geraldines now leaderless, the Desmond earldom was headed up by James Fitzmaurice, who built his support base by appealing to Irish Catholics. In June 1569, Fitzmaurice attacked an English colony placed south of Cork, and then laid siege to the home settlement of the earls of Ormond at Kilkenny, which held out. Ormond, notably shaken, returned from London to mobilise Irish support against the rebellion; he worked alongside Sir Humphrey Gilbert, the governor of Munster, in reducing Geraldine support with the use of scorched-earth policies. Fitzmaurice's allies fled home to protect their properties, leading to the collapse of the rebellion. However, rather than submit or surrender, Fitzmaurice continued his resistance in the mountains of Kerry, thereby continuing the rebellion for three further years until in early 1573 he had fewer than 100 followers. He submitted in February of that year and managed to negotiate a pardon for his life; however, by 1575 he left for France with the ambition of amassing a foreign force to lead a second rebellion. A clear winner from the rebellion was the Earl of Ormond; he was now a dominant lord in the south of Ireland and had proven himself a strong ally of the English.

Meanwhile, the Geraldines had been reduced in status, with a military force limited to twenty horsemen. In 1573, the Earl of Desmond was released from the Tower and returned to Ireland where he found the Geraldine chiefs seething with anger; they signed a pact to provide unconditional support for the earl; however, Ormond took advantage of their weak state by marching into Munster and killing a Geraldine force, which led to the Earl of Desmond bowing once more to the authority of the Crown.

A handful of years later, the Second Desmond Rebellion was initiated by the return of James Fitzmaurice, who launched an invasion of Munster in 1579. He returned with the blessing of the Pope, and his force landed at Smerwick in County Kerry in July of 1579. Within a month, however, Fitzmaurice was dead, having been shot in the chest. 'My wounds are clear, my wounds are clear,' he told his men, before dying. Leadership of the rebellion passed to John of Desmond, the younger brother of the Earl of Desmond; this, in turn, led to the earl himself joining the revolt.

The summer of 1580 saw the retaking of lost territory by the English and Ormond's troops, leading to the taking of Geraldine lands, including Carrigafoyle Castle. The rebellion was elated with the landing of 600 papal-financed troops at Smerwick in September 1580; however, within two days they were besieged, then surrendered, then were massacred. Once again, the English used a policy of scorched earth, destroying crops and animals in the Geraldine areas. The arrival of Lord Deputy Grey in 1580 led to a violent escalation, with Grey responsible for the estimated execution of 1,500 men.

By the middle of 1581 the rebellion was mostly over, with John of Desmond killed in early 1582, and the Earl of Desmond – on the run and in hiding – hunted and killed by the end of 1583. The Crown had placed a bounty of £1,000 of silver and a pension of £20 a year for whoever obtained Desmond's head; it was severed from his body and sent back to London to Queen Elizabeth. The rebellions plunged Munster into famine, with it estimated that by April 1582 more than 30,000 had died of hunger in the previous six months. By 1589, it is further estimated that one-third of Munster's population had fled and dislocated. As for the Geraldines, the outcome of the rebellions was the complete destruction of their powerbase; this time, there would be no resurrection. Munster was now overcome and was planted with more English colonists.

But despite the defeat of the Desmond rebellions, the English could not rest easy with their Irish relationship. It remained the disturbed land with the potential to erupt into open warfare, particularly due to the growing divide between the Catholic Irish and the Protestant English. The Pope's influence loomed large with the central point remaining: if the queen was a heretic, as the papacy had declared, then good Catholics had a duty to oust the Tudors. The Desmond rebellions failed in their desire to remove Tudor influence; however, the Earl of Tyrone was to have greater success.

The Nine Years' War

The biggest Irish challenge to Tudor rule came in the form of the Tyrone Rebellion, otherwise known as the Nine Years' War. The central figure was Hugh O'Neill, who had been created Earl of Tyrone in 1585; he had fought alongside the English against the rebels in the Second Desmond

Rebellion, thereby highlighting his loyalty. However, by the early 1590s, the Crown began to suspect O'Neill's intentions, which clashed with the English intention of bringing Ulster under Anglo control. Tyrone vied for the position of the provincial president of Ulster, which he would govern on behalf of the Crown; however, the position was given to the English colonist Henry Bagenal. There was bad blood between O'Neill and Bagenal; O'Neill had previously married Bagenal's sister, Mabel, which Bagenal reacted to with fury:

> that my blood which in my father and myself hath often been spilled in repressing this rebellious race, should now be mingled with so traitorous a stock and kindred.[3]

Furthermore, Bagenal believed that O'Neill had disrespected his family's honour, particularly with the stories of O'Neill's neglect of his husbandly duties, as well as the ease with which he found a mistress. O'Neill initially retained a show of loyalty to the English Crown, but after Mabel's death in 1595 he began his stance of defiance.

The Elizabethan approach to handling Tyrone was confused. The first negotiations attempted to ease Tyrone's anger, but when Elizabeth heard about the soft touch used she went into a rage and said such an approach was 'derogatory to our honour'. The new Lord Deputy sent to deal with Tyrone, Sir William Russell, summoned the Irish chief to Dublin for questioning, but then O'Neill was released and allowed to return to his home. The queen was equally displeased at the missed opportunity to have persuaded or punished O'Neill; in February 1595, he turned to outright rebellion when he joined others in the assault on Blackwater Fort.

As with the earlier Desmond rebellions, the Tudors feared the interference of foreign support for the Irish rebels; this fear was particularly pertinent during the 1590s when the Anglo-Spanish War rumbled on. Previously the Geraldines believed that attracting support from a foreign monarch would have provided their rebellion with the legs needed for long-term success, and Tyrone was keen to bring King Philip into the Irish orbit. In 1595, Tyrone wrote to Philip, offering to be his vassal, and also proposed that the Habsburg-related Archduke Albert of Austria be made Prince of Ireland. The promise of the arrival of Spanish reinforcements gave O'Neill the push needed to fight on against the English; however, any serious fighting force was not to arrive in Ireland for a further five years.

The climactic point of Tyrone's rebellion was his victory at the Battle of the Yellow Ford in 1598. 1,500 English men were killed, with hundreds more deserting in the aftermath of the battle, while their leader – O'Neill's rival Sir Henry Bagenal – was killed when he was shot in the head. The battle was England's biggest defeat on Irish territory, thereby highlighting that this rebellion could not be extinguished as easily as previous ones. The English were now on the backfoot, leading to colonists fleeing for their lives from the Munster plantation. O'Neill was now leading a nationwide revolt with the potential of establishing an independent and Catholic Irish state. In 1599, he sent a document to London outlining his demands: Ireland was to become self-governing and the Catholic Church was to be restored. One of Elizabeth's advisors, Sir Robert Cecil, commented in the margin of the document: 'Ewtopia'. However, O'Neill was closer than any previous Irish lord in making this dream a reality.

Endgame

The Tudor reaction was to assemble the largest army – almost 20,000 strong – sent across to Ireland in the sixteenth century. The man given the job of ending the war was Robert Deveraux, Earl of Essex. The stepson of the Earl of Leicester, Essex fancied his chances at being the new favourite of the queen when he entered the royal court in the 1580s; however, his ambition to become the dominant counsellor was thwarted by his rival, Sir Robert Cecil. Although Essex took part in various actions during the Anglo-Spanish War, the success of others – such as Sir Francis Drake – appeared to elude him. He was brazen and impudent; when the queen clipped him around the ear, for example, Essex reacted by reaching for his sword before being stopped in his tracks by one of his followers. The commission to head to Ireland provided Essex with the opportunity to restore his fortunes once more.

Meanwhile, Tyrone realised that he could not continue the momentum of the rebellion; he appealed to those in the Pale to join him, hoping that this would lead to the final death blow of Tudor rule in Ireland. However, the Old English within the Pale held firm to their roots, having engaged in hostilities against their Gaelic enemies in the previous decades.

The newly arrived English army was now as effective as Elizabeth hoped. The plan was to establish garrisons in the south of the island, before then taking on O'Neill's support base in Ulster. But Essex's campaign was a failure and his sizeable fighting force was reduced as the weeks wore on due to the need to garrison forts, and then hit with the spread of disease and desertion. By 1599, Essex had only 4,500 men in the field, which was far below the number needed to confront Tyrone in battle. Furthermore, Essex himself was riddled with personal problems and a general fear that he was being outmanoeuvred back home in the royal court; physically he may have been in Ireland, but his heart and mind were back in London, where he believed that his rival Robert Cecil was plotting against him. With an urgent need to return to England, Essex met with O'Neill and arranged a truce, against the wishes of the Crown. Then, having spent three months in Ireland, Essex headed back to the royal court in an attempt to plead his innocence to the queen; on arriving at Nonsuch Palace, he made his way unexpectedly and without invitation into Elizabeth's bedchamber where the queen:

> Had just a simple robe over her nightdress, her wrinkled
> skin was free of cosmetics and without her wig Essex saw
> her bald head with just wisps of thinning grey hair.[4]

Anne Whitelock writes of Elizabeth being 'speechless at the sight of the unheralded intruder',[5] with Essex flinging himself at the feet of the queen to beg for her forgiveness and for her love. However, the next day Essex was placed under house arrest and a list of charges were read against him; his exile from the court pushed him to plotting an overthrow of the queen's counsellors, which ultimately ended in the failed Essex Rebellion in 1601 and Essex's execution.

The next Lord Deputy sent to Ireland was Charles Blount, Baron Mountjoy, who was given full permission to use violent tactics to end the rebellion. Hiram Morgan writes how the 'English began to grind down the rebellious Irish with a series of close, mutually supporting garrisons which devasted the country and reduced the population to starvation'.[6] By the summer of 1601, the rebellion in Munster was over, with the English recapturing castles and subduing the population. Hope for O'Neill arrived at the end of 1601 when the long-promised Spanish troops finally appeared, with 3,500 soldiers landing at Kinsale on the southern end of Ireland. O'Neill and his allies headed south, while Mountjoy reacted fast and also marched to the location armed with 7,000 men. The rebel leaders were divided in their approach, with Hugh Roe O'Donnell attacking the English, against the wishes of O'Neill. The English, with superior cavalry, routed the Irish forces, and without any support the Spanish promptly surrendered.

Kinsale was the turning of the tide for the English, and although O'Neill continued his resistance by using guerrilla tactics, Mountjoy was able to penetrate Ulster where he employed scorched-earth tactics in destroying crops and cattle. With his homeland now in tatters, O'Neill held out until 30 March 1603, when he surrendered to the English. Little did he know, but Queen Elizabeth had died a week earlier, and so that month saw not only the end of the Nine Years' War but also the end of the Tudor dynasty.

'The English school for overseas empire'[7]

The Nine Years' War had an immense negative impact on both the Irish and the English. It is possible that more than 100,000 soldiers and civilians were killed in the Elizabethan conflicts in Ireland.[8] Around 60,000 died in the Ulster famine of 1602–3 during the end days of the war. Furthermore, all this bloodshed was costly, too; it is estimated that the Irish wars cost more than the Spanish Armada and the actions in the Netherlands combined, with the Nine Years' War alone pushing to almost £2 million. There was a huge strain on the English economy by the end of the Tudor period, which compounded the wider problems of population growth, depression and the rise of vagrancy.

This helps explain the leniency afforded to the rebel leaders in the peace settlement of 1603. O'Neill and the other leaders negotiated pardons and the return of their lands, although this came at the expense of abandoning their Irish titles and swearing an oath of loyalty to the Crown. Despite the settlement, it is clear that trust between O'Neill and the English government was irreparable, and within a handful of years the rebel leaders were plotting and considering a fresh uprising. In 1607, they left Ireland in the 'Flight of the Earls' with the aim of obtaining foreign support for an invasion; however, they were unable to find anyone to help them. The Anglo-Spanish War ended in 1604, with the new Stuart regime in Westminster and the Spanish keen to keep the peace. O'Neill's lands were confiscated, which paved the way for a new plantation in Ulster; O'Neill died in Italy in 1616, having tired himself with failed attempts to triumphantly return to Ireland.

After decades of conflict, the end of the Tudor period marked an end of an era for Ireland. The power of native Irish lords had been broken and more power had been absorbed by the Pale and central government, while Irish culture – particularly its language – was in decline. The revival of plantations in the seventeenth century saw the arrival of thousands of Protestant English, Welsh and Scottish settlers, leading to further persecution of the Catholic Irish. Many nations in Britain lay claim to being the first English colony; Wales was dominated and conquered in the late 1200s, whereas the Cornish claim goes back to the Anglo-Saxon era. All claims are valid. However, there is something particularly distinct with the Elizabethan experience in Ireland, which strongly suggests that it was the true training ground for the later British Empire.

This is supported by a multitude of historians, with Niall Ferguson arguing how 'Ireland was the experimental laboratory of British colonisation',[9] with Alan Taylor believing that this ultimately provided the English with the confidence to 'extend their colonial ambitions across the Atlantic'.[10] Many of the key figures in the subduing of the Irish in the Elizabethan period also played a large role in the Tudor expansion to the New World, as seen in the form of Sir Humphrey Gilbert, who treated the Irish with severe violence when he 'decorated the path leading to his tent with human heads'.[11] This led to the manner in which the Irish were treated, which in turn has similarities with how other peoples were handled, ranging from John Hawkins' capture of Africans to Richard Grenville's killing of American natives; they were to be punished and controlled, and therefore seen as lesser to the English. What was learned in Ireland was then used in the subjugation of those in the New World, and then later, from all around the world.

Chapter 20

The Tudor Inheritance

The passing of empire to the Stuart dynasty

The Tudor dynasty came to an end with the death of Queen Elizabeth on 24 March 1603. It had been 118 years since Henry Tudor's unexpected victory on the field of Bosworth, and during that time three generations of Tudor monarchs had obsessed over the containment and expansion of their empire. The Tudor approach to empire was, on the whole, a mixed-bag; different monarchs had distinct pressing concerns, which either enhanced or stunted the imperial drive. Henry VII spent twenty-four years retaining and strengthening his domains; however, he was curious about exploration to the New World, which led to his support of John Cabot's voyages in the 1490s. His son, Henry VIII, cared little for such schemes, preferring to enhance his imperial status by resuming wars with the French; much money was spent with little to gain and he was far more successful in centralising power within Britain itself. The reigns of Henry's successors saw the Tudor empire struggling for breath, particularly with the loss of Calais in 1558; however, this Tudor Brexit forced England to consider other alternatives across the globe. Elizabeth's reign saw the fruits of this growth of confidence, with voyages to Russia, West Africa and the Americas evidenced in the second half of the sixteenth century. Although such speculating efforts drew the attention of Spain – which almost led to the death of the dynasty in 1588 – English imperialism continued to grow, thereby encouraging future generations in the seventeenth century.

The inheritance provided to Elizabeth's successor, King James VI of the Stuart dynasty, was a mouth-watering one. Although there were considerable problems, such as war with Spain dragging on for close to two decades, as well as financial issues, James was now the monarch of a collection of peoples that stretched across the British Isles, with the potential of further expansion. He added the prosperous English

211

kingdom to his portfolio, with its seniority within the empire clearly demonstrated with James' preference of London for his royal court. England was far more united than when the Tudors found it, back when it was riven with division after fighting for generations in the Wars of the Roses; the population was greater and industry was further diversified, and power was centralised from areas such as the North and Cornwall, providing Elizabeth's successor with a solid base on which to expand. Then there were the other Celtic regions: Wales had been successfully incorporated into the English state, whereas Ireland remained a lingering problem. However, the newly agreed peace in 1603 provided hope for further exploitation of the island in the form of further colonisation in the century ahead.

More importantly, there was the growing connection of England to the wider world, such as with Russia, with North America, and with the opening markets of Asia. The tail-end of Elizabeth's reign saw the establishment of the East India Company, which would find riches in taking advantage of the Indian subcontinent in the years to come. Then, in 1607, came the foundation of Jamestown, the first successful permanent colony the New World; in the space of a handful of decades more colonies sprung up on the eastern seaboard, giving birth to what would eventually become the United States of America.

Overall, there was no clear pattern to Tudor imperialism. The Victorian historian J.R. Seeley noted how the British Empire was created 'in a fit of absence of mind', and there is enough evidence to show that there are examples of this in the Tudor century. Expansion was primarily motivated and directed by others, such as traders and explorers, with loose encouragement provided by the likes of Henry VII and Elizabeth I. But the Tudor court was keen to promote and celebrate these achievements, as highlighted in the deeds of the Elizabethan seadogs. However, it is clear that the Tudor period saw the English thinking bigger and more boldly in terms of foreign expansion than ever before; a British focus turned into a European mentality, which ultimately became a worldwide outlook. This is further evidenced in the paradigm shift required from piracy and plunder to colonisation and settlement. Although this imperial mindset was slow in developing, by the end of the sixteenth century the Tudors were more determined to become a permanent presence in different regions of the world. Yes, Sir Walter Raleigh was after a pipe-dream with his failed attempts to find El Dorado; however, he was mindful to promote Elizabeth's majesty wherever he went, believing that England was establishing allies with a long-term commitment.

Such a positive view cannot allow us to forget the sins committed by the Tudors in the pursuit of their imperial ambitions. Blood was spilled wherever they went, as with the subduing of Cornwall in the West Country, of Wales under the harsh hand of the Hanging Bishop, and notably of Ireland in which the English truly learned how to become harsh, exploitative imperial masters. In many ways, the Tudor dynasty was an apprenticeship in what later became the British Empire; the means of controlling and exploiting the world was learned during the sixteenth century.

Without the Tudors there would be no British Empire, most certainly not in the form it took. However, as demonstrated throughout this book, the Tudors themselves sustained and expanded their own specific empire. The Tudor empire was won through bloodshed at Bosworth, and it was handed over to Elizabeth's successor on her death in the early hours of the morning at Richmond Palace. King James then held the Tudor inheritance in his hands; the world was seemingly his for the taking.

Bibliography

Attreed, Lorraine, 'Henry VII and the 'New-Found Island': England's Atlantic Exploration, Mediterranean Diplomacy, and the Challenge of Frontier Sexuality'. *Mediterranean Studies*, Vol. 9, 2000, pp. 65–78. Retrieved from: https://www.jstor.org/stable/41166911

Bacon, Francis, *The History of the Reign of King Henry VII* (Hesperus Press, Jordan, 2007)

Beazley, C. Raymond, *Voyages and Travels: mainly during the 16th and 17th centuries* (Archibald Constable & Co, London, 1903)

Beckett, Andy, 'Heirs to the slaves', *The Guardian*, 2 December 2006. Retrieved from: https://www.theguardian.com/politics/2006/dec/02/past.andybeckett

Casimir, Nicholas and de Bogoushevsky, Baron de, 'The English in Muscovy during the Sixteenth Century', *Transactions of the Royal Historical Society*, Vol. 7, 1878, pp. 58–129. Retrieved from: https://www.jstor.org/stable/3677884

Cavendish, Richard, 'Marriage of James IV of Scots and Margaret Tudor', *History Today*, Vol. 53, Issue 8, August 2003. Retrieved from: https://www.historytoday.com/archive/marriage-james-iv-scots-and-margaret-tudor

Chrimes, S.B., *Henry VII* (Yale University Press, USA, 1999)

Clifford, Arthur *The State Papers and Letters of Ralph Sadler, Knight-Banneret*, Vol. 1 (Archibald Constable, Edinburgh, 1809)

Cole, Grenville A.J., 'The Narrow Seas and the Arctic route to Muscovy', *The Geographical Teacher*, Vol. 10, No. 1, Spring, 1919, pp. 4–8. Retrieved from: https://www.jstor.org/stable/40555794

Condon, Margaret M. and Jones, Evan T., 'William Weston: early voyager to the New World', *Historical Research*, Vol. 91, Issue 254, November 2018, pp. 628–646. Retrieved from: https://academic.oup.com/histres/article/91/254/628/5603429

Crooks, Peter, 'Factions, Feuds and Noble Power in the Lordship of Ireland, c. 1356–1496', *Irish Historical Studies*, Vol. 35, No. 140 (Nov., 2007), pp. 425–454. Retrieved from: https://www.jstor.org/stable/20547488

Currin, John M., 'Pierre Le Pennec, Henry VII of England, and the Breton Plot of 1492: A Case Study in "Diplomatic Pathology"', *Albion: A Quarterly Journal Concerned with British Studies*, Vol. 23, No. 1 (Spring, 1991), pp. 1–22. Retrieved from: https://www.jstor.org/stable/4050539

Currin, John M., 'To Play at Peace: Henry VII, War against France, and the Chieregato-Flores Mediation of 1490', *Albion: A Quarterly Journal Concerned with British Studies*, Vol. 31, No. 2 (Summer, 1999), pp. 207–237. Retrieved from: https://www.jstor.org/stable/4052743

Currin, John M., '"The King's Army into the Partes of Bretaigne": Henry VII and the Breton Wars, 1489–1491', *War in History*, Vol. 7, No. 4 (November 2000), pp. 379–412. Retrieved from: https://www.jstor.org/stable/26013873

Davies, C.S.L., 'Tournai and the English Crown, 1513–1519', *The Historical Journal*, Vol. 41, No. 1, March, 1998, pp. 1–26. Retrieved from: https://www.jstor.org/stable/2640143

Dunlop, David, 'The "Masked Comedian": Perkin Warbeck's Adventures in Scotland and England from 1495 to 1497', *The Scottish Historical Review*, Vol. 70, No. 190, Part 2, Oct 1991, pp. 97–128. Retrieved from: https://www.jstor.org/stable/25530509

Dunning, Chester, 'James I, the Russia Company, and the Plan to Establish a Protectorate over North Russia', *Albion: A Quarterly Journal Concerned with British Studies*, Vol. 21, No. 2 (Summer, 1989), pp. 206–226. Retrieved from: https://www.jstor.org/stable/4049926

Edwards, David, *Age of Atrocity: Violence and Political Conflict in Early Modern Ireland* (Four Courts Press, 2010)

Ellis, S.G., 'Parliaments and Great Councils, 1483–99: Addenda et Corrigenda', *Analecta Hibernica*, No. 29, 1980, pp. 98–111. Retrieved from: https://www.jstor.org/stable/25511959

Ellis, Steven G., 'The Irish Customs Administration under the Early Tudors', *Irish Historical Studies*, Vol. 22, No. 86, Sep. 1980, pp. 271–277. Retrieved from: https://www.jstor.org/stable/30008787

Ellis, Steven G., 'Henry VIII, Rebellion and the Rule of Law', *The Historical Journal*, Vol. 24, No. 3, Sep. 1981, pp. 513–531. Retrieved from: https://www.jstor.org/stable/2638881

Ferguson, Niall, *Empire: How Britain Made the Modern World* (Penguin Books, St Ives, 2004)

Fleck, Andrew, '"At the Time of His Death": Manuscript Instability and Walter Ralegh's Performance on the Scaffold', *Journal of British Studies*, Vol. 48, No. 1, Jan. 2009, pp. 4–28. Retrieved from: https://www.jstor.org/stable/25482960

Fritzinger, Jerald, *Pre-Columbian Trans-Oceanic Contact* (Google Books, 2016)

Frye, Susan, 'The Myth of Elizabeth at Tilbury', *The Sixteenth Century Journal*, Vol. 23, No. 1, Spring, 1992, pp. 95–114. Retrieved from: https://www.jstor.org/stable/2542066

Goodwin, George, *Fatal Rivalry: Flodden 1513* (Norton, New York, 2013).

Gordon, Eleanora C., 'The Fate of Sir Hugh Willoughby and His Companions: A New Conjecture', *The Geographical Journal*, Vol. 152, No. 2 (Jul. 1986), pp. 243–257. Retrieved from: https://www.jstor.org/stable/634766

Gore Allen, W., 'The Western Rebellion', *The Irish Monthly*, Vol. 75, No. 894, December 1947, pp. 529–535. Retrieved from: https://www.jstor.org/stable/20515745

Hair, P.E.H., 'The Early Sources on Guinea', *History in Africa*, Vol. 21, 1994, pp. 87–126. Retrieved from: https://www.jstor.org/stable/3171882

Hair, P.E.H., 'Attitudes to Africans in English Primary Sources on Guinea up to 1650', *History in Africa*, Vol. 26, 1999, pp. 43–68. Retrieved from: https://www.jstor.org/stable/3172137

Halperin, Charles J., 'Sixteenth-Century Foreign Travel Accounts to Muscovy: A Methodological Excursus', *The Sixteenth Century Journal*, Vol. 6, No. 2, October 1975, pp. 89–111. Retrieved from: https://www.jstor.org/stable/2539745

Hamlin, William M., 'Imagined Apotheoses: Drake, Harriot, and Ralegh in the Americas', *Journal of the History of Ideas*, Vol. 57, No. 3, July, 1996, pp. 405–428. Retrieved from: https://www.jstor.org/stable/3653947

Hanna, Warren L., 'Legend of the Nicasios: The Men Drake Left behind at Nova Albion', *California History*, Vol. 58, No. 2, Summer 1979, pp. 154–165. Retrieved from: https://www.jstor.org/stable/25157908

Harrisse, Henry, 'Did Cabot Return From His Second Voyage?' *The American Historical Review*, Vol. 3, No. 3, April 1898, pp. 449–455. Retrieved from: https://www.jstor.org/stable/1833686

Head, David M., 'Henry VIII's Scottish Policy: A Reassessment', *The Scottish Historical Review*, Vol. 61, No. 171, Part 1, April 1982, pp. 1–24. Retrieved from: https://www.jstor.org/stable/25529445

Hutchinson, Robert, *Elizabeth's Spy Master: Francis Walsingham and the Secret War That Saved England* (Phoenix, Croydon, 2007)

Hutchinson, Robert, *Young Henry: The Rise of Henry VIII* (Phoenix, Croydon, 2012)

Jones, Evan, 'Salazar's account of Bristol's discovery of the Island of Brasil (pre-1476)' (Department of History, University of Bristol, 2007). Retrieved from: http://www.bris.ac.uk/Depts/History/Maritime/Sources/1476brasil.htm

Jones, E.T., & Condon, M., 'Henry VII's letter to John Morton concerning William Weston's voyage to the new found land' (Unpublished, 2011). Retrieved from: http://hdl.handle.net/1983/1734

Jones, Evan T. and Condon, Margaret M., *Cabot and Bristol's Age of Discovery: The Bristol Discovery Voyages 1480–1509* (Cabot Project Publications, 2016). Retrieved from: https://archive.org/details/Cabotdigital/mode/2up?view=theater

Joyce, Patrick Weston, *A Concise History of Ireland*, 1910. Retrieved from: https://www.libraryireland.com/JoyceHistory/Poyning.php

Kane, Brendan, 'Being Noble in Ireland before Henry VIII', *Proceedings of the Harvard Celtic Colloquium*, Vol. 32 (2012), pp. 180–197. Retrieved from: https://www.jstor.org/stable/23630939

Kelsey, Harry, 'Did Francis Drake Really Visit California?', *Western Historical Quarterly*, Vol. 21, No. 4, November 1990, pp. 444–462. Retrieved from: https://www.jstor.org/stable/969250

Laudonniére, René Goudlaine de, *Historie nortable de la Floride: Selections* (Thomas Dawson, London, 1587). Retrieved from: https://www.proquest.com/eebo/docview/2240927220/99845039

Lee, Christopher, *This Sceptred Isle: From the Roman Invasion to the Death of Queen Victoria* (Penguin Books, St Ives, 1998)

Lethbridge Kingsford, Charles (ed), *Chronicles of London* (Clarendon Press, Oxford, 1905). Retrieved from: https://archive.org/details/chroniclesoflond00kinguoft/mode/2up

Lubimenko, Inna (1914) 'The Correspondence of Queen Elizabeth with the Russian Czars', *The American Historical Review*, Vol. 19, No. 3, Apr. 1914, pp. 525–542. Retrieved from: https://www.jstor.org/stable/1835077

Lubimenko, Inna, 'England's Part in the Discovery of Russia', *The Slavonic Review*, Vol. 6, No. 16 (Jun., 1927), pp. 104–118. Retrieved from: https://www.jstor.org/stable/4202139

Mackie, J.D., 'Henry VIII and Scotland', *Transactions of the Royal Historical Society*, Vol. 29, 1947, pp. 93–114. Retrieved from: https://www.jstor.org/stable/3678551

Maginn, Christopher, '"Surrender and Regrant" in the Historiography of Sixteenth-Century Ireland', *The Sixteenth Century Journal*, Vol. 38, No. 4, Winter, 2007, pp. 955–974. Retrieved from: https://www.jstor.org/stable/20478623

Maginn, Christopher, '"Behind Every Great Woman...": William Cecil and the Elizabethan Conquest of Ireland', *History Ireland*, Vol. 20, No. 6, November/December, 2012, pp. 14–17. Retrieved from: https://www.jstor.org/stable/23290987

Marshall, Peter, '"The Greatest Man in Wales": James Ap Gruffydd Ap Hywel and the International Opposition to Henry VIII', *The Sixteenth Century Journal*, Vol. 39, No. 3, Fall, 2008, pp. 681–704. Retrieved from: https://www.jstor.org/stable/20479000

Mason, Emma, 'Obituary: "Alwyn Ruddock"', *The Guardian*, 17 Feb 2006. Retrieved from: https://www.theguardian.com/news/2006/feb/17/obituaries.mainsection

Matusiak, John, *Wolsey: The Life of King Henry VIII's Cardinal* (The History Press, India, 2016)

Mee, Arthur, *Cornwall* (Hodder and Stoughton, Great Britain, 1967)

Merriman, Marcus, *The Rough Wooings* (Tuckwell Press, East Linton, 2000)

Middleton, Richard, *Colonial America: A History, 1585–1776* (Second Edition) (Blackwell Publications, Cornwall, 1992).

Morgan, Hiram, '"Never Any Realm Worse Governed": Queen Elizabeth and Ireland', *Transactions of the Royal Historical Society*, Vol. 14, 2004, pp. 295–308. Retrieved from: https://www.jstor.org/stable/3679322

Bibliography

Morgan, Hiram, 'Teaching the Armada: An Introduction to the Anglo-Spanish War, 1585–1604', *History Ireland*, Vol. 14, No. 5, Sep.– Oct., 2006, pp. 37–43. Retrieved from: https://www.jstor.org/stable/27725518

Morris, T.A., *Europe and England in the Sixteenth Century* (Routledge, UK, 1998)

Northrup, David, *The Atlantic Slave Trade* (DC & Heath, UK, 1994)

Oko, Adolph S., 'Francis Drake and Nova Albion', *California Historical Society Quarterly*, Vol. 43, No. 2, June 1964, pp. 135–158. Retrieved from: https://www.jstor.org/stable/25155641

Palmer, M.D., *Henry VIII: Seminar Studies in History* (Longman, Great Britain, 1971)

Payton, Philip, *Cornwall: A History* (Cornwall Editions, UK, 2004)

Penn, Thomas, *Winter King: The Dawn of Tudor England* (Allen Lane, St Ives, 2011).

Pennington, Edgar Legare, 'Sir John Hawkins in Florida', *The Florida Historical Society Quarterly*, Vol. 10, No. 2, October 1931, pp. 86–101. Retrieved from: https://www.jstor.org/stable/30084887

Phillips, Gervase, 'Strategy and Its Limitations: The Anglo-Scots Wars, 1480–1550', *War in History*, Vol. 6, No. 4, November 1999, pp. 396–416. Retrieved from: https://www.jstor.org/stable/26013967

Pinkerton, John, *A General Collection of the Best and Most Interesting Voyages and Travels, In All Parts of the World; Many of Which Are Now Translated into English* (Volume 1) (Kimber and Conrad, USA, 1810). Retrieved from: https://books.google.co.uk/books?id=7cUNAQAAMAAJ&pg=PA1&redir_esc=y#v=onepage&q&f=false

Pollitt, Ronald, 'John Hawkins's Troublesome Voyages: Merchants, Bureaucrats, and the Origin of the Slave Trade', *Journal of British Studies*, Vol. 12, No. 2, May 1973, pp. 26–40. Retrieved from: https://www.jstor.org/stable/175273

Potter, David, 'The duc de Guise and the Fall of Calais, 1557–1558', *The English Historical Review*, Vol. 98, No. 388, July 1983, pp. 481–512. Retrieved from: http://www.jstor.com/stable/569781

Quinn, David B., 'The Early Interpretation of Poynings' Law, 1494–1534', *Irish Historical Studies*, Vol. 2, No. 7 (Mar. 1941), pp. 241–254. Retrieved from: https://www.jstor.org/stable/30005898

Quinn, David B. (1961) 'Henry VIII and Ireland, 1509–34', *Irish Historical Studies*, Vol. 12, No. 48, September 1961, pp. 318–344. Retrieved from: https://www.jstor.org/stable/30005087

Quinn, David B., 'Columbus and the North: England, Iceland, and Ireland.' *The William and Mary Quarterly*, Vol. 29, No. 2 (April 1992), pp. 278–297. Retrieved from: https://www.jstor.org/stable/2947273

Raleigh, Walter, *The Discovery of Guiana* (Blackmask Online, 2001)

Randell, Keith, *Henry VIII and the Government of England* (Hodder Educational, Great Britain, 2001)

Roberts, P.R., 'The Union with England and the Identity of 'Anglican' Wales', *Transactions of the Royal Historical Society*, Vol. 22, 1972, pp. 49–70. Retrieved from: https://www.jstor.org/stable/3678828

Rodger, N.A.M., 'Queen Elizabeth and the Myth of Sea-Power in English History', *Transactions of the Royal Historical Society*, Vol. 14, 2004, pp. 153–174. Retrieved from: https://www.jstor.org/stable/3679312

Rogers, Caroline and Turvey, Roger, *Henry VII* (Third Edition) (Hodder Murray, Malta, 2006)

Rogerson, David, Samantha Ellsmore, David Hudson, *The Early Tudors, England 1485–1558,* (Hodder Murray, Great Britain, 2007)

Rowse, A.L., *Tudor Cornwall* (Cornish Classics, Exeter, 2005)

Sandman, Alison and Ash, Eric H., 'Trading Expertise: Sebastian Cabot between Spain and England'. *Renaissance Quarterly*, Vol. 57, No. 3, Autumn, 2004, pp. 813–846. Retrieved from: https://www.jstor.org/stable/4143567

Sayles, G.O., 'The Vindication of the Earl of Kildare from Treason, 1496', *Irish Historical Studies*, Vol. 7, No. 25 (Mar., 1950), pp. 39–47. Retrieved from: https://www.jstor.org/stable/30007259

Scarisbrick, J.J., *Henry VIII* (Eyre & Spottiswoode, UK, 1968)

Sinclair, George A., 'The Scots at Solway Moss, *The Scottish Historical Review*, Vol. 2, No. 8, July 1905, pp. 372–377. Retrieved from: https://www.jstor.org/stable/25517648

Stoyle, Mark, 'The Dissidence of Despair: Rebellion and Identity in Early Modern Cornwall'. *Journal of British Studies*, Vol. 38, No. 4 (Oct., 1999), pp. 423–444. Retrieved from: https://www.jstor.org/stable/175946

Stoyle, Mark, '"Fullye Bente to Fighte Oute the Matter" Reconsidering Cornwall's Role in the Western Rebellion of 1549', *The English*

Historical Review, Vol. 129, No. 538, June 2014, pp. 549–577. Retrieved from: https://www.jstor.org/stable/24474187

Sturt, John, *Revolt in the West* (Devon Books, Great Britain, 1987)

Tait, James, 'Lee, Rowland', in the *Dictionary of National Biography, 1885–1900*, Volume 32, 1892. Retrieved from: https://en.m.wikisource.org/wiki/Dictionary_of_National_Biography,_1885-1900/Lee,_Rowland#

Taylor, Alan, *American Colonies: The Settling of North America* (Penguin Books, USA, 2002)

Tillbrook, Michael, *The Tudors: England 1485–1603* (Oxford University Press, Glasgow, 2015)

Trattner, Walter I., 'God and Expansion in Elizabethan England: John Dee, 1527–1583', *Journal of the History of Ideas*, Vol. 25, No. 1, 1964, pp. 17–34. Retrieved from: https://www.jstor.org/stable/2708083

Vergil, Polydore, *Anglica Historica* (1555 edition), Retrieved from: http://www.philological.bham.ac.uk/polverg/

Wallis, Helen, 'England's Search for the Northern Passages in the Sixteenth and Early Seventeenth Centuries', *Arctic*, Vol. 37, No. 4, December 1984, pp. 453–472. Retrieved from: https://www.jstor.org/stable/40510308

Walton, Kristen Post, 'Scottish Nationalism Before 1789: An Ideology, A Sentiment, or a Creation?' *International Social Science Review*, Vol. 81, No. 3 / 4, 2006, pp. 111–134. Retrieved from: https://www.jstor.org/stable/41887280

Weatherhill, Craig (2015) 'The Anglo-Cornish War of June-August 1549', *Cornovia*. Retrieved from: https://cornovia.wordpress.com/about/the-anglo-cornish-war-of-june-august-1549/

Weir, Alison, *Henry VIII: King & Court* (Pimlico, Great Britain, 2002)

Westropp, Thomas Johnson, 'Brasil and the Legendary Islands of the North Atlantic: Their History and Fable. A Contribution to the "Atlantis" Problem'. *Proceedings of the Royal Irish Academy: Archaeology, Culture, History, Literature*, Vol. 30, 1912, pp. 223–260. Retrieved from: https://www.jstor.org/stable/25502810

Whitfield, Peter, *Sir Francis Drake* (New York University Press, USA, 2004)

Whitelock, Anna, *Elizabeth's Bedfellows: An Intimate History of the Queen's Court* (Bloomsbury, Croydon, 2013)

Wilson, A.N., 'Get off your knees!', *The Daily Mail*, 23 June 2006. Retrieved from: https://www.dailymail.co.uk/news/article–392105/Get-knees.html

Wilson, A.N., *The Elizabethans* (Arrow Books, Great Britain, 2012)

Winship, George Parker, 'Sebastian Cabot, 1508'. *The Geographical Journal*, Vol. 13, No. 2, Feb. 1899, pp. 204–209. Retrieved from: https://www.jstor.org/stable/1774362

Endnotes

Preface

1. Edward Hall's *Chronicle* cited in Philip Payton, *Cornwall: A History* (Cornwall Editions, 2004), p. 115.
2. Polydore Vergil, *Anglica Historica,* 1555.

Chapter 1: The Plantagenet Inheritance: The rise of the Tudors and their imperial domains

1. Edward Hall, *Union of the Noble and Illustre Famelies of Lancastre and York* (written in 1542). Cited in Rogers and Turvey, *Henry VII* (Hodder Murray, 2005) p. 20.

Chapter 2: The Ghost of York: Henry VII's consolidation of the North 1485–1489

1. Polydore Vergil, *Anglica Historica,* 1555.
2. Vergil, 1555.
3. Vergil, 1555.
4. Vergil, 1555.
5. Francis Bacon, *The History of the Reign of King Henry VII* (Hesperus Press, 2007), p. 24.
6. Vergil, 1555.
7. Vergil, 1555.
8. Vergil, 1555.
9. Vergil, 1555.
10. Bacon, 2007, p. 50.

Chapter 3: The French Connections: The Breton Crisis and Henry VII's French war

1. John M. Currin, "The King's Army into the Partes of Bretaigne': Henry VII and the Breton Wars, 1489–1491', *War in History*, Vol. 7, No. 4, p. 381.

2. John M. Currin, 'To Play at Peace: Henry VII, War against France, and the Chieregato-Flores Mediation of 1490', *Albion: A Quarterly Journal Concerned with British Studies*, Vol. 31, No. 2, 1999, p. 210.
3. Currin, 2000, p. 381.
4. Currin, 2000, p. 383.
5. Currin (2000, p. 385) calls the subsidy 'a fiscal failure', with only £27,000 raised out of an anticipated £75,000.
6. Currin, 2000, p. 388.
7. Currin, 2000, p. 390.
8. Currin, 2000, p. 390.
9. Currin (2000, p. 398) states that by the time of the reconciliation 'the English and the Bretons had lost their best opportunity for driving the French from the duchy'.
10. Currin, 2000, p. 403.
11. Currin, 1999, p. 210.
12. Currin, 2000, p. 407.
13. Polydore Vergil, *Anglica Historica,* 1555.
14. Vergil, 1555.
15. Vergil, 1555.
16. John M. Currin, 'Pierre Le Pennec, Henry VII of England, and the Breton Plot of 1492: A Case Study in "Diplomatic Pathology"', *Albion: A Quarterly Journal Concerned with British Studies*, Vol. 23, No. 1, 1991, p. 21.
17. Cited in Currin, 2000, p. 380.
18. Currin, 2000, p. 380.
19. Cited in Currin, 1999, p. 207.
20. Currin (1999, p. 209) notes that there were two chief objectives in Henry's foreign policy in 1488–1492: to prevent French conquests of Brittany and Flanders, and to prepare a campaign to assert his claims in France.
21. Currin, 1999, p. 210.

Chapter 4: The Disturbed Land: Henry VII's problems in Ireland in the 1490s

1. Cited in S.B. Chrimes, *Henry VII* (Yale University Books, 1999), p. 260.
2. Peter Crooks, 'Factions, Feuds and Noble Power in the Lordship of Ireland, c.1356–1496', *Irish Historical Studies*, Vol. 35, No. 140, 2007, p. 440.

3. Crooks, 2007, p. 429.
4. Patrick Weston Joyce, *A Concise History of Ireland*, 1910.
5. S.G. Ellis, 'Parliaments and Great Councils, 1483–99: Addenda et Corrigenda', *Analecta Hibernica*, No. 29, 1980, p. 103.
6. Stanihurst cited in Crooks, 2007, p. 454.
7. G.O. Sayles, 'The Vindication of the Earl of Kildare from Treason, 1496', *Irish Historical Studies*, Vol. 7, No. 25, 1950, pp. 39–40.
8. Sayles, 1950, p. 40.
9. Joyce, 1910.
10. Cited in Steven G. Ellis, 'The Irish Customs Administration under the Early Tudors', *Irish Historical Studies*, Vol. 22, No. 86, 1980, p. 274.
11. Joyce, 1910.
12. Cited in Crooks, 2007, p. 426.
13. Cited in David B. Quinn, 'The Early Interpretation of Poynings' Law, 1494–1534', *Irish Historical Studies*, Vol. 2, No. 7, 1941, p. 249.

Chapter 5: The Wild West: The Cornish rebellions of 1497

1. Arthur Mee, *Cornwall* (Hodder and Stoughton, 1967), p. 25.
2. Thomas Penn, *Winter King; The Dawn of Tudor England* (Allen Lane, 2011), p. 30.
3. Philip Payton, *Cornwall: A History* (Cornwall Editions, 2004), p. 109.
4. Polydore Vergil, *Anglica Historica,* 1555.
5. Mark Stoyle, 'The Dissidence of Despair: Rebellion and Identity in Early Modern Cornwall', *Journal of British Studies*, Vol. 38, No. 4, 1999, p. 427.
6. Stoyle, 1999, p. 436.
7. Stoyle, 1999, p. 428.
8. Francis Bacon, *The History of the Reign of Henry VII* (Hesperus Press, 2007), p. 112.
9. Vergil, 1555.
10. Cited in Payton, 2004, p. 106.
11. Payton, 2004, p. 105.
12. Payton, 2004, p. 103.
13. Payton, 2004, p. 104.
14. Payton, 2004, p. 104.

15. Stoyle, 1999, p. 435.
16. Payton, 2004, p. 101.
17. Payton, 2004, p. 106.
18. Payton, 2004, p. 106.
19. Professor Penninginton cited in Payton, 2004, p. 107.
20. Payton, 2004, p. 101.
21. Payton, 2004, p. 107.
22. Bacon (2007, p. 112) calls Joseph either a blacksmith or a farrier.
23. Payton, 2004, p. 107.
24. Vergil, 1555.
25. Vergil, 1555.
26. Penn, 2011, p. 30.
27. Bacon, 2007, p. 113.
28. Penn, 2011, p. 30.
29. Vergil, 1555.
30. Vergil, 1555.
31. Bacon, 2007, p. 113.
32. Bacon, 2007, p. 116.
33. Payton, 2004, p. 108.
34. Payton, 2004, p. 108.
35. Vergil, 1555.
36. Payton (2004, p. 109) notes: 'Curiously, the Cornish left him unharmed, a strange deference or hesitancy overtaking them which may have reflected the numbness of battle or perhaps the dread realisation that already all was lost.'
37. Bacon, 2007, p. 117.
38. Stoyle, 1999, p. 443.
39. Bacon, 2007, p. 188.
40. Bacon, 2007, p. 118.
41. Bacon (2007, p. 118) notes: 'But being advertised that the country was yet unquiet and boiling, he thought better not to irritate the people further.'
42. Penn, 2011, p. 31.
43. Vergil, 1555.
44. Bacon, 2007, p. 123.
45. Bacon, 2007, p. 124.
46. Payton, 2004, p. 111.

47. Payton, 2004, p. 113.
48. Payton, 2004, p. 111.
49. Bacon, 2007, p. 124.
50. Stoyle (1999, p. 443) notes that Warbeck gathered 3,000 men. Bacon (2007, p. 124) states that Warbeck had gathered 3,000 men by the time of his declaration as Richard IV in Bodmin. Payton (2004, p. 111) notes that the number was 6,000 by the time Warbeck reached Exeter.
51. Bacon (2007, p. 124) notes that Warbeck was unable to persuade Exeter to support him: 'they had not the wit to send to them, in any orderly fashion, agents or chosen men to tempt them and to treat with them'.
52. Vergil, 1555.
53. Vergil, 1555.
54. Stoyle (1999, p. 443) puts the figure between 300 and 400 men. Bacon (2007, p. 125) estimates 200 men.
55. Cited in Charles Lethbridge Kingsford (ed), *Chronicles of London* (Clarendon Press, 1905), p. 218.
56. Vergil, 1555.
57. Vergil, 1555.
58. Vergil, 1555.
59. Vergil, 1555.
60. Bacon, 2007, p. 126.
61. Vergil, 1555.
62. Cited in Fred W. Bewsher, *The Reformation and the Renaissance, 1485–1547* (1922), pp. 14–16.
63. Cited in Bewsher, 1922, pp. 14–16.
64. Bacon, 2007, p. 128.
65. Bacon, 2007, p. 128.
66. Bacon, 2007, p. 127.
67. Payton, 2004, p. 112.
68. Payton, 2004, p. 112.
69. Payton, 2004, p. 113.
70. Payton, 2004, p. 115.
71. Stoyle (1999, p. 435) notes: 'the disturbances cannot be fully understood unless the determination of ordinary Cornish people to preserve their own distinctive identity is also taken into account'.

Chapter 6: Brave New World: John Cabot and the early voyages to North America

1. However, it must be stated that even if Columbus had sailed for Henry VII, it would have likely ended in the same way as Cabot's 1497 voyage, due to sailing at a higher latitude.
2. David B. Quinn, 'Columbus and the North: England, Iceland, and Ireland', *The William and Mary Quarterly*, Vol. 29, No. 2, 1992, pp. 288–291.
3. Alan Taylor writes: 'to his death in 1506, Columbus stubbornly insisted that all of his discoveries lay closet to the coast of Asia'. (*American Colonies: The Settling of North America*, Penguin Books, 2002, p. 37).
4. Seneca the Younger, *Medea*, 2, 2, I. 374. 'Thule' meant a distant place beyond the borders of the known world.
5. Quinn, 1992, p. 290.
6. Quinn, 1992, pp. 290–291.
7. This was suggested by Lope Garcia de Salazar in the 1400s, as noted by Evan Jones, 'Salazar's account of Bristol's discovery of the Island of Brasil (pre 1476)' (University of Bristol, 2007).
8. Cited in Jerald Fritzinger, *Pre-Columbian Trans-Oceanic Contact* (Google Books, 2016), p. 89.
9. Thomas Johnson Westropp, 'Brasil and the Legendary Islands of the North Atlantic: Their History and Fable. A Contribution to the 'Atlantis' Problem', *Proceedings of the Royal Irish Academy: Archaeology, Culture, History, Literature*, Vol. 30, 1912.
10. Evan T. Jones and Margaret M. Condon, *Cabot and Bristol's Age of Discovery: The Bristol Discovery Voyages 1480–1509* (Cabot Project Publications, 2016), pp. 9–10.
11. Lorraine Attreed, 'Henry VII and the 'New-Found Island': England's Atlantic Exploration, Mediterranean Diplomacy, and the Challenge of Frontier Sexuality'. *Mediterranean Studies*, Vol. 9, 2000, p. 66.
12. Quinn, 1992, p. 280.
13. Jones and Condon (2016, p. 37) argue that 'there are a number of problems with this theory', noting how trade with Iceland was already beginning to decline in the second half of the 1400s without the intervention of the Hanseatic League. Also, this decline was not permanent: by the 1530s Iceland became one of England's most important fishing areas.

14. Jones and Condon, 2016, p. 16.
15. This is the claim of Professor David B. Quinn. Jones and Condon (2016, p. 16) argue against this, but due to the lack of clear evidence they do not entirely discount it, due to the continual unearthing of evidence.
16. Cited in Attreed, 2000, p. 68.
17. Jones and Condon, 2016, p. 21.
18. Cabot was reputedly a well-travelled man, even claiming to have visited Mecca (as told to a Milanese ambassador). This is supported by Jones and Condon (2016, p. 22).
19. Jones and Condon (2016, p. 25) note that these attempts to gain Spanish/Portuguese support were reported in 1498 by the Spanish ambassador Pedro de Ayala.
20. Jones and Condon, 2016 p. 26. They speculate: 'it is possible that Bristol merchants in Seville approached Cabot, or more likely were approached by him, to see if he might assist their search'.
21. Quinn, 1992, p. 293.
22. Jones and Condon (2016, p. 27) add: 'Indeed, the importance of Italy's moneymen was such that the extra-European ventures launched from Iberia might best be regarded as Italian mercantile ventures undertaken under foreign flags'.
23. Cited in Richard Middleton, *Colonial America: A History, 1585–1776* (Blackwell Publications, 1992), p. 7.
24. Jones and Condon, 2016, p. 29.
25. Jones and Condon, 2016, pp. 31–32.
26. Attreed (2000, p. 69) notes that Henry VII gave Cabot £50 for the voyage.
27. Jones and Condon, 2016, p. 39.
28. Jones and Condon, 2016, p. 39.
29. As mentioned in John Day's letters.
30. Jones and Condon, 2016, p. 36.
31. Cited in Quinn, 1992, pp. 296–297.
32. Jones and Condon, 2016, p. 43.
33. Jones and Condon (2016, p. 44) do 'not entirely rule out Bonavista'.
34. Jones and Condon, 2016, p. 44.
35. Cited in Jones and Condon, 2016, p. 44.
36. Jones and Condon, 2016, p. 44.
37. Quinn, 1992, p. 295.

38. Jones and Condon, 2016, p. 45.
39. Quinn, 1992, p. 294.
40. Jones and Condon, 2016, p. 36.
41. Cited in Jones and Condon, 2016, p. 46.
42. Cited in Quinn, 1992, p. 293.
43. Attreed, 2000, p. 69.
44. Cited in Michael Tillbrook, The Tudors: England 1485–1603 (Oxford University Press, 2015), p. 48.
45. Jones and Condon, 2016, p. 50.
46. Jones and Condon, 2016, p. 49.
47. Cited in Jones & Condon, 2016, p. 51.
48. Jones and Condon, 2016, p. 52.
49. This Ruddock claim is based on a book proposal from 1992, claim Jones and Condon (2016, p. 55).
50. Emma Mason, 'Obituary: 'Alwyn Ruddock'', *The Guardian*, 2006.
51. Jones and Condon, 2016, p. 52.
52. Jones and Condon, 2016, p. 52.
53. E.T. Jones and M. Condon, 'Henry VII's letter to John Morton concerning William Weston's voyage to the new found land' (Unpublished, 2011).
54. Margaret M. Condon and Evan T. Jones, 'William Weston: early voyager to the New World', *Historical Research*, Vol. 91, Issue 254, 2018.
55. Condon and Jones, 2018.
56. Condon and Jones, 2018.
57. Attreed, 2000, p. 78.
58. Jones and Condon, 2016, p. 61.
59. Attreed, 2000, p. 73.
60. 1501 document cited in Attreed, 2000, p. 73.
61. Jones and Condon, 2016, p. 62.
62. Attreed, 2000, p. 77.
63. Jones and Condon, 2016, p. 66.
64. Attreed, 2000, p. 71.
65. Attreed, 2000, p. 72.
66. Jones and Condon (2016, p. 66) note that William Clerk sued Hugh Eliot. Also Francisco Fernandes fell out with Eliot over debt issues.
67. Francis Bacon, *The History of the Reign of Henry VII* (Hesperus Press, 2007), p. 130.
68. Jones and Condon, 2016, p. 67.

69. Jones and Condon, 2016, p. 68.
70. Jones and Condon, 2016, p. 69.
71. Jones and Condon, 2016, p. 70.
72. Jones and Condon, 2016, p. 53.
73. Middleton, 1992, p. 7. Also, Attreed (2000, p. 66) assesses the patent provided in 1501, noting how it shows 'a sensitive and moral approach towards the native population, ordering the punishment of who raped or abused them'.
74. Middleton, 1992, p. 12.
75. Quinn cited in Tillbrook, 2015, p. 48.

Chapter 7: Warrior King: Henry VIII's arrival on the European stage

1. Cited in Rogerston *et al*, *The Early Tudors, England 1485–1558* (Hodder Murray, 2007), p. 81.
2. Cited in Rogerson *et al*, 2007, p. 81.
3. Polydore Vergil, *Anglica Historica,* 1555.
4. John M. Currin, 'To Play at Peace: Henry VII, War against France, and the Chieregato-Flores Mediation of 1490', *Albion: A Quarterly Journal Concerned with British Studies*, Vol. 31, No. 2, 1999, p. 207.
5. Cited in Rogerson *et al*, 2007, p. 86.
6. Thomas Penn, *Winter King: The Dawn of Tudor England* (Allen Lane, 2011).
7. Cited in Rogerson *et al*, 2007, p. 89.
8. Cited in Rogerson *et al,* 2007, p. 90.
9. Edward Hall's *Chronicle* cited in Philip Payton, *Cornwall: A History* (Cornwall Editions, 2004), p. 115.
10. Cited in Robert Hutchinson, *Young Henry: The Rise of Henry VIII* (Phoenix, 2012), p. 162.
11. Hutchinson, 2012, p. 164.
12. Cited in Hutchinson, 2012, p. 165.
13. John Matusiak, *Wolsey: The Life of King Henry VIII's Cardinal* (The History Press, 2016), p. 109.
14. Matsuiak, 2016, p. 122.
15. C.S.L. Davies, 'Tournai and the English Crown, 1513–1519', *The Historical Journal*, Vol. 41, No. 1, March, 1998, p. 4.
16. Matsuiak, 2016, p. 122.

17. Matsuiak, 2016, p. 125.
18. Rogerson *et al*, 2007, p. 151.
19. Kristen Post Walton, 'Scottish Nationalism Before 1789: An Ideology, A Sentiment, or a Creation?', *International Social Science Review*, Vol. 81, No. 3/4, 2006, p. 114.
20. Polydore Vergil, *Anglica Historica, 1555.*
21. Cited in David Dunlop, 'The "Masked Comedian": Perkin Warbeck's Adventures in Scotland and England from 1495 to 1497', *The Scottish Historical Review*, Vol. 70, No. 190, Part 2, 1991, p. 110.
22. Dunlop, 1991, p. 120.
23. Vergil, 1555.
24. Vergil (1555) describes how James initially suggested the marriage match; Dunlop (1991, p. 125) states that it is 'highly misleading' that James raised it.
25. Richard Cavendish, 'Marriage of James IV of Scots and Margaret Tudor', *History Today*, Vol. 53, Issue 8, 2003.
26. Cavendish, 2003.
27. George Goodwin, *Fatal Rivalry: Flodden 1513* (Norton, 2013), p. 39.
28. Cited in Gervase Phillips, 'Strategy and Its Limitations: The Anglo-Scots Wars, 1480–1550', *War in History*, Vol. 6, No. 4, 1999, p. 401.

Chapter 8: Peacemaker: Thomas Wolsey's diplomatic direction

1. John Matsuiak, *Wolsey: The Life of King Henry VIII's Cardinal* (The History Press, 2016), p. 127.
2. T.A. Morris, *Europe and England in the Sixteenth Century* (Routledge, 1998), p. 160.
3. Cromwell cited in C.S.L. Davies, 'Tournai and the English Crown, 1 513–1519', *The Historical Journal*, Vol. 41, No. 1, March, 1998, p. 24.
4. Cited in M.D. Palmer, *Henry VIII: Seminar Studies in History* (Longman, 1971), p. 16.
5. Cited in Rogerson *et al*, *The Early Tudors, England 1485–1558* (Hodder Murray, 2007), p. 153.

Chapter 9: Expanding the 'Imperiall Crowne': The enlargement of Britain in the 1530s

1. Cited in P.R. Roberts, 'The Union with England and the Identity of 'Anglican' Wales', *Transactions of the Royal Historical Society*, Vol. 22, 1972, p. 49.

2. Roberts, 1972, p. 50.
3. Peter Marshall, '"The Greatest Man in Wales": James Ap Gruffydd Ap Hywel and the International Opposition to Henry VIII', *The Sixteenth Century Journal*, Vol. 39, No. 3, Fall, 2008, p. 684.
4. Cited in Marshall, 2008, p. 690.
5. Marshall, 2008, p. 690.
6. James Tait, 'Lee, Rowland', in the *Dictionary of National Biography, 1885–1900*, Volume 32, 1892.
7. Preamble cited in Roberts, 1972, p. 52.
8. Cited in Roberts, 1972, p. 52.
9. A.O.H. Jarman, *Cymru 'nrhano Loegr, 1485–1800, Seiliau Hanesyddol Cenedlaetholdeb Cymru* (Cardiff, 1950), p. 97.
10. Roberts, 1972, p. 61.
11. Steven G. Ellis, 'Henry VIII, Rebellion and the Rule of Law', *The Historical Journal*, Vol. 24, No. 3, Sep. 1981, p. 518.
12. 'The Chronicle of the Grey Friars: Henry VIII', in *Chronicle of the Grey Friars of London Camden Society Old Series: Volume 53*, ed. J.G. Nichols (London, 1852), pp. 29–53. *British History Online* http://www.british-history.ac.uk/camden-record-soc/vol53/ pp. 29–53
13. David Edwards, *Age of Atrocity: Violence and Political Conflict in Early Modern Ireland* (Four Courts Press, 2010), p. 59.
14. Ellis, 1981, p. 519.
15. Brendan Bradshaw (1979) deems the formation of the kingdom a 'liberal revolution'; cited in Christopher Maginn, "Surrender and Regrant' in the Historiography of Sixteenth-Century Ireland', *The Sixteenth Century Journal*, Vol. 38, No. 4, 2007, p. 961.
16. Cited in Keith Randell, *Henry VIII and the Government of England* (Hodder Educational, 2001), p. 86.
17. Cited in Rogerson *et al*, 2007, p. 137.
18. Cited in Rogerson *et al*, 2007, p. 137.

Chapter 10: The Rough Wooing: Henry VIII's attempt to subjugate Scotland in the 1540s

1. David M. Head, 'Henry VIII's Scottish Policy: A Reassessment', *The Scottish Historical Review*, Vol. 61, No. 171, Part 1, April 1982, p. 16.
2. Head, 1982, p. 6.

3. Head, 1982, p. 17.
4. Head, 1982, p. 17.
5. George Sinclair, 'The Scots at Solway Moss, *The Scottish Historical Review*, Vol. 2, No. 8, July 1905, p. 372.
6. Cited in Sinclair, 1905, p. 373.
7. Keith Randell, *Henry VIII and the Government of England* (Hodder Educational, 2001), p. 128.
8. J.D. Mackie, 'Henry VIII and Scotland', *Transactions of the Royal Historical Society*, Vol. 29, 1947, p. 112.
9. Cited in Head, 1982, p. 20.
10. Sinclair, 1905, p. 376.
11. Sinclair, 1905, p. 376.
12. Cited in Arthur Clifford, *The State Papers and Letters of Ralph Sadler, Knight-Banneret*, Vol. 1 (Archibald Constable, Edinburgh, 1809), p. 70.
13. Marcus Merriman, *The Rough Wooings* (Tuckwell Press, 2000), p. 144.
14. J.J. Scarisbrick, *Henry VIII* (Eyre & Spottiswoode, 1968), p. 626.
15. Alison Weir, Henry VIII: King & Court (Pimlico, 2002), p. 480.
16. Weir, 20002, p. 480.
17. Cited in Weir, 2002, p. 485.
18. Cited in Michael Tillbrook, *The Tudors: England 1485–1603* (Oxford University Press, 2015), p. 95.
19. Randell, 2001, p. 131.
20. Randell, 2001, p. 131.

Chapter 11: An Anglo-Cornish War: A different perspective of the 1549 Prayer Book Rebellion

1. Craig Weatherhill, 'The Anglo-Cornish War of June-August 1549' (*Cornovia*, 2015).
2. Weatherhill, 2015.
3. Weatherhill, 2015.
4. Philip Payton, *Cornwall: A History* (Cornwall Editions, 2004), p. 115.
5. Payton, 2004, p. 121.
6. John Sturt, *Revolt in the West* (Devon Books, 1987), p. 13.
7. Payton, 2004, p. 121.
8. Rose-Troup cited in A.L. Rowse, *Tudor Cornwall* (Cornish Classics, 2005), p. 258.
9. Sturt, 1987, p. 15.

10. Sturt, 1987, p. 15.
11. Mark Stoyle states that contemporaries dubbed the disturbance of 1548 the 'Cornish Commotion' ('"Fullye Bente to Fighte Oute the Matter": Reconsidering Cornwall's Role in the Western Rebellion of 1549', *The English Historical Review*, Vol. 129, No. 538, 2014, p. 550).
12. Rowse, 2005, p. 262.
13. Payton, 2004, p. 122.
14. Payton, 2004, p. 123.
15. Cited in Payton, 2004, p. 123.
16. Rowse, 2005, p. 263.
17. Rowse, 2005, p. 263.
18. W. Gore Allen, 'The Western Rebellion', *The Irish Monthly*, Vol. 75, No. 894, December 1947, p. 531.
19. Rowse, 2005, p. 263.
20. John Winslade's wife, Jane, was half-sister to William Kendall, who was killed for his involvement in the Exeter Conspiracy in 1538.
21. Gore Allen, 1947, p. 531.
22. Rowse, 2005, p. 264.
23. Sturt, 1987, p. 24.
24. Sturt, 1987, p. 26.
25. Sturt, 1987, p. 31.
26. Sturt, 1987, p. 33.
27. Cited in Sturt, 1987, p. 47.
28. Sturt, 1987, p. 89.
29. Sturt, 1987, p. 57.
30. Weatherhill, 2015.
31. Sturt, 1987, p. 64.
32. Sturt, 1987, p. 76.
33. Cited in Payton, 2004, p. 123.
34. This place continues to be referred to as Woodbury Common, rather than Aylesbury Common. However, Rose-Troup dismissed this more than a century ago, and this was re-emphasised by Sturt (1987).
35. Weatherhill, 2015.
36. Cited in Sturt, 1987, p. 85.
37. Gore Allen, 1947, p. 535.
38. Cited in Payton, 2004, p. 124.

39. Weatherhill, 2015.
40. Weatherhill, 2015.
41. Sturt, 1987, p. 99.
42. Payton, 2004, p. 124.
43. Sturt, 1987, p. 101.
44. Weatherhill, 2015.
45. Sturt, 1987, p. 100.
46. Cited in Payton, 2004, p. 125.
47. Weatherhill, 2015.
48. Cited in Weatherhill, 2015.
49. Cited in Rowse, 2005, p. 267.

Chapter 12: Tudor Brexit: The imperial implications of losing Calais in 1558

1. Both statements cited in C.S.L. Davies, 'Tournai and the English Crown, 1513–1519', *The Historical Journal*, Vol. 41, No. 1, March, 1998, p. 12.
2. David Potter, 'The duc de Guise and the Fall of Calais, 1557–1558', *The English Historical Review*, Vol. 98, No. 388, July 1983, p. 483.
3. Potter, 1983, p. 491.

Chapter 13: 'The Discovery of Russia': England's Russian connections and the Northeast Passage

1. Cited in Eleanor C. Gordon, 'The Fate of Sir Hugh Willoughby and His Companions: A New Conjecture', *The Geographical Journal*, Vol. 152, No. 2, 1986, p. 245. The Venetian ambassador was Giovanni Michiel; the letter was written in London on 4 November 1555.
2. The year 1527 is provided in the form of a letter – 'Declaration of the Indies' – from Thorne to Dr Edward Lee (later the Archbishop of York).
3. Cited in Helen Wallis, 'England's Search for the Northern Passages in the Sixteenth and Early Seventeenth Centuries', *Arctic*, Vol. 37, No. 4, December 1984, p. 453.
4. Cited in Wallis, 1984, p. 453.
5. Cited in Wallis, 1984, p. 455.
6. Alison Sandman and Eric H. Ash, 'Trading Expertise: Sebastian Cabot between Spain and England', *Renaissance Quarterly*, Vol. 57, No. 3, Autumn, 2004, p. 815.

7. Taylor cited in Walter I. Trattner, 'God and Expansion in Elizabethan England: John Dee, 1527–1583', *Journal of the History of Ideas*, Vol. 25, No. 1, 1964, p. 22.
8. Trattner, 1964, p. 23.
9. Nicholas Casimir and Baron de Bogoushevsky, 'The English in Muscovy during the Sixteenth Century', *Transactions of the Royal Historical Society*, Vol. 7, 1878, p. 58.
10. Cited in Casimir and Bogoushevsky, 1878, p. 63.
11. Gordon, 1986, p. 244.
12. Cited in John Pinkerton, *A General Collection of the Best and Most Interesting Voyages and Travels...* (Kimber and Conrad, 1810), p. 15.
13. Cited in Pinkerton, 1810, p. 15.
14. Cited in Pinkerton, 1810, p. 15.
15. Pinkerton, 1810, p. 15.
16. Gordon, 1986, p. 245.
17. Cited in Gordon, 1986, p. 243.
18. Casimir and Bogoushevsky, 1878, p. 59.
19. Inna Lubimenko, 'England's Part in the Discovery of Russia', *The Slavonic Review*, Vol. 6, No. 16 (Jun., 1927), p. 110.
20. Wallis, 1984, p. 456.
21. Gordon, 1986, p. 245.
22. Gordon, 1986, p. 246.
23. Gordon, 1986, p. 247.
24. In 1556, the two ships were recovered to sail them back to London. However, they only made it as far as the Norwegian coast, when in a storm both ships sank; this included the bodies of Sir Hugh Willoughby and his men. However, Willoughby's journal did not make it back to England, due to being packed on a different ship.
25. Casimir and Bogoushevsky, 1878, p. 60.
26. Casimir and Bogoushevsky, 1878, p. 60.
27. Cited in Grenville A.J. Cole, 1919, p. 7.
Cole, Grenville A.J., 'The Narrow Seas and the Arctic route to Muscovy', *The Geographical Teacher*, Vol. 10, No. 1, Spring, 1919, p. 7.
28. Cited in Casimir and Bogoushevsky, 1878, p. 61.
29. Cited in Casimir and Bogoushevsky, 1878, p. 62–63.
30. Cited in Casimir and Bogoushevsky, 1878, p. 63.

31. Casimir and Bogoushevsky (1878, p. 64) write of Chancellor's return as being a 'public curiosity'.
32. Cited in Casimir and Bogoushevsky, 1878, p. 64.
33. Cited in Casimir and Bogoushevsky, 1878, p. 65.
34. Casimir and Bogoushevsky, 1878, p. 67.
35. Casimir and Bogoushevsky, 1878, p. 69
36. Casimir and Bogoushevsky, 1878, p. 69.
37. Casimir and Bogoushevsky, 1878, p. 69.
38. Cole, 1919, p. 7.
39. Cited in Cole, 1919, p. 7.
40. Casimir and Bogoushevsky, 1878, p. 69.
41. Lubimenko, 1927, p. 111.
42. Inna Lubimenko, 'The Correspondence of Queen Elizabeth with the Russian Czars', *The American Historical Review*, Vol. 19, No. 3, Apr 1914, p. 528.
43. Lubimenko, 1914, p. 529.
44. Cited in Casimir and Bogoushevsky, 1878, p. 84.
45. Casimir and Bogoushevsky, 1878, p. 111.
46. Cited in Casimir and Bogoushevsky, 1878, p. 71.
47. Cited in Casimir and Bogoushevsky, 1878, p. 72.
48. Cited in Casimir and Bogoushevsky, 1878, p. 73.
49. Lubimenko, 1914, p. 533.
50. Cited in Casimir and Bogoushevsky, 1878, p. 81.
51. Casimir and Bogoushevsky, 1878, p. 128.
52. Casimir and Bogoushevsky, 1878, p. 128.
53. Charles J. Halperin, 'Sixteenth-Century Foreign Travel Accounts to Muscovy: A Methodological Excursus', *The Sixteenth Century Journal*, Vol. 6, No. 2, October 1975, p. 98.
54. Halperin, 1975, p. 99.
55. Lubimenko, 1914, p. 536.
56. Cited in Cole, 1919, p. 7.
57. Sandman and Ash, 2004, p. 841.
58. Sandman and Ash, 2004, p. 841.
59. Cited in Wallis, 1984, p. 456.
60. Wallis, 1984, p. 457.
61. Chester Dunning, 'James I, the Russia Company, and the Plan to Establish a Protectorate over North Russia', *Albion: A Quarterly Journal Concerned with British Studies*, Vol. 21, No. 2 (Summer, 1989), p. 207.

62. Dunning, 1989, p. 206.
63. Lubimenko, 1927, p. 110.

Chapter 14: The Birth of the English Slave Trade: The 1560s voyages of Sir John Hawkins

1. Cited in Andy Beckett, 'Heirs to the slaves', *The Guardian*, 2006.
2. Cited in Beckett, 2006.
3. A.N. Wilson, 'Get off your knees!', *The Daily Mail*, 2006.
4. Edgar Legare Pennington, 'Sir John Hawkins in Florida', *The Florida Historical Society Quarterly*, Vol. 10, No. 2, October 1931, p. 86.
5. P.E.H. Hair, 'Attitudes to Africans in English Primary Sources on Guinea up to 1650', *History in Africa*, Vol. 26 1999, p. 55.
6. Pennington, 1931, p. 88.
7. Cited in Hair, 1999, p. 60.
8. Cited in Hair, 1999, p. 57.
9. Ronald Pollitt, 'John Hawkins's Troublesome Voyages: Merchants, Bureaucrats, and the Origin of the Slave Trade', *Journal of British Studies*, Vol. 12, No. 2, May 1973, p. 28.
10. Cited in C. Raymond Beazley, *Voyages and Travels: mainly during the 16th and 17th centuries* (Archibald Constable & Co, 1903), p. 44.
11. Cited in Beazley, 1903, p. 44.
12. John Sparkes cited in Beazley, 1903, p. 51.
13. Cited in Beazley, 1903, p. 80.
14. Cited in Beazley, 1903, p. 48.
15. Cited in Pennington, 1931, p. 95.
16. René Goudlaine de Laudonniére, *Historie nortable de la Floride: Selections* (Thomas Dawson, 1587).
17. Pennington, 1931, p. 100.
18. John Hawkins, 'An Alliance to Raid for Slaves' (1587) cited in Northrup, David Northrup, *The Atlantic Slave Trade* (DC & Heath, 1994), pp. 70–71.
19. Hawkins cited in Northrup, 1994, pp. 70–71.
20. Hawkins cited in Northrup, 1994, pp. 70–71.
21. Cited in Beazley, 1903, p. 97.
22. Cited in Beazley, 1903, p. 100.
23. Cited in Beazley, 1903, p. 100.
24. Cited in Beazley, 1903, p. 102.

25. Cited in Beazley, 1903, p. 84.
26. Pennington, 1931, p. 88.
27. Hair, 1999, p. 67.
28. Hair, 1999, p. 49.

Chapter 15: The King of California: Sir Francis Drake's Claim to Nova Albion

1. Warren L. Hanna, 'Legend of the Nicasios: The Men Drake Left behind at Nova Albion', *California History*, Vol. 58, No. 2, Summer 1979, p. 159.
2. Peter Whitfield, *Sir Francis Drake* (New York University Press, 2004), p. 25.
3. Hanna, 1979, p. 161.
4. Adolph S. Oko, 'Francis Drake and Nova Albion', *California Historical Society Quarterly*, Vol. 43, No. 2, June 1964, p. 135.
5. Cited in Hanna, 1979, p. 162.
6. Cited in Oko, 1964, p. 138.
7. Cited in Oko, 1964, p. 136.
8. Cited in Oko, 1964, p. 146.
9. Harry Kelsey, 'Did Francis Drake Really Visit California?', *Western Historical Quarterly*, Vol. 21, No. 4, November 1990, p. 462.
10. Kelsey, 1990, p. 444.
11. As Kelsey (1990, p. 444) notes: 'Even today, after four centuries of research, nearly every important aspect of the voyage is a matter of uncertainty, contradiction, and dispute – the dates of departure and return, the route taken, the numbers of men and ships involved, the places visited, the wonders encountered'.
12. Hakluyt cited in William H. Hamlin, 'Imagined Apotheoses: Drake, Harriot, and Ralegh in the Americas', *Journal of the History of Ideas*, Vol. 57, No. 3, July, 1996, p. 408.
13. Drake's nephew cited in Hamlin, 1996, p. 409.
14. Drake's nephew cited in Hamlin, 1996, p. 409.
15. Drake's nephew cited in Hamlin, 1996, p. 409.
16. N.M. Penzer cited in Oko, 1964, p. 147.
17. Hamlin, 1996, p. 409.
18. Hanna, 1979, p. 159.

Chapter 16: American Dream: Elizabethan England heads out to North America

1. Alan Taylor, *American Colonies: The Settling of North America* (Penguin Books, 2002), p. 94.
2. Cited in Richard Middleton, *Colonial America: A History, 1585–1776* (Blackwell Publications, 1992), p. 13.
3. Cited in Niall Ferguson, *Empire: How Britain Made the Modern World* (Penguin Books, 2004), p. 4.
4. Taylor, 2002, p. 123.
5. Cited in Taylor, 2002, p. 123.
6. Anna Whitelock, *Elizabeth's Bedfellows: An Intimate History of the Queen's Court* (Bloomsbury, 2007), p. 220.
7. Whitelock, 2007, p. 220.
8. Taylor, 2002, p. 118.
9. Cited in William M. Hamlin, 'Imagined Apotheoses: Drake, Harriot, and Ralegh in the Americas', *Journal of the History of Ideas*, Vol. 57, No. 3, July, 1996, p. 412.
10. Taylor, 2002, p. 124.
11. Middleton, 1992, p. 10.
12. Taylor, 2002, p. 124.
13. Middleton, 1992, p. 12.
14. Middleton, 1992, p. 12.

Chapter 17: Day of the Dog: How the Spanish Armada almost ended the Tudors

1. Cited in Susan Frye, 'The Myth of Elizabeth at Tilbury', *The Sixteenth Century Journal*, Vol. 23, No. 1, Spring, 1992, p. 98.
2. Christopher Lee, *This Sceptred Isle* (Penguin Books, 1998), p. 186.
3. Cited in Ronald Pollitt, 'John Hawkins's Troublesome Voyages: Merchants, Bureaucrats, and the Origin of the Slave Trade', *Journal of British Studies*, Vol. 12, No. 2, May 1973, p. 39.
4. Hiram Morgan, 'Teaching the Armada: An Introduction to the Anglo-Spanish War, 1585–1604', *History Ireland*, Vol. 14, No. 5, Sep. – Oct., 2006, p. 39.
5. Robert Hutchinson, *Elizabeth's Spy Master: Francis Walsingham and the Secret War That Saved England* (Phoenix, 2007), p. 210.
6. Morgan, 2006, p. 40.

7. Morgan, 2006, p. 41.
8. Cited in Frye, 1992, p. 97.
9. Frye (1992, p. 95) outlines the questions regarding Elizabeth's speech and whether it actually happened. After all, there were no reliable eyewitnesses and the words first appeared decades later in 1623 in a letter written by Leonel Sharp.
10. Cited in Hutchinson, 2007, p. 235.
11. Cited in N.A.M. Rodger, 'Queen Elizabeth and the Myth of Sea-Power in English History', *Transactions of the Royal Historical Society*, Vol. 14, 2004, p. 157.
12. G.D. Ramsay cited in Michael Tillbrook, *The Tudors: England 1485–1603* (Oxford University Press, 2015), p. 205.

Chapter 18: The Search for the City of Gold: Sir Walter Raleigh's quest to find El Dorado

1. Cited in Andrew Fleck, '"At the Time of His Death": Manuscript Instability and Walter Ralegh's Performance on the Scaffold', *Journal of British Studies*, Vol. 48, No. 1, 2009, p. 18.
2. Cited in Fleck, 2009, p. 9.
3. Fleck, 2009, p. 9.
4. Walter Raleigh, *The Discovery of Guiana* (Blackmask, 2001), p. 11.
5. Anna Whitelock, *Elizabeth's Bedfellows: An Intimate History of the Queen's Court* (Bloomsbury, 2007), p. 259.
6. Raleigh, 2001, p. 3.
7. Raleigh, 2001, p. 35.
8. Raleigh, 2001, p. 1.
9. Regarding Whiddon, Raleigh writes: 'to my great grief I left buried in the said island [Trinidad] after my return from Guiana, being a man most honest and valiant' (2001, p. 7).
10. Raleigh, 2001, p. 7.
11. Raleigh, 2001, p. 8.
12. Raleigh, 2001, p. 8.
13. Raleigh, 2001, p. 8.
14. Raleigh, 2001, p. 8
15. Raleigh, 2001, p. 17.
16. Raleigh, 2001, p. 19.
17. Raleigh, 2001, p. 19.
18. Raleigh, 2001, p. 21.

19. Raleigh, 2001, p. 34.
20. Raleigh, 2001, p. 28.
21. Raleigh, 2001, p. 20.
22. Raleigh, 2001, p. 8.
23. Raleigh, 2001, p. 21.
24. Raleigh, 2001, p. 22.
25. Raleigh, 2001, p. 22.
26. Raleigh, 2001, p. 19.
27. Raleigh, 2001, p. 23.
28. Raleigh, 2001, p. 31.
29. Raleigh, 2001, p. 31.
30. Raleigh, 2001, p. 35.
31. Raleigh, 2001, p. 3.
32. Raleigh, 2001, p. 37.
33. Raleigh, 2001, p. 27.
34. Raleigh, 2001, p. 5.
35. Cited in Fleck, 2009, p. 5.

Chapter 19: Elizabethan Ireland: The training ground for the British Empire

1. Both cited in Hiram Morgan, '"Never Any Realm Worse Governed": Queen Elizabeth and Ireland', *Transactions of the Royal Historical Society*, Vol. 14, 2004, p. 295.
2. Niall Ferguson, *Empire: How Britain Made the Modern World* (Penguin Books, 2004), p. 55.
3. Cited in *The Dictionary of Irish Biography*, 'Bagenal (O'Neill), Mabel', 2009. Retrieved from: https://www.dib.ie/biography/bagenal-oneill-mabel-a6953
4. Anna Whitelock, *Elizabeth's Bedfellows: An Intimate History of the Queen's Court* (Bloomsbury, 2013), p. 315.
5. Whitelock, 2013, p. 315.
6. Morgan, 2004, p. 307.
7. Alan Taylor, *American Colonies: The Settling of North America* (Penguin Books, 2002), p. 123.
8. Morgan, 2004, p. 308.
9. Ferguson, 2004, p. 57.
10. Taylor, 2002, p. 118.
11. Taylor, 2002, p. 127.

Index

Warbeck, 33-35, 40-43, 54-59, 70,
82, 89-90, 121
Wars of the Roses, 1-6, 9-10,
14-15, 17-18, 25, 38, 46, 49,
89, 101
Western Rebellion (Prayer Book
Rebellion), 120-130
Weston, Weston, 74, 76-78, 80
White, John, 171, 178-181

Willoughby, Hugh, 137-143,
145, 152
Wolsey, Thomas, 86-87,
93-98, 102

Yellow Ford, battle of, 202, 207
York, 17-18, 98, 111, 113
Yorkists, 1-5, 9-10, 12-22, 25, 34,
38-39, 46, 51, 55-56